BRIDGWATER
WITH AND WITHOUT THE 'I

By Roger Evans

First printed – November 1994

Reprinted – May 1995

Published by R. Evans
9 Sussex Close, Bridgwater
Somerset TA6 5PA
Telephone: (01278) 455190

Printed by LPL Print Service
14 Castle Street, Bridgwater,
Somerset TA6 3DB
Telephone: (01278) 429738   Fax: (01278) 424043

ISBN 0 9525674 0 7

TO MY WIFE LORNA

AND OUR CHILDREN

Introduction

If you want to offend a Bridgwater person, send them a letter addressed to "Bridgewater". Most Bridgwater born and bred natives take umbrage at this misspelling since the lack of the middle 'e' is seen to be one of the peculiarities which sets this Somerset town apart from the rest.

This obsession with the 'e' reflects just one part of the character of Bridgwater and its people. They are different to the people from other towns. I suppose any one from any town in England could say that about their own home town. But where else would one find the world's largest night time carnival? And what makes Bridgwater people so fanatical about this peculiar pastime?

Then there's the strong tradition of live local theatre. Drama, pantomime and operatic societies flourish much as in any other town of a similar size. But add to that the carnival concerts, with some six hundred performers on stage every evening of this two week spectacular, and you've beaten any other town hands down.

In this publication, I have tried to capture the character of Bridgwater, the character of those that shaped its history and to chronicle the events that have shaped it over the centuries. I have tried to address the questions so often raised by my fellow townsmen. Where was the castle? How big was it? Is it true that .....? And so on.

Today the town is best known for its carnival, its fair, the Cellophane manufacturing plant with its towering chimney and for its surrounding wetlands, now increasing in national environmental importance. Historically, Bridgwater is best known as the home of its most famous son, Admiral Blake and for the Battle of Sedgemoor, the last battle on English soil.

Other periods of historic significance go unnoticed. The battle for Bridgwater Castle; the sailing of Bridgwater's Emanuel on Frobisher's voyage to find the North West passage; and how many know that Bridgwater was once important enough that Henry VlII gave it county status.

Bridgwater's real development started in medieval times when its position as a river crossing consolidated its significance and ensured its future. Bridgwater's role as a port brought significant growth and its industrial development in later years consolidated its dominant position in the area. These aspects of the town are covered herein.

Bridgwater people have always shown an interest in the other Bridgewaters, the ones overseas which are spelt without dropping the 'e'. Most locals know that there is one in the States and one in Australia. There are in fact seventeen others, many named after our own town and I have included a section on these Bridgwater namesakes.

The town, steeped in history and tradition, and its people are far more interesting than most would realise. That is, of course, unless one journeys into its records and archives and discovers for oneself the characters and events that shaped its history and development. This book is an attempt to make that journey an easy and enjoyable one. It is meant to be an easy read, and not an academic historical document, in the hope that more people will read it and benefit from the experience. I trust the reader gains as much pleasure in exploring its pages as I did in their preparation.

Celtic and Saxon days

In the beginning

Little is known of Bridgwater before the days of the Saxon Chronicles. It would appear that it started as a collection of small wattle houses lived in by the early Britons. Its position on the River Parrett is due to there being a ford across the river at a point which was a crossing on an old British trackway. Even in those early days the name of the river, Y-Parwydd, was recognisable with today's version.

It is unlikely that there was any settlement where Bridgwater now stands much before Roman times, certainly not of any significance. When our present town bridge was being built back in 1883, a piece of Phoenician ring money was found. This could indicate a pre-Roman trading presence.

It is believed that the Romans took control of a small Celtic settlement that was to become Bridgwater and called it Uzela or Uxellam. We know of a Roman presence from coins found in the area. The place would have been of little interest to them other than as one through which they would frequently pass when sailing from their area headquarters at Ilchester to the mouth of the Parrett, which they knew as Uxella Aestuarium, and beyond.

They certainly had a settlement at Combwich and Puriton which both served as outposts of their coastal defence system. Combwich and Crandon Bridge (known locally as the Silver Fish) served as Roman river ports. They were concerned with possible invasions from South Wales which made these outposts significant. There followed a period of stability under the Romans during which they brought peace and order to the land. The communities in this area were able to settle down to farming. The only weapons required in these times were those to defend against the still present wolves.

The Saxon invasion

With the withdrawal of the Romans, the Britons reverted back to their tribal way of life based on smaller communities. Hill-forts such as that at Cannington were re-occupied. The Saxons took advantage of this weaker position and gradually migrated towards this area between A.D. 450 and 600. Certainly by A.D. 658 they had not yet reached the Bridgwater area albeit those living here, if anyone was at that time, were no doubt aware of their presence to the north and west.

The Britons had been pushed into Wales and the South West. The Saxons had a word for foreigners or strangers; it was wealas or Welsh. The Britons called themselves the Cymri or comrades. Modern day Welsh is derived from the mother tongue of the Britons at that time and thus would have been the language used in and around Bridgwater.

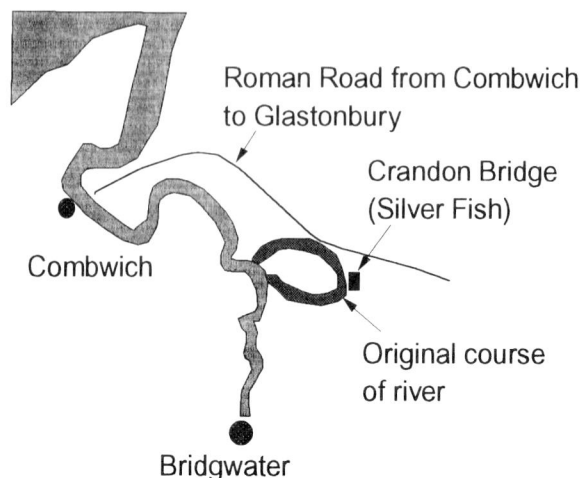

Roman Road from Combwich to Glastonbury

Crandon Bridge (Silver Fish)

Combwich

Original course of river

Bridgwater

The arrival of Centwine

It was probably in AD 682 that Centwine, a king of the West Saxons, drove the Britons to the North Somerset coast. Having moved increasingly westward, he had restricted the British presence in this area to the wetlands either side of the Polden hill ridge and then pushed them on across the Parrett almost certainly at Bridgwater or Combwich. Having pushed his boundary forward, he set up outposts at Cannington and one at Bridgwater on its east bank.

A Saxon Soldier

Ufer being the Saxon word for bank, we therefore have the origin of Eastover (from 'east ufer') and Westover.

In the year A.D 800 the Saxon chronicles were published and we know from them that Bridgwater was then known as Bruggie or Bruge, being the Saxon for fording place or bridge. Other theories suggest that it is derived from the Old Norse *Bryggja* meaning quayside or from the Old English *Brycg* being a gang plank running from ship to shore, either of which fits in accurately with Bridgwater as a significant landing place.

At this time Bridgwater was really no more than the best point at which to cross the river. It is at a point where the river narrows down in width for the first time in its fourteen meandering miles up from the sea. Also, as you continue upstream, it is a long way again before a similar opportunity arises. Apart from the river being narrower at this point, perhaps more significant is that here the mud is much less of a problem than elsewhere. The crossing therefore became a strategic point where routes crossed between the Polden and the Quantock hills.

The Danes invade

During the ninth century, Bridgwater witnessed the unwanted presence of the Danes. They frequently forced their way up the river on their raids. In A.D. 878 they landed at Combwich resulting in a major battle at Cannington. These raids of the Danes continued until Alfred finally settled the score by defeating the Danes at Edington. Many of the Danes are believed to have hidden at Bridgwater after their defeat.

In the years leading up to 1066, a Saxon, Earl Merleswain was in control. He was a Christian and it was probably he who built the first church here on the site where St. Mary's now stands. He owned much land

North Petherton Hundred

Pawlett

Puriton

Bridgwater

Wembdon

Sydenham

Hamp

Dunwear

North Petherton

Creech St.Michael

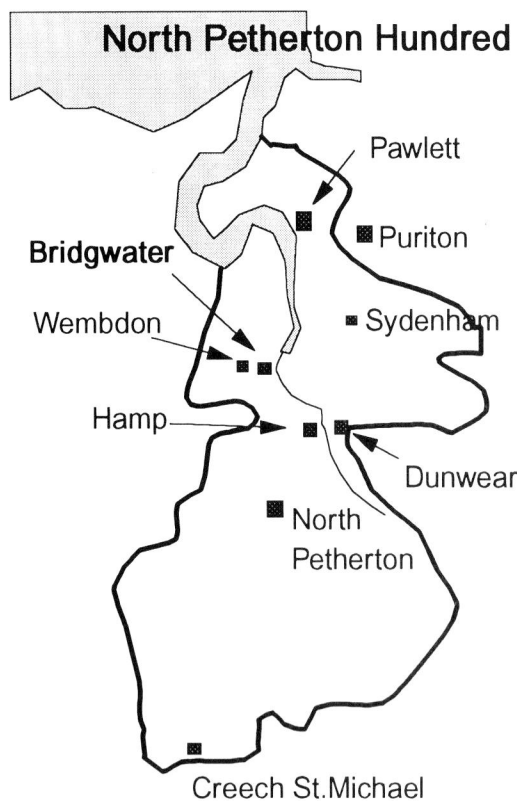

throughout the country and at the time was the Sheriff of Lincolnshire.

Bridgwater by now was still just a cluster of Saxon farmsteads. Apart from metal for tools and salt for preserving meat, the community was self-sufficient. It grew its own corn and meat and had a plentiful supply of wool which would have been dyed using local and natural colorants in the making of yarn for weaving.

The North Petherton hundred

The size and significance of Bridgwater at this time can be gained from its position within the North Petherton hundred. The Saxons had a way of dividing their land for the purposes of taxation and control. A 'hundred' was the area of land on which one hundred extended families would live, the extended family covering any number of generations living at the same time. The land per family was a hide and varied in size from say 40 to 140 acres dependant on its quality. Bridgwater was part of the North Petherton hundred. Thus we can assume that it was less significant than North Petherton (which was the minster or mother church) and had no more than a handful of families.

The Norman conquest, Walter de Douai

The Saxon way of life continued until the Norman invasion in 1066. William the Conqueror then gave control of Merleswain's empire to one of his close supporters, Walter de Douai. The settlement was henceforth known as The Bridge of Walter going through the following stages to the current day's spelling:-

Brugie - the Domesday Book entry, Brycg in old English
Brigewaltier - 1194, Briggwalter - 1201, Brug, Bruggewate, Bruggewaut - 1297, Brugewalt, Bruggewate - 1315, Brugie Walter, Bruggewater, Bruggewaterre, Briggewater, Bryggewater, Brugewater, Brygewater, Brigwater, - all at various times during the 15th century.

These details we know from various works starting with the Domesday Book on which work began around 1080 and a plethora of medieval wills, particularly around the 15th century. These wills tell us a great deal about the wealthier inhabitants of the town and their dependence on the Grey Friars and friars of St. Johns hospital for their spiritual needs.

The Domesday Book showed that Bridgwater consisted of five hides, thus we can assume there were five extended families. The arable land was sufficient for ten ploughs and supported 13 villeins, a peasant who is tied to his lord and pays dues or services to him in return for his land, 9 bordars and five cottagers who between them had eight ploughs. The term plough in this case can be misleading because the Saxons referred to carts as ploughs, the ploughs being called 'zuls'. By comparison, North Petherton had land for 30 ploughs, so it was roughly three times the size of Bridgwater.

The Domesday book shows Bridgwater and numerous other lands belonging to "Walscin". This was the popular name for Walter of Douai, a bit like using Harry for Henry. Walter de Douai was a Fleming, as were many who came over with William the Conqueror. Douai can be found just to the south of Lille in France close to the Belgian border.

The land given to Walter made him one of the most powerful and influential in Somerset. His area of responsibility was that enclosed by the Parrett and the Axe from river mouth to source, lands which included Burnham, Brean, Huntspill, Pawlett and Wembdon. No doubt his role would have been a military one defending the area against invaders. To help him in that role he commanded a keep at Castle Cary. Despite his responsibilities he never actually lived in the town but settled instead in Bampton, Devon having done little or nothing for the town of Bridgwater itself, other than to give it his name and effectively give away its church. During his period of control he gave the town's church and the tithes therefrom to the monastery at Bath.

On his death the township passed to his son, Robert of Bampton and after him by marriage to the Paynel or Pagnall family whose name lives on in Penel Orlieu. Fulk Pagnel, Walter's great grandson, granted the church to Marmoutiers, near Tours in France.

The neighbouring areas of Chilton Trinity, Otterhampton, Charlynch and Enmore were the property of Roger of Courcelle whilst the King had Cannington, North Petherton and Chedzoy with the Church of Rome holding Puriton.

Domesday book entries

Bridgwater

Walfcin ten Brvgie. Merlfuain tenuit T.R.E. 7 geldb p.v.hid.Tra.e.x.car. In dnio st.lll.car.7 v.ferui.7 xlll.uilti 7 lx.bord 7 v.cotar cu.vlll.car.Ibi molin redd.v.fol. 7 x.ac pti.7 c.Ac filuae minutae.7 xxx.ac pafturae. Qdo recep.ualb.c.fol.Modo.v11.lib.

Walscin holds Bridgwater. Merleswain held it before 1066. It paid tax for 5 hides (extended families) and had land for 10 ploughs. In Lordship were 3 ploughs and 5 slaves. There were 13 villagers, 9 smallholders and 5 cottagers with 8 ploughs. A mill which paid 5 shillings had 100 acres of woodland, 10 acres of meadow and 30 acres of pasture. Value when acquired was 100 shillings and has now increased to £7.

Sydenham

Witts ten de Ro.una v trae in Sideha. Cheping tenuit T.R.E. Tra.e.l.car. Ibi.xv.ac.pafturae. Valet.xv.denar.

William holds 1 virgate (a quarter of a hide) in Sydenham from Roger. Before 1066 it was held by Cheping (a Saxon lord). There is land for 1 plough with 15 acres. Its value was 15 pence.

Hamp

Ipfa aeccla ten Hame. T.R.E.geldb p una hida. Tra.e.llll.car. In dnio.e.l.car.7 llll.ferui.7 l.uitt 7 vll.bord cu.l.car.Ibi.xv.ac pti.7 lll.ac filuae minutae.

Before 1066 taxes were paid on 1 hide with land for 4 ploughs. In lordship was 1 plough and 4 slaves. There was also 1 villager and 7 smallholders with 1 plough, 15 acres of meadow and 3 acres of wood.

King John and William Briwer

William Briwer

In 1180, the estate of Bridgwater passed over to Lord William Briwer, a close friend and hunting partner of King John, himself a regular visitor to the town. There were royal visits on at least five occasions between 1204 and 1210. The tales of Robin Hood have made us all aware of what a wicked man King John was and in contrast what a fine fellow was his brother, King Richard.

This view was probably not shared in Bridgwater. Who needs a King who spends all of his time gallivanting around Europe on some religious crusade, causing a drain on the taxpayer? On the other hand what a fine fellow is his brother who regularly visits our town taking advantage of the local hunting. How the money rolls in when his retinue come to town, and how grateful are the townsfolk for the other privileges he has bestowed on them. Somerset was after all his favourite county.

Bridgwater however can defend itself against a bias towards King John. It was William Briwer who delivered the ransom for the release of Richard the Lionheart.

Granting of borough status

On June 26th, 1200, in Chinon near Tours in France with William Briwer at his side, King John granted Bridgwater free borough status. This put an end to serfdom and allowed burgage rent to be collected by the borough provosts or reeves.

Up to this time anyone who worked the land had to give occasional days to the local lord. This would most likely be at the very time the serf really needed to be seeing to his own plot. The end of serfdom meant they could get away with a payment, probably equivalent to a days pay. The going rate was a shilling per burgage per year and the penalty for non payment was to have the doors of one's premises sealed until settlement was made.

This was far more convenient for all concerned and the tax was collected by the provosts or reeves who had their own seals. The design of the seal for the Bridgwater provosts depicted two men pulling a rope on a single masted ship. Seals were an important feature in those days when so few people were able to read or write.

Provost's or Reeve's Seal

During the 13th century the burgesses also had their own circular seal. This showed a castle standing on a four arched stone bridge with the river below. The legend on the seal read "Sigillum commune de Brigwalter", the seal of the Bridgwater community. By 1464 the seal had altered in that the bridge had six arches and was of wood. The inscription had also altered to "Sigillum commune ville de Bridgwater". A further change in 1478 replaced the castle door with a portcullis over a leopard's head. Further small changes took place right up to the 19th century.

Apart from greater freedom for the locals, the lord of the manor also benefited from free

borough status by more tenants being attracted to the town. Bridgwater thus increased in rentable value many times over.

The borough court.

The charter allowed the burgesses, a limited number of privileged businessmen, to hold their own court to deal with local criminal and civil cases. The court met monthly on a Monday presided over by the lord's steward.

Many of the cases were much as today; trespass, debt, fraud and even environmental issues were on the agenda. On this latter point there were regular cases regarding people not keeping ditches clear or indiscriminately disposing of waste including animal offal.

Short measure was a popular one, as was trading in the street too close to an existing trader. There was little in the way of written law. Many of the offences were basically those of not conforming to tradition or practice. Regrating was another offence associated with market trading which occurred when one bought an item at one

price and then sold it a higher price, totally unacceptable! Imagine the impact that legislation would have on today's stock market!

Among the punishments that the court dished out were fines at one extreme and imprisonment at the other. There were, in between, alternative forms no longer practised such as pillorying and tumbrelling.

Being punished by the tumbrel or cucking-stool (not to be confused with ducking stool) involved sitting on a wooden stump from which one was not allowed to move whilst the public hurled various insults and missiles. To be punished in this way usually meant that you had committed an offence that would be unacceptable to the general public and thus the hurling of missiles and insults could be quite aggressive.

The pillory was worse. For this the offender was bolted in without the opportunity to duck when the need arose. At least two pillories existed, one within the castle and one without. The borough archives show an example of a lady punished by pillory for failing to re-site a dung heap quickly enough and another for disturbing the peace. It didn't take much to experience the wrath of the court. The pillory and stocks were certainly in use as early as 1378 and as late as 1782 when they were moved back to their earlier position roughly outside the Town Hall. That was their position in the 17th century until their temporary move for the best part of forty years to the Cornhill in 1744.

Apart from the pillory in the castle, there was also a ducking stool, a gallows and a prison.

The execution of Lord Stafford

One person executed in the castle was its keeper at the time, Lord Stafford. He had been involved in a battle at Danesmore in 1469 and was deemed not to have entered the fray with sufficient commitment. Edward IV issued instructions for Lord Stafford's arrest and subsequent execution. This took place in the grounds of the castle on August 17th.

The town was relatively small in those days. It had four gates, each of which had its own caretaker and was secured at night. These gates had heavy arches built of the fawn coloured Ham Hill stone. Three of them each had an iron hook from which a heavy gate was hung for night time security. Between the gates the town boundaries were basically ditches or rows of houses.

The town was governed by the Gild Merchants, a group of influential businessmen with extraordinary privileges. These included having the first option on any newly available goods, certainly for the first three weeks of their availability. Only after then did they become available to the general public. Only Gild members and local taxpayers were allowed to trade without toll within the town. All others had to pay their dues and naturally those payments went straight to the gild members. Being a member also entitled one to trade anywhere else in the country, except London, without paying tolls. Fairs were an exception to this rule and must have been welcome by those outside the Gild as an opportunity to get in first. This practice continued until June 18th, 1468 when a new charter was granted to the town and henceforth the rules for trading were not so rigid. The original site of the Guildhall was the present position of the Town Hall.

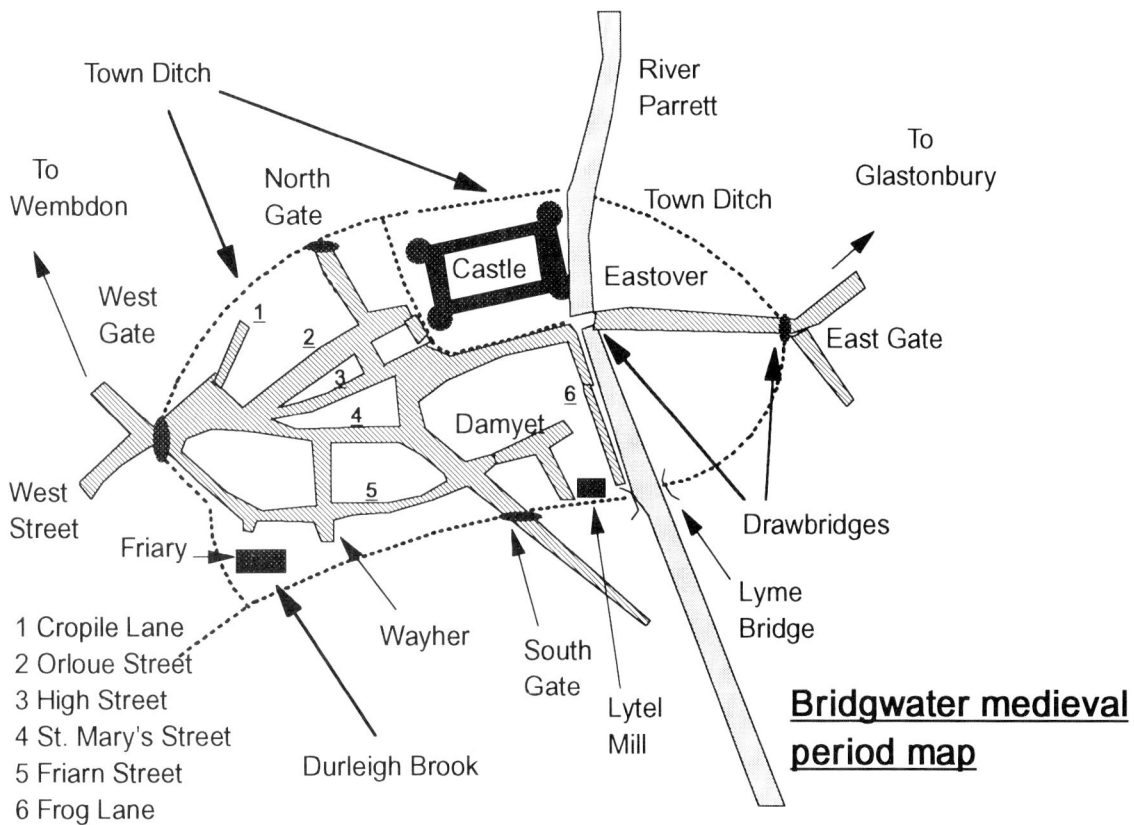

Bridgwater medieval period map

Town Ditch
River Parrett
To Wembdon
North Gate
Town Ditch
To Glastonbury
West Gate
Castle
Eastover
East Gate
West Street
Damyet
Drawbridges
Friary
Lyme Bridge
Wayher
South Gate
Lytel Mill
Durleigh Brook

1 Cropile Lane
2 Orloue Street
3 High Street
4 St. Mary's Street
5 Friarn Street
6 Frog Lane

The town in those days revolved around three focal points. The first of these was the gild which governed the town and upheld justice. The others were the church for moral and spiritual guidance and the market which involved everyone in the township.

We can more or less tell the size of the town at this time. Records from 1444 indicate the population at 1600 and the town was wealthy enough to have its own piper to liven up official occasions. The greatest number of houses were in Eastover with 58, St. Mary's Street with 51, then Friarn Street with 43. The High Street counted as two streets in those days, these being North Street with 39 houses and South Street with 25. Then came Castle Ditch 25, Fore Street 20, West Street 19, Orloffe Street and Damyate with 18 each.

Bridgwater's first mayor

The court now met weekly, still on a Monday, and was presided over by the mayor, this being a new position granted with the charter. Bridgwater's first mayor in 1469 was John Kendall. Whilst the way the town was governed may have changed, the individuals with the power remained much the same and included John Kendall. This form of government for the borough under the chairmanship of the town mayor was to remain until local government reorganisation which took effect on March 31st, 1974. This pattern of elected members, plus aldermen elected for life from within their own ranks, was unchanged for over five hundred years. Only the numbers qualifying to vote at the elections of those members was to change. I was privileged to serve as an elected councillor for the old borough in the years immediately before reorganisation. The changes brought about in 1974, whilst no doubt offering greater efficiency in the long term, regrettably left Bridgwater without even a parish council. Whilst Bridgwater became the centre of Sedgemoor, it was no longer master of its own destiny.

Bridgwater Castle

Bridgwater Castle

King John also allowed William to fortify the town with a castle which was built between 1200 and 1210. With walls 12 to 15 feet thick it was surrounded on three sides with a 30 foot moat, or fosse as they were sometimes called, and on the fourth side by the river. The moat on the north side was known as the Common Ditch, the other two sides being the Castle Ditch.

If the castle was still standing today, its boundaries would run along the river from Chandos Street to the Town Bridge with Fore Street forming the south side - the moat on the south side actually ran below the shops on the Castle Street side of Fore Street. Castle Moat, from York Buildings across the top of King Square, formed the higher west

The Watergate entrance to the castle

side and the final side ran down to the river, almost along the site of Chandos Street.

There were only two entrances. The Watergate, part of which can still be seen on the West Quay, was the entrance from the river and was protected on either side by towers being smaller versions of those on the corners of the castle. The castle bailey entrance, which was the main access point and opened out onto the town market was where York Buildings now stand. Thus to get the feel for this entrance, walk from the Cornhill up into King Square. As you pass the dental surgery on your right, imagine a large arched castle entrance is in front of you with its drawbridge down and portcullis raised to permit your access. Either side of the gated entrance was a barbican or tower built to defend the entrance. Pass on into King Square and you're in the castle grounds within its ten feet thick and thirty feet high walls of red Wembdon sandstone. And you've just trodden the same path of those who visited the castle all those centuries ago including many kings and queens.

As you stand in King Square, you are in what used to be the higher part of the castle grounds, the upper bailey. Running across in front of you, more or less along the line of the offices on the river side of King Square, was an inner wall which separated the upper bailey from the lower. The lower bailey was the ground which ran down to the river. Thus the castle was split into two within its walls. This allowed the defenders to lose ground if necessary and fall back within the confines of a smaller and more defensible area. As you look down Castle Street, there is a very definite drop in the road which

Plan of Bridgwater Castle

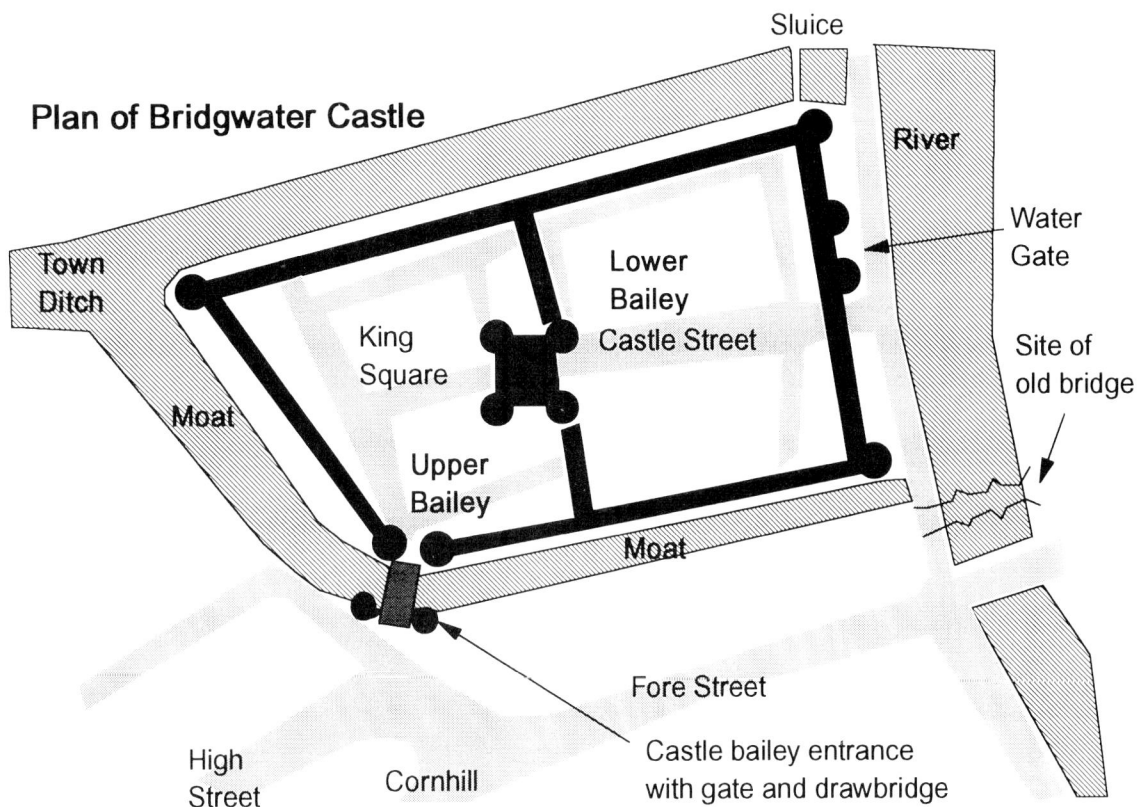

Plan of Bridgwater Castle — labels: Sluice, River, Water Gate, Site of old bridge, Town Ditch, Lower Bailey, Castle Street, King Square, Moat, Upper Bailey, Moat, Fore Street, High Street, Cornhill, Castle bailey entrance with gate and drawbridge

clearly indicates the line between the two baileys.

The castle, at about 10 acres in total, was of sufficient size to hold 1200-2000 troops under normal circumstances and up to 3000 in times of strife. It was a royal residence in that King John used it on frequent occasions and throughout its life the residents were supporters of the king.

In style it was much like other castles of that period with rounded towers at each corner and smaller half round towers in between. Built of red Wembdon sandstone, decorative features were incorporated through the use of fawn coloured Ham stone. Buildings within the walls had green glazed roof tiles. The castle had vaults used originally as dungeons but these were later to become bonded cellars for wine which had been

cleared by the nearby Customs House in Bond Street.

Inside its walls there was the church of St. Mark (looked after by the brethren from St. Johns hospital), a bell tower, dovecote and the great hall. This was Mortemere's Hall situated in the very centre of the grounds and used for entertaining by the castle governor who would sit at one end on a raised platform or dais. Royal personages or other influential visitors would share this table on their visits

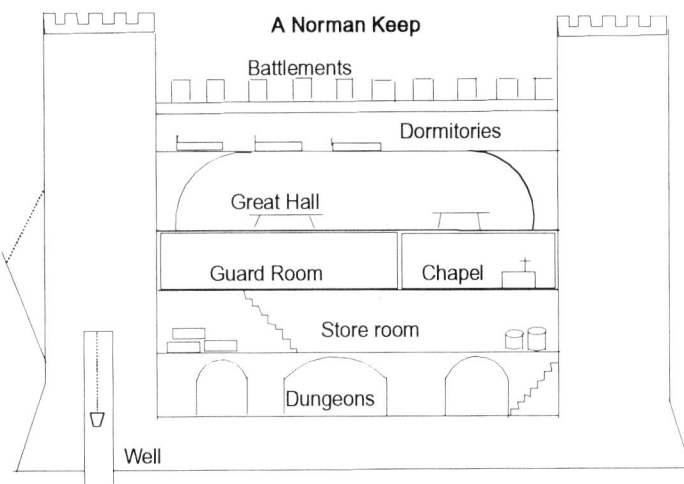

A Norman Keep — labels: Battlements, Dormitories, Great Hall, Guard Room, Chapel, Store room, Dungeons, Well

The Cornhill market place looking up through what is now York Buildings to the castle entrance

to Bridgwater. For the troops there was an armoury, smithies and stables.

On the death of the younger William Briwer, the male line finished and the castle passed to the eldest of five daughters, Graecia Broase, the wife of William de Broase, a Welsh baron.

In 1233, Alienora, a daughter of King John, took up residence in the castle, albeit the castle stayed in the ownership of the Broase family. Graecia's son, also called William, was killed by Llewellyn Prince of Wales. Maud, the eldest of his 4 daughters, inherited the castle and thus the Broase regime ended with the castle now becoming the property of the Mortimer family into which Maud had married. The Mortimer family became the dominant family in Wales and thus Bridgwater's castle spent most of its time governed by a constable in the owners absence.

In 1424, the property changed families once again when Anne Mortimer married Richard Earl of Pembroke and so the castle became a property of the crown.

During the days of King John it was from Bridgwater Castle that hunting parties set forth into the Forest at North Petherton. Deer and other forms of game were plentiful and hunting was carried out by both hawk and hound. During King Henry Vll's reign, Lord Daubenny frequented the castle as its governor and took advantage of the hunting, whilst entertaining many of his friends into the bargain.

Outside of the castle, the rest of the town spread only a short distance further. Durleigh brook formed one natural defensive boundary and there was a wall from the West Gate (where Westgate House now stands) and the North Gate at the top of Angel Crescent.

Lord Daubenny's hunting party

A poem in George Parker's 1877 'Ancient history of Bridgwater' depicts the flavour of hunting parties and life within the castle. It relates a the tale of Lord Daubenny and the event which led him to take the Lady Arundel for his bride in 1486.

There was a park at Petherton
Where stately trees did grow
You ne'er the like could look upon,
For noble buck or doe.

In fourteen hundred eight-six,
The young Lord Daubenny
A wondrous hunting match did fix,
For governor was he.

Henry now wore King Richard's crown,
He nobly did attain;
One battle brought the tyrant down,
Which Daubenny helped to gain.

He was then active and was bold,
And fear he never knew;
His diary many records told,
He prized his bow of yew,

Which he had won when very young,
When knights had met to see
A match which bards had ably sung
Of skilful archery.

To be the foremost was his pride,
In daring deeds led he;
His fame was echoed far and wide,
For acts of chivalry:

To join the hunt, to view the sights
Which he would then display,
Both lords and ladies with their knights
Assembled on this day.

Bridgwater Castle opened wide
Its sturdy gates to all;
It was the young Lord Daubenny's pride
To fill the spacious hall.

Sir William Stanley proudly came
With lady, knight and shield;
Fame placed its stamp upon his name,
On famous Bosworth's field;

Courtenay, the Earl of Devon, too,
And Arundel of Kent,
With other knights and men as true,
Who were for pleasure bent.

Their 'squires attended in their train,
Their daughters young and fair;
Some sighed Lord Daubenny's heart to gain,
His reputation share.

As o'er the drawbridge on that day
Caparisoned they passed.
So grand and gaudy the display,
It scarce could be surpassed.

The gates oped wide to friend or foe,
So noble Daubenny willed;
The outer ballium to its end
With spectators was filled.

The loud huzzahs, marks of delight,
The very air now rent,
As the sun's dazzling rays of light
Shone on the pageant.

Heraldic banners lifted high,
Of various forms were seen,
With colours to attract the eye,
Of azure blue or green.

Long-bearded men, each armed with lance,
All men of martial deeds,
In compact line were in advance,
Mounted on mettled steeds.

The stirrup-top formed a lance rest,
O'er which a cross was strung;
A silver belt lashed o'er the breast,
From which a bugle hung.

Lady and knight, each side by side,
Soon followed in the track;
Each lady's grey pranced in its pride,
The bold knights' steeds were black.

The bits and stirrups looked as gold,
The bridles white as snow;
On either side walked yeomen bold,
With quiver and with bow.

Next came the earls, whose stern looks tell
Of haughty, proud disdain,
Whose summons thousands could compel
To follow in their train.

Close in their rear a few renowned
For valour in war's field,
Who had, when danger sternly frowned,
With courage borne their shield -

Who had in difficulties shared,
And won distinguished place,
But now, with hearts and arms prepared,
Were eager for the chase.

Was ever seen such gay parade?
The multitudes remark,
As they surveyed the calvacade,
In Petherton's wide park.

They soon were formed within its bounds,
Its groves of sylvan green;
The huntsman, with the deep-toned hounds,
In various groups were seen.

The rough-haired staghound, with an eye
Keen as the arrow's flight,
With graceful form fitted to fly,
Yet showing muscled might.

The sleek-haired hounds, with pendent ears,
To sweep the morning dew;
Their look sagacious appears
Their height and colour true.

The spotted beagles scattered round,
An active little pack,
With nose already to the ground,
With tail curled o'er the back.

Another group must not escape,
Our notice in the wood;
The greyhounds tall with slender shape,
Held in their leashes stood.

In the amusements of the day,
All ranks of persons shared;
Some here, some there, wandered away,
For any game prepared.

When the nobility were seen,
The huntsmen gathered round,
And with their bugles tasselled green,
Rung out a cheering sound.

The various hounds the signal caught,
As each would each outvie;
In sympathy, by practice taught,
They joined the chorus cry.

Scarcely the ladies could prepare,
No time allowed to flag;
With sudden spring from covert lair,
Rushed out an antlered stag.

Boldly he took a look around,
His enemies he heard;
And off he bounded o'er the ground;
Swift as a feathered bird.

The law of chase was then allowed,
The foremost hounds whipped back;
Now they, in eager circle crowd -
Then off, the gallant pack!

Well off, well off, my merry hound,
Oh, what a joyful spring!
The huntsman said, "Hark to that sound!
It makes the forest ring."

Now mettled steeds away pursue;
It calls the fleetest pace;
The sportsmen and the ladies too
Dash forward in the chase.

Through brake and glade, o'er hill and dale,
Away from man's abode;
No check from danger would avail -
With energy they rode.

The frightened stag, o'er briar and brook,
With speed of lightning goes;
His way toward the Quantocks took,
Where the wild heather grows.

The scent lay well, the dogs pursued
Unerring in his track;
A few with lasting strength endued,
Led on the pressing pack.

United now what music went,
In chorus of alarm,
So much the closer was the scent,
The louder was the charm.

The hill-top gained, the stag he stood
As watchful as a bird,
With ear bent towards a neighbouring wood,
The fearful sound he heard.

Quickly he turned by other ways
To reach once more the plain -
Took his straight course o'er rugged braes
To reach his lair again.

The leading sportsmen flushed with heat,
Kept up a fleeting pace,
And little dreamt they soon would meet
The object of their chase.

Too soon, for in a narrow glen,
As ancient records tell,
But a short distance from the men
Rode Lady Arundel.

Down came the stag from upper ground,
With furious pace he came,
The sportsmen heard the rushing sound,
And trembled for the dame.

One minute more, his branching head
The lady's steed would meet;
Within that minute he lay dead
and prostrate at her feet.

Another wreath from smiling fame
That arrow gained, I trow,
It with a true precision came
From young Lord Daubenny's bow.

He caught a glimpse of danger near,
And strung the fatal dart,
With practised hand and vision clear,
He sent it to the heart.

The bugles join in reveille,
They hear the stirring round;
Attendants move the stag away,
As sportsmen gather round.

The Lady Arundel was young,
The blush was on her face;
Her hair the theme of every tongue,
Her beauty and her grace.

The chase was run on Crispin's day,
If chroniclers must guide,
And ere could follow Easter-day
She was Lord Daubenny's bride.

Such feasting and such joyous glee
We never must forget,
It happened then what all would see -
Valour and beauty met.

Long did Bridgwater Castle ring
With sounds of revelry,
And years to come bards they would sing,
Of gallant Daubenny.

St. John's hospital, the Grey Friars and early town bridges.

St. John's Hospital and the Augustine Friars

Lord Briwer continued his building work with an Abbey at Dunkeswell and a castle at Torquay. Locally he built the hospital of St. John the Baptist, an Augustine Priory, in 1216, a gift which was confirmed by Bishop Jocelin in 1219. The hospital was originally founded in 1213 and a copy of the charter can be found in the register of Bishop Beckington.

The grant was for 5 acres of land in order to maintain 13 poor and infirm persons plus pilgrims and religious persons passing through the town with some notable exceptions. For some reason the friars were excused from tending to the needs of lunatics, lepers, pregnant women and those with contagious diseases. Their main purpose was to provide food and lodgings for travellers, care for the sick and educate the young, mainly of the poor.

The hospital, known as 'The House of Augustine Friars' was based at the eastern end of Eastover (thus giving St. John's Street its name). If today you cross Broadway from St. John's Street to Eastover, then you cross the actual site of the hospital. For those old enough to remember the Queen's Head public house, that marked the spot. Its position was partly within the town and partly without, an arrangement aimed at the late night traveller.

Within the hospital grounds there was a church dedicated to St. Katharine, 112 feet long, an infirmary, refectory, dormitory, chapter house or office, cloister for exercising, parlour and Bridgwater's first school. The garden included space for herbs and vegetables, a fish pond for Friday meals and a graveyard. In 1286, a licence was granted for the cutting of a channel to the river in order to clear the waste from the privies on each incoming tide. We know that in the same year there was a causeway which ran from the hospital to the Polden Hills which became known as the Long Causeway and went through Sydenham Manor, Horsey and Crook to Crandon.

Whilst the original purpose of the hospital was to care for the sick and the traveller, by 1298 Geoffrey, the prior, had bound himself to maintain 13 scholars who lived within the grounds. The funding for their education came from Robert Burnell, the Bishop of Bath and Wells and Chancellor of England, from the income of the rectories of Morwentow and Wembdon.

These thirteen lads lived and ate in the friary but took their education in the town, being excused religious duties. In return, seven poor scholars from the town were fed at the friary. The hospital continued to support thirteen boys until at least 1535.

The priory's 13th century seal was a vesica, or pointed oval shape, just less than three inches by two, showing Our Lady with the child on a parapet of a four-arch bridge over a river. To her left is St. John with Agnus Dei on a roundel and to her right is St. Paul with sword and book. The incomplete inscription apparently reads *"S' commune hospitalis sancti Iohanni Baptiste de .... altera"*.

Records show that between 1329 and 1336, Sir John Popham of Huntworth was assisting the hospital by way of grants. New buildings were added in 1350 and 1450.

A medieval hospital of the **Order of St. John**

For a place whose purpose was to provide hospitality, it was not without its troubles. In 1381, there was religious unrest throughout the country. This was at the period of the Wat Tyler rebellions. These troubles had kept themselves mainly in the South East of the country with the exception of a few isolated outbreaks. Wat Tyler, having been executed in London, the government soon put the word out as to his death and the crushing of the rebellion. This was enough to quell most potential trouble spots with exceptions in York, Scarborough and Bridgwater. Locally this manifested itself with St. John's hospital coming under attack by a extremely ugly mob on June 19th and 20th. At the time, St. John's took all the local tithes and even appointed the vicar of St. Mary's.

The attackers were headed by a priest named Nicolas Frompton and Thomas Engilby, a yeoman. Frompton apparently claimed the legal right to the vicarage belonging to the Knights of St. John. He had spent time in London and had seen the way the Knights of St. John had been treated there. Hurrying back from London, he raised a mob of fourteen men captained by Engilby. They forced an entry to the house of the Knights, seizing William Camel, the master of the premises, making him transfer the premises and the profits therefrom to Frompton. Whilst there, they destroyed a number of bonds detailing the debts owed to the hospital by a various locals and committed the master to signing a £200 ransom promise.

Having finished their work at St. Johns hospital, they attacked several houses in the town and broke open the gaol. Engilby then took his mob to East Chilton and Sydenham where they burnt the rolls of the manors of Sir James Audley and John Cole.

At Ilchester Gaol, they removed Hugh Lavenham and Walter Baron, beheaded them and had their heads placed on spears on Bridgwater's town bridge.

Those involved were tried for their part in the violence. Engilby, who on hearing the news from London of the crushing of the rebellion fled the district, was condemned to death. But within a month he had amazingly been granted a free pardon. Nothing is known as to what happened to Frompton.

17

Medieval arch from St. John's

The brethren themselves, who wore long robed gowns with an embroidered black cross, were not so perfect either. In 1463 the bishop found it necessary to send in his auditor to investigate complaints of misbehaviour by the brethren. Enough of them required punishment to justify the construction of a dungeon including stocks in which to correct the errant brothers.

It was a busy year for the bishop. He also found it necessary to investigate claims of miraculous cures at Wembdon. St. Johns spring, a well, supplied water which somehow came to be associated with wondrous cures. For a time Wembdon became a local Lourdes and the faith of its visitors helped to bring in a regular income for the local church. The bishop had severe doubts about the legitimacy of the claims but lacked the confidence to interfere.

St. John's Hospital lasted until the Dissolution albeit parts of it survived until at least 1703. One piece still surviving is an ornate window arch which for many years served as an ornament at the entrance to Hamlin's garage in Monmouth Street.

The Grey Friars of Friarn Street

In 1230, William Briwer's son of the same name opened the Grey Friars or Friar Minor's Franciscan priory in Friarn Street. Land was donated in 1246 for their use and records of 1278 show the king granting permission to Richard de Plessy, the keeper of the parks, for five oak trees to be taken from the North Petherton forest for their use as timber at the friary. Further grants were made in 1284.

Francis of Assisi was born in 1182 and his influence spread rapidly across Europe. The younger William Briwer was obviously sufficiently influenced by their doctrine to build the Friarn Street premises for these Franciscan Friars. A large parcel of land went with the premises including low lying meadows beyond Durleigh Brook. On this they sited their 210 feet long friary, described in medieval records as 10 steppys in length. In Silver Street there is an old arched doorway believed to be the sole relic of the old priory.

For three hundred years they practised poverty, chastity and prayer and dedicated themselves to improving the lives of others, especially the sick and destitute.

By their example, they earned themselves the respect and admiration of the community. They were able to take confessions, make wills and carry out various other duties normally associated with the 'official' parish priest. This resulted in them being less popular in some quarters than others, but it would have been a foolish man who would have criticised them for fulfilling the religious obligations, such was their popularity with the public at large. They were easily distinguished from the Augustine Friars by their long grey gowns with cowl and cloak, girded with a cord. Travelling barefoot, they took no money, only gifts of food and other

Trivett's Bridge

bodily requisites. They travelled the whole county serving the community and preaching the gospel in their own popular way.

During the 14th century, the friars were only allowed to preach under licence. Records show Maurice de la More being granted his in 1332, William de Anne in 1333 and Richard Aunger in 1353. One of the most famous of the friars was Brother John Sumner or Somer who made his name as a much respected astronomer. One of his successes was to write an astronomical calendar for Joan, the Princess of Wales, wife of the Black Prince.

Both the hospital of St. John and the Grey Friars lasted until 1536 when they were closed under Henry Vlll's Suppression of the Monasteries Act.

Records also show that there was a "Hospital of St. Giles" from some time in the fourteenth century until 1539 which started as a leper colony, eventually becoming a hospital. Its site was probably just outside the old west gate.

Early town bridges

In the days of William Briwer, the town's bridge was a timber one. Briwer set about building a three arched stone crossing but his death in 1227 put paid to its completion. It was not until the reign of Edward 1 that Sir Thomas Trivett completed the task with a donation of 300 marks, affixing his arms of a trivet to the coping of the bridge.

For many years there were houses on the bridge. Heavy traffic, particularly military vehicles, along with the effect of the strong tides, eventually did much damage and repairs were necessary in 1532 and again in 1678.

Fairs, Markets and the Wool Trade

Medieval markets

Markets were necessary not only as a way for the population to trade in the necessities of life, but also as a means of generating revenue for the local manor or castle. The middle of the 13th century saw Bridgwater with 13 stalls and 5 shops along with just over 300 burgages. Records even show three Jews as living in the town. Two were licensed for up to a year but the third was fined for trespass.

Traders included goldsmiths, wine merchants and the various trades associated with the cloth and wool industry. There were tuckers, dyers, spinners and drapers, weavers and shuttle makers.

Medieval fairs

Fairs in Bridgwater have always been a good way of raising revenue for both the traders and the local authority. One of the earliest records we have is that of an eight day fair granted by King John through William Briwer in 1200. This fair started on June 24 each year but as the numbers of traders dwindled, it died a natural death around 1357.

Other fairs had taken its place by 1358. The smallest of these was on Ascension day when cherries were in season. It appears to have lasted until around 1900 and by the 18th century was specialising in shoes and cloth.

The Midsummer horse and shoe fair on June 24th was held originally in George Lane and then moved to Dampiet Street and lasted until just before World War ll. The Bridgwater Herald report for 1831 referred to it as the smallest of the fairs with trade in beef and lamb but predominantly cart horses.

The second Thursday in Lent was the Lent Fair, granted by charter in 1468, when oranges were sold. The Bridgwater Herald report for 1831 described that year's fair as the best for a long time with cows, calves, cheese, bacon and cloth all trading well. There was also a Christmas Fair trading in the same produce on December 27th or 28th.

The summer horse fair was held in Eastover. It was instigated to raise funds for St. John's chapel and lasted until the earlier part of this century. The horses would be trotted up and down Eastover to show their form. Those brought in by the gypsy community would be ridden bare back by the gypsy children using a single rope halter. This was a sure fire way to demonstrate to a potential buyer how easily the animal would respond to its new owner.

The same technique can be witnessed today on the morning of the first day of St. Matthew's Fair, the biggest by far of all the Bridgwater fairs and of course the only one that survives today.

St. Matthew's fair

A new charter was granted on February 16th, 1613 for St. Matthew's fair, albeit we know it was actually established in 1404.

St. Matthew's Fair, or Bridgwater Fair as it is commonly known was the great high spot of the social calendar for the people of Bridgwater and surrounding area.

The fair, originally held on St. Matthew's day September 21st, now starts on the last Wednesday in September and lasts for 4 days. It was a one day fair until 1857 when a local act was passed making it a three day event. In 1919 the weather was so disastrous that

The old market or High Cross on the Cornhill

the traders had been unable to make a decent return on their trading and they were granted an extra day. This was the Saturday and the fair has had four days ever since.

Today it is more significant as a funfair than as a traditional fair for trading in sheep and ponies. The pleasure side of the fair was an addition around 1852 and has grown in significance ever since and the fair has now become the third largest in England.

Quantock round up

Until recent years there was a spectacular scene on the Quantock Hills on the Saturday before the fair when the Quantock ponies were rounded up and driven down into the villages such as Nether Stowey and Holford.

Unfortunately this spectacle became too popular as a tourist attraction and the custom had to cease. Scores of ponies galloping through the narrow streets of these villages

were never going to mix with the 'townies' who went to view them.

The trading part of the fair is complete on the first day but for many it is still the most significant and interesting aspect of the whole event. The stalls which now line the sides of West Street use the same places previously reserved for the sheep sales when both sides of the street were lined with hurdled pens.

From its inception until more recent years, Bridgwater Fair had a far greater social significance than today. It was very much the exception for local people to go beyond the bounds of their own town or surrounding villages. Those living in the country would rarely go farther than the nearest market town. Life was hard enough without losing valuable time on unnecessary travel.

Major social events in the calendar were therefore a matter of great excitement and social significance. They were a chance to

21

get up to date with the news, meet friends rarely otherwise seen and to listen to people from other parts whose stories would be fascinating if only for being different to the otherwise very parochial and mundane news. Harvest festivals, saints days and the like were all causes of mounting excitement, but nothing compared with Bridgwater Fair.

As well as the social aspect, there was of course a commercial side to the event. A far wider range of products would be available than local tradesmen would ever be capable of displaying. It was like having a departmental store visit once a year. For those from outside the town it justified taking lodgings for the duration. It also justified taking a horse and cart since it would not be unusual to buy a years supply of cloth, boots, pans or the like.

To give some idea of the size and significance of the fair, one could expect to find more than a hundred shoemakers trading their wares. In one year they actually exceeded a hundred and fifty. Whilst agricultural sales were the mainstay, hardware, haberdashery, millinery, toys and various food products ensured the turnover was considerable. With so much money to be spent there were inevitably problems with vagabonds and pickpockets. The local constabulary would therefore be increased with volunteers to ensure the number of incidents was kept to a minimum.

King of the Beggars

One example of the problems encountered comes from the early part of the eighteenth century. Bampfylde Moore Carew (1690-1798) was born a gentleman but preferred the life of a Romany gypsy. The Bampfyldes were for years the squires at Lee near the valley of the Rocks at Lynton and the Carews were the squires at Crowcombe until succeeded by the Trollope-Bellews.

Carew was very popular within the gypsy community and was often called the King of the Gypsies although King of the Beggars was more accurate. He was a master of disguise and an accomplished confidence trickster.

Vicars were favourite targets and some were duped by him as many as three times, each time in a different disguise. Well-practised, he organised a group of con men to come to Bridgwater fair where, disguised as cripples, blind and various other unfortunates, they tore at the very heart strings of the more fortunate who so generously gave to those less well off.

The mayor of the town and his fellow burgesses recognised them for the con men that they were and had them arrested for fraud. They were locked up over night to await their trial in the morning. It was never intended that they should be brought to justice, just frightened enough to never return to Bridgwater again.

Under the mayor's instructions, the gaoler was informed to tell them of their likely fate. In the morning they would be taken for trial before the mayor who had a wicked reputation where people who masqueraded as cripples or blind were concerned. Having put the fear of God into them, he accidentally on purpose failed to secure the lock up. Realising their opportunity, they made their escape. The cripples threw away their crutches and departed with wings at their heels. The blind miraculously saw again and sped into the night with amazing visual powers and the mayor and his friends watched the whole proceedings with much pleasure under cover of the night's darkness.

The trade in human labour

St. Matthew's fair was, like many other fairs at the time, also the place where agricultural workers would go to hire themselves out for the coming year. Men and women lined up in rows waiting to be purchased for their particular skill. Their occupation was easily recognised by the tools of their trade which they carried with them. The carter's whip, the shepherd's crook and the milkmaid's stool all lined up with their owners. It must have been a trying time especially for those beginning to age and consequently looking less of a bargain to the potential hirer.

Equally it must have been a trying time for wives who had not kept their husbands happy. It was not unknown for husbands to sell their wives at these fairs. Indeed there is one local parish register which records such an event. The wife's arrangement with the new husband appears to have been much more successful than with the first, the marriage being blessed with several children.

Of traction engines and mashed potatoes

During the earlier part of this century, there was a ruling that the fairground showmen could not move onto St Matthew's field on a Sunday. They would arrive in West Street and wait there for midnight to arrive. At the allotted hour, the showmen with their enormously heavy traction engines would pull up onto the fairground.

At that time the fair ground was used for most of the year as allotments, the holders of which knew well in advance they would have to clear out their crops before the fair arrived. Each year they were given a month's notice to be off their allotment by the week before the fair. That was when the steam rollers would be sent in to flatten the site.

Potatoes were one of the more popular crops that they grew and these had to be cleared from the ground before they were 'mashed in situ'. In a wet season, a not unusual occurrence around fair time, the crops would be left until the last minute. It was therefore not unusual to see the allotment holders digging frantically as midnight approached Once the steam rollers moved in, they would get down to business with no further delay.

The annual trade in human labour at Bridgwater Fair

That is, of course, unless it was one of those really wet years when, on more than one occasion, a traction engine became irretrievably bogged down in the mud. In such cases no amount of assistance from other engines would shift it and the only thing to do was to wait for drier weather.

Amusements and cheapjacks

Many of the original funfair attractions have left the scene. The steam operated fairground organs are now museum pieces. The circus comes in its own right on a different occasion. The cheapjacks are no longer allowed to trade. These perhaps are not missed other than by the fools who fell for their trickery. Their usual modus operandi was to have a small collapsible table from which they would sell perhaps boxes of matches. They could convince anybody that the box they were about to buy contained some valuable item such as a gold watch or a pound note. Needless to say those who paid the inflated price ended up with just a box of matches. If the law arrived, then the table disappeared along with the cheapjack.

I remember much of the old fashioned entertainment that existed at the funfair when I was a child. Apart from the obvious rides and side shows, the gypsies were also an attraction. There used to be a beer tent run by Mr. Cavill from the Hope Inn. It was on the fairground, not far from the Horse and Jockey, an attraction to those buying and selling at the fair. My perception as a child was that the young gypsy men could be guaranteed to have a fight once they had taken their fill at the two licensed premises.

These fights were fascinating to watch because of the ritual to which the combatants adhered. First the argument would begin. It didn't matter what the subject was, any reason would do to justify the fight that was to come. Then a circle of gypsy families would form penning in the two adversaries and at the same time keeping out the Gorgios, the gypsy name for non-gypsies.

Within the confines of the circle, the disrobing process would start. Jackets off, very formally, sleeves rolled up, very carefully and tidily, braces taken off the shoulders and left to drape around the buttocks. Then as if by an unsounded signal, the fight would begin. No dirty stuff here, just unadulterated bare knuckle fighting within the circle. The fights were fast and furious and over in a matter of seconds. They were very private affairs albeit conducted in public. There was never any danger of the fracas spreading. The gypsies took care of their own and had their own code of behaviour within which the fights took place.

Then there were the striptease tents and boxing booths. The latter took with them their regular boxers who would challenge any local from the crowd. They always found a volunteer, much to the pleasure of the crowd who would then go in to see how the local lad faired against the hardened 'pro'. The result didn't really matter if the truth was known. Most of the time, unknown to the audience, the so called local lad was actually one of the travelling band of pugilists.

This wasn't the only con that was going on. My father worked on the fairgrounds for many years and in my childhood he would take me to the fair and fix me up with work on one or more of the small stalls. The hoopla was one example. My role here was to reach over the stall when the owner's back was turned and slip the hoop over the prize. The hoop was a 'just fit'. It was almost impossible to do legitimately but by reaching over it could be done. I would then jump and shout with joy, loudly declaring I'd won a prize. The stall owner, grinning from ear to ear and sharing my pleasure would willingly pass me my prize. Off I'd go, delighted with my reward. he also would be delighted with the crowd that this attracted to his stall only too willing to part with their money. Once they'd spent and passed on, I'd return my winnings and repeat the process. This pastime would benefit me by two shillings and sixpence for a two hour session. Not bad for a lad still at junior school.

Apart from the fairground itself, West Street also had a busy time. The numerous drinking houses did a great trade and entered into the atmosphere by bedecking the fronts of their premises with bunting and streamers. Circuses and travelling theatres added to the attraction and there would be a number of these present each year.

Development of the wool trade

Bridgwater's trade developed in the 1300's with the expansion of the wool industry and remained a significant part of local exports until the 16th century. Edward lll recognised that much English wool was being exported and then processed abroad.

The expertise in wool processing and dying was stronger on the continent than at home. He recognised that the nation would benefit if the extra value was added in England. Towards that end, he bought in the skills from the continent. Many of these foreigners, mostly Flemings around 1330, settled in Somerset which consequently developed into a stronghold for quality woollen products. Bridgwater became famous for its woollen serge, the quality of which would match any in the world. There was also a coarse woollen Bridgwater cloth called Ratteens.

Taunton and Dunster were the other two centres of excellence. The quality of Somerset woollen products was such that inevitably imitations began to appear. They lacked the quality of the original and were sold rolled up to avoid detection. It became necessary for legislation to be introduced forbidding the sale of Somerset named products in the rolled up form. They were only to be sold open in order that the superior quality could be witnessed. Records show

that in 1388 at least three drapers from Taunton were selling rolled cloth illegally at Bridgwater Market.

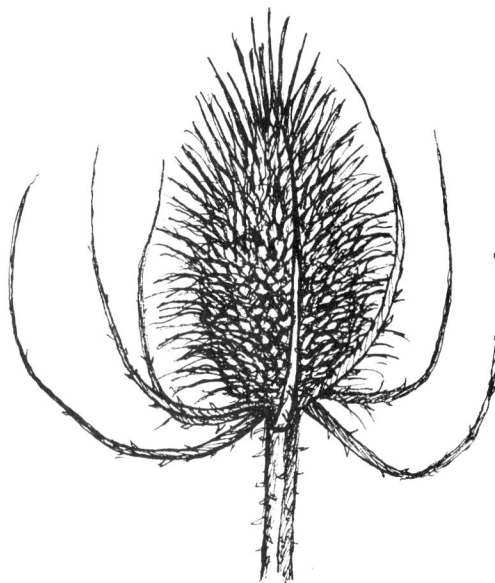

One spin off of the woollen fabric trade was the small industry of teasel growing . This practice continued right into the first part of the twentieth century. The teasels were grown for finishing the fabric and were popular outside of the Somerset area particularly in areas such as Lancashire and Yorkshire. The hooked prickles of the flower heads were used to raise the nap on cloth. Isle Abbots and Isle Brewers (named after Bridgwater's William Briwer) were other favourite spots for this crop.

There was little money to be made for most of the workers in the wool and cloth trade, although the clothiers themselves made a very profitable living. It was the wealth that they developed which left Somerset with such a legacy of fine churches, as good as any county in the nation.

The mass of workers unfortunately did not share the benefits. Many of them worked independently in their own cottages. Although they were in theory their own masters, the hours were long and hard if a reasonable living was to be made.

The supply chain worked like this. The shepherds sold their wool to the clothiers. They took it to the cottagers who cleaned, combed and spun their supply. From there it went to the fuller whose job it was to remove any natural resin in the wool and shrink it. Then after dying, off to the weavers it went, still under the control of the clothier.

Within the confines of the castle, various trades were practised within the woollen based economy. There was a fulling mill (where cloth was cleansed and beaten to make it thicker), tuckers, dyers and card makers. All of these skills were also practised outside of the castle where there were at least 30 others involved in these trades and included goldsmiths and mercers, traders in cloth.

When these various roles are considered along with the extent of the woollen trade in Somerset in those earlier centuries, we can start to understand why there are still so many Somerset families whose names reflect their origins. Weaver, Dyer, Mercer, Tucker and the less obvious Fuller all have their beginnings in this aspect of local industry.

It was the volume of trade in cloths and wool which led to the construction of the Langport Slipway (between the town bridge and the library) in 1488. The trade declined steadily through the 16th century and inevitably the industrial revolution in the Midlands and the North took its toll. By 1800 the woollen industry in the local area had died out.

Leland's visit

Leland was an employee of the King who travelled the country documenting his opinion of various town around the country and, fortunately for us in 1538 he visited Bridgwater and gave us a very detailed description of how the town appeared.

Leland's report on Bridgwater in 1538

The way or I came into Bridgwater was causid with stone more than half a mile. Entering into Bridgwater I passed by a chapel of St. Salvior standing on the ripe of the haven. Then I entered into a suburb and so over a bridge under which runneth a brook that risith a 4 miles of by West at Bromefelde. The south gate of the town joineth hard onto this bridge.

The town of Bridgwater is not walled nor hath been by any likelihood that I saw. Yet there be four gates in the town named as they be set. The walls of the stonehouses of the town be instead of the town walls. I rode from the south gate in a pretty street a while and then I turned east and came to the market place. The farrest street and principal show of the town is from westgate to eastgate. That part of the town that standeth on the west side of the bridge and haven is three times as big as that that standeth on the east side. The castle sometime a right fair and strong piece of work but now all going to mere ruin standeth hard beneath the bridge of the west side of the haven.

In the Est part of the town is onely the House, late College of St. John, a thing notable, and this house standeth partly without the est gate. This college had prestes that had the apparell of secular prestes, with a cross on the breste, and to this house adjoined an Hospice for poor folks".

The troubled days of the Seventeenth Century

Of Blake, Monmouth, the Gunpowder Plot and the siege of Bridgwater Castle

The seventeenth century was probably the most violent and restless period in the nation's history. It was time of persecution, hatred and fear, full of superstition, intrigue and deceit. Bridgwater was as involved as any other town in the country.

In 1605 we had the Gunpowder Plot from which our carnival originates. Then the Civil War of 1645 in which Blake played such a prominent role and during which Bridgwater's castle fell to Cromwell's forces. The West Country featured strongly in the Civil War, indeed the first battle of the war was at Marshall's Elm and the last at Langport. And last but not least we had the Monmouth Rebellion and the 1685 Battle of Sedgemoor.

For the most part, Blake's battles and the Duke of Monmouth's story took place well away from Bridgwater, yet these two individuals had such an impact on the town and are so closely identified with it that they deserve sections of their own which appear later in this book. In the same way, the Gunpowder Plot from which our carnival originates, was an important seventeenth century national issue, yet the carnival itself is more of a twentieth century phenomenon and thus belongs in a later section. The siege and destruction of Bridgwater Castle likewise justify a chapter of their own. For the time being we will confine ourselves to other aspects of the 17th century.

A record in St. Mary's church register for 1683 gives a flavour of how politics and religion divided the community. The entry, presumably by the vicar, refers to the recently departed mayor in a very disrespectful way. *"Whoever judges this man a lover of the church or anything that relates to it knows not the man. This man afterward carry'd himself with that insolency and tyranny to all sorts of people that the inhabitants, whether churchmen, Presbyterian, or other, joyn'd together to ring out the belles for joy at his departure into Ireland, where he was preferred, and where it is thought he was poysonid.".* The mayor was clearly not a popular man and the vicar doesn't come across as too charitable either!

In another report of 1683, exactly two years before the Monmouth rebellion, Lord Stawell reported he had sent for the Mayor and searched various premises for arms. The Nonconformists were active and had become a target for the King's attention. Stawell found the *'Fanatic's house of worship, being round like a cockpit and able to hold four hundred'.* He arranged for the contents to be taken to the Cornhill to make a fourteen foot high bonfire with pulpit and cushions perched on top.

Somerset Trade Tokens

During the 17th century, as if the country didn't have troubles enough, trade became difficult because of a lack of suitable coinage. During Saxon times a penny weighed 24 grams, a penny weight. By the days of Queen Elizabeth 1, these had shrunk in size to the point where it was a job to spot them in the bottom of one's purse.

From early times coins had been made of silver but to compensate for inadequate suitable coinage, tradesmen and publicans introduced brass coinage of their own, trade tokens as they were known. These were also difficult to trade with and were only recognised by those who issued them and could only be exchanged for trade goods.

Although these tokens were officially outlawed, there was little that king or country could do to stop their usage. Queen Elizabeth introduced copper coins, predominantly farthings, which helped the situation but they were quite unpopular. These coins and the trade tokens coincided with the almost complete disappearance of gold and silver coins.

By 1649 tradesmen issued their own coins, a practice which lasted until 1672 when Charles II introduced a new range of coins and banned other forms to control the situation. During this period, local coins travelled no distance at all, little more than two or three streets.

Listed below are some of the Bridgwater examples of this period. Each item represents a trade token used as a coin. The individuals were named on their own tokens and many described the nature of the business in words or by design. Those marked with the asterisk (*) indicate where Bridgwater has been spelt with the extra 'E', an indication of the acceptability of either spelling at that time.

- Bridgwater farthing 1666. This had the town coat of arms on one side with a five arched bridge and the castle. Variations on this had flags on the towers and six arches.

- * Alexander Atkins 1654.

- John Bone 1656 depicting a hand held woolcomb

- * John Crapp 1659 & 1670.

- Edward Dawes Brasier 1657

- Joseph Franklin 1666, depicting a wool comb, perhaps a fuller by trade.

- William Goodridge 1669 depicting a ship, perhaps a ship's chandler.

- Robert Haviland 1652 showing a merchant's mark.

- John Hunt 1651

- John Linton 1656-59. The Salters Arms, a public house.

- William Page 1669

- John Palmer 1664. The Drapers Arms.

- * Edward Pettitt 1654

- Christopher Roberts 1664, covered cup.

- John Rogers 1669. A sword standing erect between two wings with the town's high cross on the reverse side.

- James Safforde 1658

- * William Seally 1652 & 1654

- * William Serlland 1654

During the years 1787 - 1817 trade tokens made a return due to the scarcity of copper and the proliferation of forged coins. Bridgwater introduced its own halfpenny with the motto "For change not fraud". It had the town arms of castle and three arched bridge on one side with "Issued by Holloway and Son & Post Office" on the other. Around the edge were the words "On demand we pay 1/2d".

Another resurgence in the late nineteenth century saw a number of local houses producing tokens which were used mainly in the playing of pub games. Houses issuing these included the Alexandra Hotel in St. Mary's Street, the Bath Bridge Inn, Beaufort Arms, Bristol Arms Hotel in the High Street, the British Flag, Cross Rifles, Crown Inn, First and Last, the Devonshire Arms which used to be in Eastover, Hope Inn, Lions Club, Three Crown Inns and the White Hart Hotel. Many of these token lingered in use until the start of the second world war.

Smuggling and contraband

The general lawlessness of the seventeenth century and the problems with legitimate trade were reflected in the smuggling and contraband practices which were rife.

The War of Expansion in the nation had led to high excise duties in the wake of which came much smuggling.

Bridgwater, as a port, had responsibility for collecting duty on most types of imports for a considerable stretch of the Somerset coast, as far down even as Minehead. This meant that the duty collection officer had to travel quite far afield for those days. One local officer, Daniel Yates, complained on one occasion that the ship "Encrease" from Virginia on June 6, 1679 landed 60 hogsheads of tobacco before he was able to get there and claim the duty, which he did on the remaining 125 hogsheads.

This conjures up a picture of a customs man arriving an hour or so too late and therefore missing the opportunity. It appears he had no powers to penalise the ship's captain for landing the first 60 hogsheads. That was considered fair game. One can imagine ships unloading as fast as was humanly possible to beat the custom's man.

Another example around the same time tells how George Atwell, again a Bridgwater man, informing the collection officer that a wagon load of cloth, big enough to require twelve oxen and four horses to pull it, was being unloaded at Giles Russell's house without duty being paid. Again it was a case of what the eye doesn't see, the heart (or custom's man) won't grieve.

On one occasion, the government sent in two excise surveyors, William Culliford and Arnold Browne. They were sent to Bridgwater to establish the size of the problem. Those who they identified and interviewed as culprits admitted to 101 tuns of wine and brandy and 2357 packages of Irish linen in less than 3 years. The town was searched and contraband found all over the place. The report on the affair referred to the custom's collectors as drunken and dishonest and the surveyor as seldom or never sober!

The siege of Bridgwater Castle

The siege of Bridgwater Castle

Late in the spring of 1645, the Prince Rupert summoned a meeting of justices loyal to the crown at Bridgwater Castle. His purpose was to co-ordinate their activities and ensure there would be sufficient support for the Royalist cause in that part of the West Country. The inhabitants of the castle had shown a loyalty to the crown for generation after generation but it has to said that whilst those who controlled the castle were Royalists, the towns people themselves were divided in their loyalties and were for the most part supporters of the Parliamentarian cause.

In July of that same year, Parliamentary forces arrived in Somerset led by General Sir Thomas Fairfax, Lieutenant-General Cromwell and Major General Massey. The presence of these eminent leaders reflects the strategic importance of Bridgwater at this time.

Lord Goring took his Taunton based royalist forces to Langport in order to engage the Parliamentarian troops. His venture was unsuccessful and his troops being well beaten were forced to retreat to Bridgwater and the shelter of the castle. Fairfax's troops followed on but were first allowed two days rest just on the Bridgwater side of Westonzoyland, a short distance only from where the famous Battle of Sedgemoor was later to be fought.

Whilst here, under Holborne's leadership they captured Sydenham Manor, a Royalist occupied estate which still survives in the centre of the Courtauld's factory. Weldon meanwhile occupied Hamp and Parliamentarian ships in the channel intercepted Royalist ships carrying supplies to Colonel Wyndham, the Governor of Bridgwater Castle.

Lady Wyndham's pot shot

While the troops rested, Fairfax and Cromwell, on July 12th, went on a reconnaissance mission to Bridgwater Castle. As they surveyed the defences, the high-spirited and outspoken wife of Colonel Wyndham, the governor of the castle, stood on the ramparts where she bared her breast as an insult to Cromwell and fired a shot in Cromwell's direction. The shot felled an officer at his side.

Despite the endeavours of Mrs. Christabella Wyndham, Fairfax and Cromwell found the information they required and returned with sufficient knowledge of the layout of the castle and its surrounds to formulate a plan for its capture. The castle was well defended with 1800 troops and forty or more guns. It also had a massive moat which, unbeknown to them, was twenty five feet deep.

Cromwell and Fairfax moved their forces into positions around the castle with much help from the locals who had faired poorly under the castle management.

Cromwell's close encounter with the bore.

The course of English history could have taken a very different turn during these moves. The boat, which the two generals were using to cross the river near the village of Dunwear, was caught by the tidal bore that makes the River Parrett so treacherous as it sweeps its way rapidly up the river. Their small craft was almost overturned and its occupants just managed to safely maintain their positions.

An early but unsuccessful attempt was made to storm the castle by night. The attempt was abandoned when it was discovered that the surrounding moat was significantly deeper than originally envisaged.

The plan had been to make a large number of 'faggots' from sticks and branches. These would be dumped into the moat in sufficient numbers to allow the troops to walk across them safe from the moat if not the Royalists. The depth of the moat however was sufficient that the faggots made no impact.

Storming the castle

Several days later, on July 20th, it was decided to storm the castle. Cromwell's troops were positioned in St. Johns and Castle Fields where the storming party spent the evening parading around East Bower and Horsey.

Massey was to take the south side as a diversionary tactic. Lieutenant Colonel Hewson was to attack from the north east. Before getting to the castle, the parliamentarian forces first had to capture Eastover which was defended by a ditch and raised bank. At two in the morning, Eastover was stormed using floating bridges to cross the ditch along Castle Fields.

Captain Reynolds crossed the ditch at St. Johns and gained control of the east gate and Eastover, taking some 600 prisoners in the process. His troops fought all the way to the river pushing Sir John Stawell's royalists back across the bridge which was then barricaded and the drawbridge raised.

At the Cornhill and around St. Mary's Church, the Royalist were coming under fire from their own captured guns.

The town bridge became the next significant barrier. Fairfax decided to regroup his troops and give them a chance to recover ready for the next major assault. Parliament then attacked from all sides with heavy fire forcing the Royalists back within the town walls in the south and south west of the town.

The fighting was heavy and eventually the gates fell. One side of the castle was taken but not the innermost parts. Many of the royalist troops captured were easily persuaded to take a new oath and swear their allegiance to Parliament.

The razing of Eastover

Colonel Wyndham fought back bravely, firing into the Eastover area, much of which was soon aflame. All but three or four houses were razed to the ground.

The following day, Fairfax's troops prepared to storm the castle again but not before Fairfax had granted safe passage to the women and children within. They were given two hours notice to evacuate. Eight hundred were to take advantage of the offer including the intrepid Mrs. Wyndham, Lady Stawell (whose husband, the former Governor of Taunton Castle, was so active in the battle), Lady Hawley and Mrs. Warre.

Early the next day the attack recommenced and the besiegers redoubled the cannonade. Soon fires, many started by the townsfolk themselves, took a hold all over the town fanned by the high winds.

Wyndham saw defeat and destruction as inevitable and, perhaps somewhat optimistically, offered terms for surrender.

Wyndham conceded and sent Sir John Heale, Sir Hugh Wyndham, Mr. Waldron, Mr. Warr Major Sydenham and Mr. Speke as hostages.

By the evening of July 23rd it was all over. 1500 soldiers and 120 officers were taken prisoner. In addition at least two months supply of food and ammunition, 5,000 weapons, 36 cannon and £100,000 of various valuables were taken. These had been placed in the castle by the landed gentry for safe keeping. It had been inconceivable that the castle should be capable of being captured.

Fairfax's letter to Parliament

Five days later, at 8 p.m., Thomas Fairfax wrote the letter shown on the next page to William Lenthall, the Speaker of the House of Commons.

Bridgwater had been the last significant royalist stronghold in this part of the West Country. Any royalist supporters remaining in these parts were effectively isolated with no lines of communication to the rest of the country. The town itself had suffered badly. Eastover, in effect, had ceased to exist. Westover, the Cornhill and surrounding areas had suffered badly from the fires. Even the town bridge had been breached at its centre to permit the introduction of a drawbridge as part of the castle's defences.

Excavations in the Barclay Street area in 1877 involved the removal of a high mound of earth in which were found human bones, bullets, swords and various other weapons from the civil war.

The destruction of the castle

The year following the battle, Parliament agreed to the dismantling of the castle. Locals still insist that this was Cromwell's way of getting his own back at Mrs. Wyndham for the pot shot that so nearly changed the course of history.

And so in November 1646, a troop of horse came to the town to dismantle the castle according to the instructions of the 'county committee'. The locals joined in enthusiastically, wanting to go beyond just dismantling the castle and finishing off the surrounding defence works. This the troops would not allow and a battle broke out between them and the locals led by Henry Cheeke. The result was several killed, even more injured and the people and the parliament being polarised by the oppressive manner of the troops.

Mr. Speaker, I dispatched hence letters of yesterday to the counties of both kingdoms, which gave some account of God's blessing on our endeavours in the storming of Bridgwater. On Monday (July 21st) morning last, we gained that part of the town which lies this side of the river, and therein above six hundred prisoners, divers officers of quality, and two pieces of ordnance. The enemy fired that part of the town wherein we were; and the next day (July 22nd) burned down all the houses except two or three. Yesterday, perceiving an obstinate resolution in the enemy not to yield the town, I was forced to use those extremities for the reducing of it, which brought on a parley; and, in short, to yield the town upon no other terms than quarter. We entered the town this day (July 23rd), finding great store of arms and ammunition; thirty-eight pieces of ordnance; above a thousand prisoners, and among them divers persons of great quality, as you will perceive by the list inclosed. I have not much time to spend here, and therefore shall dispose the command of it for the present to Colonel Rich, as Governor, wherein I doubt not of your approbation; and I believe the Commissioners of the Army will offer something further concerning him, and for the future settlement of the place. He is a gentleman of known and integrity; and his regiment at present with Major-General Massey: and I will, I believe, with God's blessing, give you a good account of it. There was found in the town a commission from Prince Charles for . . . .Phillips, a gentleman of this county, to raise a regiment of Clubmen, which I send to you by Mr. Peters. I am very desirous to give some encouragement to the soldiers for their many services, and especially for the honest and sober demeanour towards the prisoners in the town, in repairing the violence and injury, which has somehow brought dishonour upon most of the armies in this kingdom; which gives encouragement to them in the like for the future. I make no doubt they will be well satisfied in what I shall do, and I assure you will be done with as little burden to the state as may be. I beseech to take into your consideration the necessities of the army, for a speedy supply of money, clothes, and other provisions; wherewith the bearer, Master Peters, will more particularly acquaint you more largely on all particulars of this late action, that I can now write. Your most obedient servant, Thomas Fairfax.

In George Parker's book 'The Ancient History of Bridgwater' published in 1877, he prints a poem in dialect which was written by a Westonzoyland labourer. It gives the labourer's account of the siege at Bridgwater and gives the impression that the author witnessed events at first hand as a reluctant Cromwellian conscript. Since the poem is in dialect, I reproduce it here. To help the reader who may struggle with the dialect, Weston was the name by which Westonzoyland was commonly known, 'zoger' is soldier

In Weston field I earn'd my bread
In sixteen forty five;
A very quiet life did lead,
Vor my family did strive.

And when I war at work one day
A turning up zome ground,
I heard a noise which made me start:
It waran an awful sound.

Aye, zich a crashing sound it war,
I never shall forget;
I dro'd away my spade, by gor,
And away then I did zet.

And as I cum'd nigh Oller drove
I zeed zome zogers run;
I clim'd a tree, and there above
Thought I shud zee some fun.

Oh, how the Red Coats tackled on,
And tothers atter hied;
They soon war cum, soon war gone;
It zeem'd war's opening tide.

A company at length appeared,
And stop'd the tothers' flight,
And then they turned, and then they cheered,
And vow'd that they would fight.

And twarden long they had to stay,
Vor General Cromwell cum,
And never war there such a day;
Twar cruel death to some.

Zome Zogers fall'd by musket shot,
Zome spiked wi a long spear,
And zome into the ditches got,
Where their heads did only peer.

I cling'd to middle of the tree -
The leaves war very thick -
And twar a lucky job vor me,
Vor I feel'd faint and sick.

To see the blood and hear the groans,
Twar savages outright;
Thick as hail the splinter bones;
It war an awful sight.

At last the Royalists gi'd in;
The prisoners vall'd down,
The rest retreated in a din
Towards Bridgwater town.

I climmered down from off the tree;
A voice said there's a chap;
Cromwell he catched a sight o' me,
And ordered me to stap.

Then down upon my knees I vall'd;
He said, "My man, stand op;
Twarden to kill thee that I called;"
My head spin'd like a top.

"Wut list?" zaid he. "I will," said I;
And list I did there right,
And made a vow till I did die
Vor Cromwell I wud fight.

I noed my life war at a stake,
My very brains did ring;
At that time vor my own self's sake
I'd a promised anything.

Vrom there we march'd to Weston Moor
And then the trumpet zound;
That night wi ly'd upon a floor,
And that war the bare ground.

I zend home to my family,
And told em twar my doom -
A general's servant I shud be,
Vor I war Cromwell's groom.

He zaid he'd make a man o' me,
Vor that he wud be bown;
War pleased, he said, to see the way
I rub'd the hosses down.

He war a fuss-rate man, I know,
Wud do what he did dare;
But as for they about em, tho',
Their ways I cud not bare.

They long'd, they said, to kill the King;
Twar that vor they war bent,
And then zome arguments would bring
About zome Parliament.

Now in my heart I loved the King;
His laws wud I obey,
And hated beyond anything
Such wicked men as they.

But I war in their clutches now,
And bown to act my part,
And tho' my mouth war forced to bow
It warden from my heart.

"Come, join in chorus," they did cry
When mornings they did sing;
Inward I vowed when I did die
Shud be to sarve my King.

We marched to Chedzoy; there we ly'd,
And noed not what to do;
To teake Bridgwater they had tried,
But Bridgwater men war true.

They war no traitors, no, not they,
And wud stan firm, they zaid;
We heard about em day be day,
Brave Wyndham was their head.

He had a wife war good and brave,
One day she fired a shot;
Vor Cromwell twar the closest shave
That ever he'd a got.

When Okey cum our force war strong;
Twar whispered then about
They'd seize Bridgwater afore long,
And set em to the rout.

Fairfax and Cromwell talk'd one night
Whilst I the hoss rubbed down;
They zaid the next day they'd go right
Into Bridgwater town.

That night no sleep I never found,
Altho' the moon did shine,
Vor living in Bridgwater town
War some old friends o' mine.

Jest avore day away I sot,
Before the cock did crow;
I thought thinks I, I'll blow their plot,
And let the townsmen know.

When at the gate they cried out, "stop!
Or else I'll make thee spin;"
I tould the zogers what war op,
And zoon they let me in.

Right glad war they to hear my tale;
Wi warmth my hands they shook,
And when they found the facts war real
To the Castle I war took.

I told em all, the drums did beat,
And they begun to arm;
The news it spread droo every street,
The town was in alarm.

Brave Wyndham talk'd em into tears
To do as they were bid,
"And now," said he, "dree hearty cheers!"
Dree hearty cheers they gid.

And soon the roaring guns we heard
Towards the eastern side;
The more they roared the more we cheered,
Our guns, too, they reply'd.

The tug of war it cannot last;
It cum wi awful might;
We know'd our fated die was cast,
Like dragons we did fight.

They ring'd the bells, burn'd houses down,
Like phrenzy volks they were;
File atter file marched droo the town
The dangers vor to share.

But when the wild dragoons cum op
Droo Eastover at last
I noed that Fate had filled the cup,
All hopes or chance was past.

At last I zeed how it wud be,
That they wud gain the day;
I took't a chance war offered me,
And scampered far away.

I never fear'd their hue and cry;
They sought for me in vain.
I lived to see old Cromwell die,
And good King Charlie reign.

With all their errors or mishaps
It always seemed to me
Bridgwater men were plucky chaps
As ever I did see.

Admiral Blake

Admiral Blake's childhood

Bridgwater's most famous son has to be Robert Blake, hero of the civil war and one of England's naval legends. He was born in Bridgwater in August 1598 in the house which is now home to Bridgwater's Blake Museum. His baptism was on September 27th in St. Mary's Church and the font used on that occasion survives even now. Blake was the eldest son of Humphrey Blake, a local merchant dealing mostly in overseas trade.

Robert Blake's mother, Sarah, gave birth to at least 13 children between 1598 and 1619, four of them dying in infancy. She must almost have given up hope of a daughter for it was not until 1616 that Bridget entered the world, all the other children being boys. Needless to say the house in Blake Street had servant quarters at the back. Not only was it necessary with so many children but Humphrey Blake senior was certainly sufficiently affluent to afford them.

Blake's home was virtually on the banks of the River Parrett. His father's involvement in trade meant that Robert Blake was inevitably to grow up close to the ocean going ships which came to the town and its dominant castle.

Bridgwater and the Spanish Armada

Indeed Bridgwater was steeped in the mariners way of life and had a close affinity with the sea. Was it not a Bridgwater seaman on board one of Humphrey Blake's vessels who first sighted the Spanish Armada? That must have been an awesome sight to witness the slow movement up the English Channel of two hundred and fifty ships carrying 30,000 soldiers and 125,000 cannon balls. Thanks to the Bridgwater mariner's observation, Sir John Popham was able to deliver the intelligence to Her Majesty's Secretary of State and the English fleet was made ready. And when battle took place, the Bridgwater bark 'William' with its crew of thirty under the command of Captain John Smyth was there to represent the town.

Bridgwater was well known for its sea faring men and their qualities at sea. Cabot on his voyages of discovery selected his crews from Bristol and Bridgwater men. Even Frobisher on his 1578 voyage to find the North West passage to Cathay took a Bridgwater vessel, The Emanuel, as part of his fleet of 15 ships.

Quantock connections

The Blake family in general were certainly well established amongst the better off in the town. They originally came to the town from the Quantocks where Robert Blake's great grandfather Humphrey had property at Over Stowey and his uncle likewise at Tuxwell. His mother had inherited land almost next door at Plainsfield. The Blake family tomb can still be found amongst the Quantock churches including Humphrey's at Aisholt. It was Blake's grandfather, also called Robert, who had left Plainsfield to start an import-export business in Bridgwater. By 1580 he had four ships trading abroad.

No doubt Robert Blake would have spent much of his early years with his relations on the hills and equally much of it would have been close to the ships and the river. Whether or not his later involvement with the sea dates back to those childhood days is debatable. Perhaps it was the moors which most influenced him.

Blake was educated at King James Grammar School until the age of 16 when he went to St. Albans' Hall, and then Wadham College at Oxford where he gained several honours. Appropriately Wadham College had another connection with the county, its founder was a Somerset man who started the establishment only six years before Blake's arrival. We know that whilst there he had a great love of fishing and wild-fowling, suggesting perhaps a greater interest in the moors and wetlands whilst at home than the hills and the river. Those close to him also knew of his quiet anti-Royalist feelings even before national feelings had begun to stir.

Blake goes into business

After nine years at Oxford, Blake returned to Bridgwater where his father, now close to financial ruin following the Spanish Wars, was dying. He passed away the following year and Blake assumed his new role as head of the family.

After selling part of the estate, there was still sufficient to keep the rest of the family and to pay for a reasonable education for his younger brothers and sister. During the years that followed, Blake had to abandon his literary learnings but developed in its place a love of politics and public affairs. It was an unhealthy business that Blake inherited. The war with Spain, and in the following year another with France, had depleted overseas trade to the point where there were few ocean going ships to be seen in Bridgwater.

Blake disappeared from the town from about 1629 to 1638. The most likely theory is that he went into trade working closely with his brother George and sister Bridget who had both moved to Plymouth from where George ran his own import-export business. It appears that during this time he spent several years in Holland. His return to Bridgwater coincided with his mother's death in 1638.

A reconstruction of the original appearance of Blake's house. Courtesy Chris Sidaway

Entry into the Civil War.

The country as a whole was divided between those who supported the catholic king and those who supported the more puritan parliament. Those who failed to practice their religion the catholic way were hounded by those who did. Many Protestants were punished for their convictions, amongst them Humphrey Blake, the brother of Robert. His persecution for his religious ways was sufficient for him to emigrate to America. There he settled in Carolina, his son Joseph becoming Lord-Proprietor in that state, following in the family's footsteps where commerce and politics were concerned. Amongst Humphrey Blake's 'crimes' was his failure to report to the authorities that John Devenish, who had been the vicar of St. Mary's for almost thirty years, had been preaching on weekdays and holding bible lessons in his home. Robert Blake was thus bound by his personal experiences to have strong anti-Royalist feelings.

Blake enters Parliament

Against this background, he stood for parliament in 1640 and was returned on his first attempt. The number of burgesses at this time, being those entitled to vote, was a mere twenty four. His career in the house, however, was short lived.

One of the shortest sittings ever was terminated by an irate King Charles who was not getting the financial contributions he demanded from his government. It was a long enough experience for him to develop a friendship with the likes of Cromwell and others in the Reform Party.

Blake returned to Bridgwater and at the next election was defeated by Colonel Wyndham, the governor of the castle and a staunch Royalist. There was clearly a score to be settled but that would come later. Wyndham, in the meantime, was to lose his parliamentary seat. A government enquiry found him to

have been associated with a monopoly involved in the manufacture and supply of soap.

Blake set about organising and training troops for the Parliamentarian cause. His first military successes against the Royalists were to come at Bodmin, Lansdowne near Bath and at the siege of Bristol, successes which resulted in him gaining the rank of Lieutenant-Colonel.

The Battle for Bristol

The siege at Bristol was a significant event in the Civil War. Colonel Popham had taken Bristol for Parliament with the help of some 500 Somerset militia. Blake was certainly involved in the action. Meanwhile the Cornish Royalists had taken Taunton, Dunster and Bridgwater. The Parliamentarian forces at this time were too preoccupied with holding Bristol to be able to help out the Somerset towns.

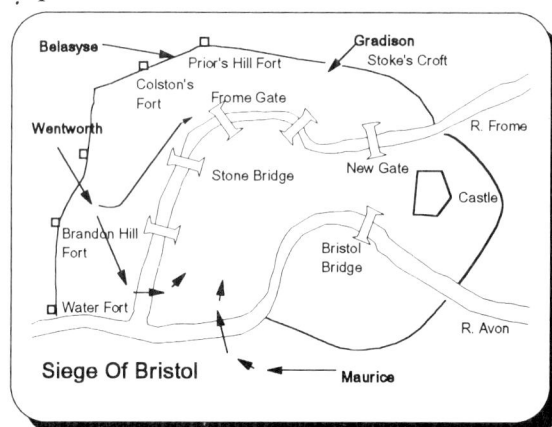

Siege Of Bristol

Blake's role at Bristol was to hold Prior's Hill Fort, one of the defensive positions that surrounded Bristol Castle. It was in fact the most exposed and vulnerable point. The area being defended lay in a stretch of land between the Rivers Frome and Avon, cleft in the join of the two. There were three defensive fronts, the River Frome with its wide defensive wall, the River Avon and on the landward side, Bristol Castle.

Thus it was that on July 26th, 1643 Blake was in the thick of it defending his outpost near Bristol Castle. The Royalist forces attacked on a number of fronts with varying success. An attempt to break through the defences near Blake's position was thwarted when the Royalists, having successfully taken a defensive ditch, realised that they had left their scaling ladders behind. The momentum was lost and Blake was able to counter attack with his troops outside of their defensive position, successfully holding the fort.

Meanwhile to the south and out of Blake's view the Royalists were fairing much better. They successfully breached the defences and were able to get through the inner walls forcing the surrender of the castle and the Parliamentarian forces. Blake however, along with Captain Husbands who was defending the Brandon Hill Fort, was unaware of the surrender until informed by the Royalist forces. At first he was reluctant to accept the news, there being no obvious signs of a Royalist success and no obvious damage to the defences. Bristol had taken only four days to fall but through no fault nor lack of effort on the part of Blake.

The siege of Lyme.

Blake somehow returned to the Parliamentary forces and with his troops increased to 1500, the time seemed right to return to Bridgwater and settle the old score with Colonel Wyndham. The castle governor was ready for the expected attack and thus Blake moved on to Lyme Regis in April 1644 where he was more successful defending it against the troops of Prince Rupert.

Blake along with two other colonels, Thomas Ceely the local mayor and John Were, found himself defending the small town of Lyme. It was an almost impossible place to defend but at least they had 1,000 troops to fulfil the task. These troops had been harassing nearby Royalist towns, burning where appropriate and depriving of stores and victuals where ever possible. The Royalists had to react and Prince Maurice, Rupert's brother duly arrived with 6,000 men with which to take Lyme and put paid to this Parliamentarian stronghold.

The 1,000 men defending Lyme was increased to 1,500. This was a massive number compared with the 1,800 who had defended Bristol, a much larger proposition. But it in no way matched the 6,000 who waited outside for the assault. There is a story that at this time Blake, the "Bridgwater Bruiser", made an offer to Prince Maurice to settle the matter in hand the gentleman's way. "You send out twelve of your best men and I'll send twelve of mine!"

When the battle for Lyme started, the Royalists failed singularly in their attempts to breach the defences. The people of Lyme had a determination about them due in part no doubt to Blake's leadership. Whilst the two other colonels outranked him, it was Blake's influence which was strongest and Blake's name with which the victory at Lyme is associated. He had a religious passion and conviction which was infectious. Those serving with him had no doubt of what they had to do and the just cause they served. They were also well provisioned with supplies coming in by sea where the Parliamentary army had control.

Those outside the town serving the Royalist princes were less committed. The Cornishmen would sooner have been home

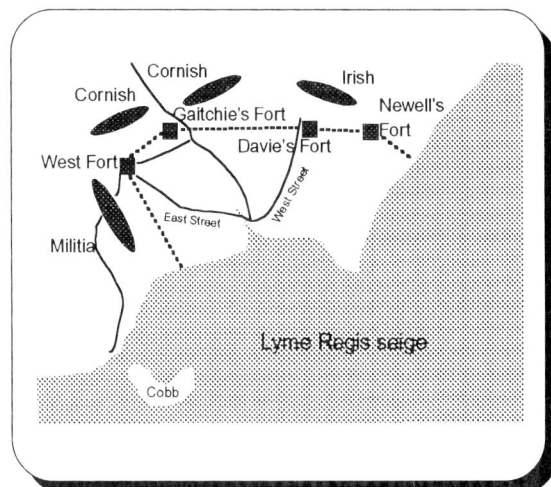

Lyme Regis seige

knowing that a threat existed to their own county from Plymouth. The Irish contingent had come to fight Catholics not Protestants. There was a marked difference in attitudes which must have told at the end of the day.

The siege lasted a week before the Royalist attempted an unsuccessful all out assault. Then after a week's respite, they attacked again in numbers, this time taking the defenders by surprise. Hundreds breached the defensive wall before the garrison rallied to regain their defensive positions on the outer wall. Hundreds of Royalist were cut off inside the town at the end of fierce and bloody battle. Blake held on.

The Cobb bombarded

After some weeks the Royalist forces realised that the key to taking Lyme was in gaining control of the Cobb, the harbour which had proved so important to Blake in ensuring a continuous supply of food and munitions for the garrison. Gun positions were set up and the Cobb bombarded. Virtually all the vessels along the quayside were destroyed. The Royalists realising the partial success of this manoeuvre, repositioned their guns to more effective use. Both Blake and Were received wounds but not sufficient to keep Blake from his duties.

An attempt to draw Royalist forces away from the town proved unsuccessful. The plan was to convince the Royalists that several hundred men from the garrison were being taken down along the coast to Charmouth from whence an attack on the Royalists would be made. The Royalists seeing what was happening would take a number of their troops away from the siege to thwart the venture. The defenders in the garrison could then sally forth and attack the Royalist positions knowing their numbers were reduced. However the Royalists failed to rise to the bait and they in turn took advantage of the depleted numbers in the garrison to trigger their next offensive. An eight hour

battle ensued with heavy loss of life but with Lyme still holding its own. Supplies continued to come in by sea under cover of darkness.

It was not until June 15 that Prince Maurice finally withdrew his troops on hearing the news that Parliamentary forces were on their way under the command of Colonel Essex.

Siege of Taunton

The next highlight in Blake's career came in capturing Taunton from the Royalist and then successfully holding it against three consecutive sieges. Colonel Wyndham was once again his adversary .

In July 1644 Taunton was given up rather too easily by the Royalists under the command of Colonel Reave. Having heard of the advancing Parliamentarian troops, he negotiated a rapid surrender permitting his troops to withdraw to Bridgwater Castle. His surrender came so readily that he was later tried and executed for cowardice.

Whilst this was going on, Blake was scouring Somerset for further volunteers. Essex had actually come to the West Country for the same purpose but had no ability at all to rally recruits to the cause. Apart from being an outsider, he lacked Blake's skills of leadership. Thus it was Blake who acted as recruiting officer. Having increased the numbers around him, he was obliged to release them to Essex who left Blake in the position of governor of Taunton Castle, its previous inhabitants now being safe within the walls of Bridgwater Castle.

The war elsewhere in the country was going well for the Royalists. Gains were made in Cornwall and the Midlands. Somerset remained a problem for the king with Blake holding Taunton, a key position in the county. Colonel Wyndham at Bridgwater Castle was ordered to take 3,000 troops and recapture Taunton Castle. Blake was there with only about 1,000 men but it was a very defensible position and numbers weren't everything as the experience at Lyme had already shown. The weeks went by with Wyndham's men besieging the castle and Blake taking every opportunity to sally forth and harass the Royalist encampment as best he could.

Whilst Taunton as a site may have had only limited strategic importance, Blake recognised the value of it being held for Parliament. As long as he could hold out, his presence there was tying up at least three times as many Royalist troops. His determination was absolute. As food supplies in the town diminished so the skirmishes around the town reduced. The Royalists attacked twice unsuccessfully but on the third attempt gained sufficient ground to push Blake back into the confines of the castle. Wyndham demanded the total surrender of Blake's forces promising no mercy if his demands were not accepted.

Blake was unmoved and told Wyndham to do his worst. The siege continued for some weeks until fresh Parliamentary forces arrived causing Wyndham to withdraw to the relative safety of Bridgwater Castle. Blake maintained control of Taunton and used its central position as a base from which to skirmish and hassle the king's cavaliers.

In April, 1645 Sir John Berkeley led a disastrous attempt, suffering heavy losses, to take Taunton where Blake had spent much of the winter reinforcing its defences ready for just such an event. Berkeley's only solution was to keep the town under siege. Meanwhile the Parliamentarian forces had been reorganised into the New Model Army, a far more effective fighting force than had previously been available, due mainly to the changes in leadership. One result of this was the new force commanded by Fairfax which had set out to relieve Taunton.

Blake's stand had served as a beacon to the cause whilst the Parliamentary forces reorganised. It was important now that Taunton should not fall to the Royalists. The damage to morale could have proven irreversible. Taunton became a focal point of Parliamentary attention.

The Royalists, realising their time was running out, put in another concerted effort. Early in May, they bombarded Blake's defences for four days gradually taking Taunton street by street until Blake and his troops were forced back into an area immediately around the castle. The Royalist commander, Hopton, demanded Blake's surrender which in true Blake style was turned down.

Food and munitions for Blake's troops were in desperately short supply but Blake commented that whilst he still had four pairs of boots, he still had three square meals. His ability once again to maintain the morale of his men had meant Taunton was held against the odds until a Parliamentarian force under Fairfax arrived to relieve the besieged town. The Royalists once more retreated to the safety of Bridgwater Castle.

The fall of Bridgwater Castle

It was at this time that Bridgwater Castle was besieged and taken by Cromwell's forces. Blake had no involvement in these activities in his home town, the details of which have been covered in greater detail in an earlier section.

The siege of Dunster Castle

In the October, after the fall of Bridgwater, Fairfax ordered Colonel Blake and Colonel Sydenham to besiege Dunster Castle, still held by the Royalists. It was in fact held by Colonel Francis Wyndham, the brother of the former governor of Bridgwater Castle.

Francis Wyndham was a different kettle of fish. He had more resolve and ability than his brother. Dunster was not going to fall too readily. It had been well provisioned, had its own supply of water and was a well fortified position on a difficult to attack steep sided hill. Blake had only 600 troops at his disposal. Battles going on elsewhere in the West Country left Blake with no hope of support should he himself come under attack which inevitably happened. The Royalist Colonel Finch with a force of 1,800 relieved the siege of Dunster without too much difficulty. No one could accuse Blake of cowardice, his previous encounters with the Royalists had proven his mettle, but the sheer difference in numbers made it prudent to withdraw .

The following weeks saw the Royalists capitulating throughout the West Country as town after town fell to the Parliamentarian forces. Blake was ordered to Barnstaple where Sir Hardress Waller was besieging the castle. Waller was to go to Exeter leaving the job to Blake. Once those in the castle realised that it was Blake himself who had come to finish the job, it appears they decided it was time to give up.

This left Blake free to return to Dunster and this time Dunster Castle fell just as easily as Barnstaple. The Royalist forces had capitulated completely in the West but the news had not got through to the isolated Dunster Castle. The Parliamentarian forces besieging the castle passed the news on but those defending the castle were reluctant to accept its truth. Eventually Blake arrived with confirmation and the Royalists, trusting his integrity completely, surrendered the castle.

Blake returned to Bridgwater to become, somewhat reluctantly I suspect, its M.P.

Blake, General-At-Sea joins the Irish campaign

In 1648 there was a second but smaller civil war. It was much shorter and far less significant than the first. During it, however, the navy became split with at least eleven ships being part of a Royalist mutiny. The Earl of Warwick, who was the Lord High Admiral, had the task of regaining control of the fleet. The eleven had sought refuge in a Dutch harbour making it diplomatically difficult for open action. Warwick regained some of the deserted fleet but had to abandon the rest. Many construed his actions as an indication of lack of commitment to the Parliamentary cause and a sign of weakness. It was decided to reorganise the navy and Warwick was not to be part of its future.

The committee controlling military affairs were nervous of appointing a single person to control the navy. What if he proved unfaithful? They were also unable to convince themselves that there was anyone capable enough in the navy in whom they could put their trust. They therefore appointed three army men of proven loyalty and ability as Generals-At-Sea, Richard Deane, Edward Popham and Robert Blake. All three were West Country men and had all fought together in 1645.

Richard Deane was a Plymouth timber trader and must have had dealings with Robert Blake and his brother George before the war. Popham too was an old friend of Robert Blake. The fact that all three were so close was probably no coincidence.

The navy reorganises

One of the first changes introduced by the three Generals was that they were given the power to promote the men within their own ranks. Previous practice meant that most appointments were politically founded rather than based on merit. The new practice was important in renewing confidence and morale in the wake of the mutiny. The ships that survived the mutiny were of course still based over in Holland under the command of Prince Rupert. These ships and privateers of various nationalities were playing havoc with English merchant shipping in the Channel. This gave the reorganised navy its first task to perform.

Thus it was with a somewhat depleted and ill prepared navy that the three set about the task. It was decided that Popham, the most experienced of the three, would take part of the fleet and head to sea with the purpose of minimising the damage at the hands of Prince Rupert. Blake and Deane stayed behind in order to prepare the rest of the fleet in the shortest possible time scale. This was no mean feat. Those responsible for provisions and repairs needed the likes of the commercially minded Blake to ensure there was no undue delay. And so with Blake's usual commitment and drive, the fleet was made ready and set sail to join Popham.

The siege of Kinsale.

The opinion was that Prince Rupert was now probably sheltering in Kinsale harbour in County Cork. It was Parliaments intention to invade Ireland at about this time and Prince Rupert's presence there was most undesirable. When the three generals arrived at Kinsale, sure enough the mast of Prince Rupert's fleet were clearly visible and included the largest three of his ships. It was decided that Blake would remain and blockade the harbour. Prince Rupert was not to be allowed out and interfere with the plans for a land invasion.

Deane, meanwhile, was to return to Plymouth and make ready for the transportation of the land forces while Popham was to continue on to London and organise things from there.

Blake's first problem came with a violent storm which left him no alternative but to seek shelter at Milford Haven. It must have been a most unpleasant duty being tossed around at sea for weeks on end whilst blockading a harbour and with no opportunity to land. The chance to shelter at Milford Haven and later at Lundy was a welcome respite. Not so for Blake however, whose only concern was that in his absence Prince Rupert may flee from Kinsale harbour and sail away unobserved. To his relief on returning to Kinsale, the same storm that had given Blake such problems had also kept Prince Rupert tied down.

Months were spent off Kinsale with only occasional opportunities to take ships as prizes. Meanwhile the plans to invade Ireland had taken a different course. All action was to the north and east, Blake had no involvement.

Cromwell realised he was not making the best use of Blake's skills and knew that he must be frustrated in his now less than demanding role. He sent a letter to Blake offering him the elevated position of Major-General of Foot, a position which Blake turned down saying he would retire rather than accept the position. Blake's commitment now was visibly and unquestionably to the navy. This was a tremendous boost to those who served under him and who now saw in Blake the first man in their experience who was totally committed to them and their welfare.

The months went by and Blake continued the blockade of Kinsale. Cromwell's troops were progressing deeper into the south of Ireland. By the time he had taken Wexford, it was clear that Rupert would soon have to surrender or make a break for it. Once more the wrath of the Irish Sea forced Blake to shelter at Milford Haven. Unfortunately for Blake, this time Prince Rupert seized his opportunity to escape and in October 1649 he made for Portugal to organise the Royalist cause. To Blake's delight he was awarded the task of tracking down Prince Rupert and neutralising his impact on the Commonwealth.

Blake in Portugal

Blake followed Prince Rupert's fleet and found them in the safety of Lisbon harbour. Blake's approach was met by cannon fire from the fortifications around the harbour. His only recourse was a tactical withdrawal and he sought permission from the King of Portugal to use a bay not too far from Lisbon for shelter and fresh water. This was granted but only on the condition that Blake was not to abuse the hospitality; any hostilities had to take place outside of Portuguese waters.

All Blake could do was to sit and wait for Prince Rupert to make a move. Meanwhile he sought advice from Parliament. Whilst he awaited his reply, relationships with Portugal deteriorated and Blake was obliged to put to sea from where he sank or captured any vessel he considered may have been able to help the cause of Prince Rupert.

Blake's request for advice was answered by Parliament sending a fleet with Popham to assist Blake with the clear instructions to sink Prince Rupert's fleet wherever they may be and no matter what the consequences were in terms of offending the Portuguese.

Months passed with little activity on either side. Supplies for those at sea were running short. A large part of the fleet was despatched to Cadiz for fresh supplies. With a diminished fleet waiting at the mouth of the Tagus, Prince Rupert finally made a run for it. His ships numbered some forty five, Blake's were reduced to just nineteen. Despite the imbalance of numbers, Blake's tactics and greater commitment resulted in the breakout attempt being unsuccessful and Prince Rupert's ships being forced into the Tagus.

Weeks later, with the state of provisions being even worse and Parliament complaining about the high cost of keeping such a force off Portugal, the largest part of the fleet sailed for England leaving Blake with just three ships to keep up the blockade.

Prince Rupert made another attempt with the help of a fog to provide cover. Blake's vigilance once more proved the better of Prince Rupert. Blake's lead ship fired at Rupert's flag ship, breaking its mast forcing the Royalist fleet to retreat once more.

Meanwhile a Portuguese merchant fleet had returned from Brazil giving Blake the opportunity to raise some cash by its capture. Seven ships of the Brazil fleet were taken by Blake. The battle to gain control took well over three hours of hard fought battle. Not only was Robert Blake in the thick of it, but his brother Benjamin was also in control of one of the English ships. Benjamin had played his role in the Civil War in the Parliamentary Army. It is not known when he changed his allegiance and joined the navy, but no doubt it was his brother Robert who was part of the attraction. Another of Blake's brother had played a role in the Civil War;

Admiral Robert Blake

Samuel was killed in a skirmish at Combwich and was buried at Pawlett church.

The attack on the Brazil fleet left no opportunity for Blake to negotiate with the Portuguese. There was no way now that the Portuguese would insist on Prince Rupert leaving the River Tagus. Blake split his ships into three groups. Some went back to England to be replenished for further duty, a limited number were left to keep an eye on Prince Rupert and Blake took the rest to track down French ships which had been creating problems for British shipping. Blake soon located one of the French frigates which readily surrendered more to Blake's reputation than to any actual overpowering. Indeed the French frigate outgunned the English vessel by 40 guns to 32.

Prince Rupert's escape

Blake returned to Cadiz to hear the news that Prince Rupert had escaped and was now believed to be somewhere in the Mediterranean. He set out on the trail capturing any French vessels he could on the way. From one of these he learned that the Royalist ships were somewhere off the Spanish coast. Blake's ships captured one and forced another to beach itself before the remaining four reached the Spanish harbour at Carthagena.

His approach to the port was met with cannon fire. Both Blake and the local governor wrote to the King of Spain for instructions. It was known that the King felt it necessary to consolidate good relationships with the Commonwealth government. The Royalist captains decided their best chance was to make a dash for it under cover of darkness. And so three nights later they made their attempt to steal past Blake. The venture was a complete disaster, all four ships were wrecked on the rocks around the harbour without a shot being fired. To Blake's disappointment neither Prince Rupert nor two of his best ships were amongst them.

Information from those taken prisoner suggested Rupert was now down in the Canaries. He did in fact make it to the West Indies and a few years later sold off the remaining ships.

The Royalist fleet was effectively destroyed but more importantly, Blake had established in the minds of the Mediterranean nations that the new Parliamentary government was a force to be reckoned with and its navy was best treated with the greatest of respect. After almost a year at sea, Blake returned to England with the only threat to English shipping now coming from privateers. The closest of these were the Royalists based in the Scillies and the Channel Islands.

Blake at the Scillies

After a short rest in Somerset, Blake received orders to go to Plymouth from where he was to take a number of ships to the Scillies. The islands were under the control of a Royalist governor, Sir John Grenville. He had set up a number of Royalist privateers who were capturing large numbers of Dutch merchant shipping plus the odd Parliamentarian vessel. The problem for the Dutch was such that they sent a small flotilla under the command of Lieutenant Admiral Tromp. This Dutch presence posed a threat to Parliament and it was Blake's role to put an end to the privateers activities.

When Blake arrived in the Scillies, Tromp was already there but showing no signs of action. Grenville was on the island of St. Mary's which was well defended and would prove difficult to take.

Blake's decision was initially to ignore the main island and take the two lesser ones of Tresco and Bryher. This would give him effective control of the whole area including the approaches to St. Mary's. Tresco had two harbours, one well defended, the other not so.

An early morning assault by the army was put into effect under a cover of sea mist, the plan being to take the smaller harbour on Tresco. Unfortunately the army were no seamen and half the force managed to land on the wrong island whilst the rest bounced around until sea sickness rendered them useless. The following morning Blake sent in a force of seamen who could fight just as well as any soldier and after fierce fighting the island was taken.

Blake then offered Grenville surrender terms that he really could not refuse. Despite that it took a full month to agree. Safe passage was guaranteed for all plus payment for their losses and thus the Scillies came under Parliamentary control. The Dutch ships returned to Holland knowing that one thorn in their side had been removed.

Blake returned to England where Cromwell declared he was needed with the army to help put down a rebellion in Scotland. Before Blake had chance to become effective in a role he would have preferred not to take, news came that Popham had died from a fever. Blake was to return to the sea as the sole active General-At-Sea, Deane being in Scotland. The problems with the Irish and the Scots were now subsiding, the Channel Islands were to be Blake's next challenge.

Blake in the Channel Islands

Just like the Scilly Isles, the Channel Islands were being used by Royalist privateers. Blake was to flush them out. The main problems he would face were the autumn weather and the strong running tides. Blake sailed from Weymouth on October 15th, 1651 with 2,000 infantry and horse. On arrival at Jersey, he immediately offered surrender terms to Sir George Carteret, the Royalist commander. Carteret declined hoping that either the weather or the French would come to his rescue.

The weather was poor the whole time Blake was there and delayed any attempts to land. After one unsuccessful attempt, Blake's ships sailed up and down the south west coast of Jersey for a complete rain sodden day. Blake knew that as long as he patrolled the coast threatening to land, Carteret's troops would have to travel on shore to shadow their movements. The weather and the boredom would lower their morale and resolve. Come evening time they should be at a low enough ebb to be easily overrun.

Well after night had fallen, and two hours after high tide, when a landing was not suspected, Blake put his forces ashore. Carteret's men took the best part of an hour to get themselves reorganised. The foot troops fled and only a small part of his horse were ready to defend the island. The fighting was fierce but relatively short lived. In under an hour it was all over.

Blake's tactics again had been the deciding factor. His timing, unexpected as it was, his knowledge of the effect of a long day in poor weather for troops on foot, his understanding of the tides and his ability to raise his own forces to a peek at just the right time, all contributed to his ability.

War with the Dutch

With the Civil War apparently settled, Blake's attention was to turn to the Dutch and their refound supremacy at sea. During the period of the English Civil War, both Holland and England had built their fleets up to around eighty men of war.

The Dutch had a more significant number of armed merchantmen. Parliament decided that to keep the Dutch under control, especially in English waters, all foreign shipping would have to lower their flags as a submissive act and also permit the English captains to search their ships for contraband or other items which fell under the category of that which could legitimately be confiscated. This was totally unacceptable to the Dutch and so Tromp set sail with fifty two ships to force the issue.

In May, 1652 Tromp's fleet, reduced to forty four, eight having failed to keep up, were met by Blake with thirteen men of war and Major Nehemiah Bourne with nine. Tromp knowing the English rule in respect of lowering the flag, deliberately kept his raised despite warning shots across his bows from Blake's flag ship. A red flag of war was raised and fired upon. Battle immediately commenced during which Blake, outnumbered two to one, captured one of the Dutch fleet and forced the rest to retire. It was an humiliation for Tromp and an outstanding success for Blake.

Following the skirmish, war was inevitably declared on July 8th, 1652. Blake was put in control of the English fleet which totalled over a hundred and ten ships in a state of readiness. He sailed with at least eighty ships to attack whatever Dutch shipping he could find. To that end he headed north for the Dutch fishing fleets.

Meanwhile further south, Sir George Ayscue with a small squadron of about twenty attacked a fleet of Dutch merchantmen, capturing seven and forcing several others ashore around Calais. This action attracted the attention of Tromp with a fleet of eighty plus. The Dutch pinned Ayscue down for the best part of a week but the winds never permitted an all out attack. When they finally picked up, they were the wrong way for an assault on Ayscue and so Tromp headed north in search of Blake.

There is a story told which relates the feelings that Blake and Tromp had for each other. Tromp, it appears, during the Dutch Wars always had a broom strapped to the mast of any ship on which he sailed. This he claimed was there to sweep the English navy from the sea. Blake however, not to be outdone by this gesture, had a whip strapped to his 'with which to beat them back again'.

Storm in the Shetlands.

Blake reached the Shetlands and soon spotted a Dutch fishing fleet protected by twelve Dutch war ships. Three were sunk during the battle, the others all captured. Of these Blake added six to his fleet and sent the other three back to Scotland. Tromp eventually arrived in the Shetlands late in July. He received information regarding the whereabouts of Blake's fleet and immediately set out for the battle. By early evening a tremendous gale had arisen. It was one of the worst gales that any of the Dutch seamen had ever experienced. After two days the storm had blown itself out and Tromp was able to assess the damage. Of his original fleet of a hundred and two vessels, thirty four were left. At least sixteen were wrecked on the rocks of the Shetlands or went down in the storm. The remainder of the fleet were scattered, some as far away as Norway.

Blake meanwhile had found reasonable shelter. However whilst Blake managed to keep his entire fleet, every vessel had received some form of damage. The effect of the storm had been so great that neither side had the stomach for a fight. Tromp however had lost as many ships as could be expected from a major sea battle and the largest part of those that survived were scattered far and wide.

Blake's decision to position himself at the Shetlands had been a quite deliberate one. He knew that in the event of bad weather he could position his ships in relative safety whilst denying the enemy the same facility. He knew that Tromp would have to go to the Shetlands to await the arrival of the Dutch East India fleet. Blake was ready to do battle or let the weather do it for him.

De With pursues Blake.

Blake moved south but avoided any further conflict with the Dutch. His fleet needed time to recover from the storm damage acquired in the Shetlands. An opportunity however presented itself for Blake to help the Spanish in their war with the French. The Spanish had been besieging Dunkirk for some weeks. The French were close to giving in but hoped that the arrival of a small fleet of French ships would help their cause. Blake learning of the situation, found the French fleet on its way and captured it. While this was going on, Commodore Adrianszoon de Ruijter successfully got the Dutch ships home. Tromp was in disgrace and was forced to resign. His command was given to Cornelius de With. The two parts of the Dutch fleet were now brought together and de With set out to find and destroy Blake.

Both de With and Blake were now at sea with about sixty five ships apiece albeit Blake's were the better equipped. The morale of the English was also much better. Whilst Blake's ability to motivate needs no more emphasis, the ill-tempered de With was most unpopular with his men who more than anyone else wanted the return of Tromp.

When the two fleets eventually met in the English Channel, there was a wait of three days before the Battle of Kentish Knock could commence. Once again bad weather conditions prevailed with the Dutch contending with the open sea while the English fleet were able to take shelter. On September 30th they finally met for battle.

As on previous occasions, Blake's tactics proved decisive. Before the battle commenced, Blake allowed a third of his fleet to lag behind giving the Dutch the chance to pick them off. At the end of a two hour battle, the Dutch had lost three ships captured, had three seriously damaged and nine had disappeared, some possibly sunk. Two days later de With called on his fleet to

renew the battle, the weather having improved. Without exception every captain in the Dutch fleet refused and with de With accusing them all of cowardice, they returned to Holland. De Ruijter was amongst the captains present. Quite possibly he was still the most influential despite his now more subordinate position.

The return of Tromp

There was no choice for the Dutch government but to recall Tromp. He rapidly set about rebuilding the Dutch fleet and, without any consent from his government, pressganged and commandeered to his hearts content. When the time was right for the Dutch merchant fleet to once more run the gauntlet down the English Channel, Tromp sailed with them. The total fleet was five hundred strong including one hundred men-of-war.

The battle off Dungeness Point

Blake had been less successful replenishing his fleet. In the wake of the success at Kentish Knock, complacency had set in with the English Parliament and it was proving hard for Blake to obtain provisions for his fleet or indeed to pay his seamen who were already owed six months pay. Thus it was that Blake had a fleet of just forty when he met the powerful Dutch fleet off Dungeness Point.

The outcome was almost inevitable with the total imbalance of numbers. The English were beaten back and to some extent saved by the weather. Losses were heavy and an enquiry was called. Several English captains under Blake's command were rewarded for their heroism. Others were accused of failure to fulfil their duties and were deprived of their commands. Amongst those punished this way under Blake's hand was his own brother Benjamin who quietly, along with four others, eventually got their commands back. Whilst some were undoubtedly guilty of cowardice, others were only guilty of disagreeing with Blake's tactics and openly said so. This position was unacceptable to Blake who demanded nothing but the fiercest loyalty.

It was probably Tromp at the end of the day who can take the credit for the survival of this significant part of the English fleet. When the opportunity existed to press home the defeat and finish off Blake's forty or so ships, Tromp held back. His orders were to ensure the safe passage of the Dutch merchant fleet and when the opportunity to finish Blake presented itself, he sailed off with the merchant ships, saw them through the channel and then awaited the arrival of the next merchant fleet requiring escorted passage home.

Blake rebuilds the fleet

Blake recognised his task was now to rebuild the fleet and the confidence of its men. He arranged for hospitals to be set up specifically for wounded seamen and for hospital beds to be reserved in London's hospitals in readiness for those who would suffer in the forthcoming war. All ranks received pay rises and indeed their back pay. Conditions generally were improved but still not sufficiently to entice enough volunteers to man the number of ships required.

Again it was necessary to draft in men from the Commonwealth army. Whilst they were no sailors, they did release sailors for the duties involved in handling a ship when the battle raged and indeed they were credible fighting men in their own right and spent much of their spare time on board training for battle. Blake saw the need to make the arrangement a permanent one and can thus be credited with the introduction of the marine commandos that we know today.

The battle with Tromp.

By February 1653, Blake had a fleet ready for sea and ready to meet Tromp with his fleet of returning Dutch merchantmen. When the two fleets spotted each other in the Channel in the early hours of the morning, Tromp's fleet of about eighty was neat and compact whilst Blake's sixty or more ships were well scattered. Tromp seized the opportunity and turned his ships for a head on conflict with the closest section of the English fleet, the rest of it being separated as much as seven miles away. The fighting was fierce, the English standing their ground particularly well. They may have been outnumbered but their gun power was the greater, the discipline was good and the will to win the stronger.

Tromp was unable to take advantage of his apparently stronger position and Blake lost not a single ship. De Ruijter elsewhere in the battle was more successful, capturing some English ships only to lose them later. When the Dutch fleet, running short of munitions, made off in order to return to protecting the merchant fleet, twelve of their ships had been lost to just the one English vessel. Three English ships had however been rendered unfit for further service without repair.

Blake seriously wounded

Whilst the low English losses may give the impression that the going had not been particularly tough , the hundreds of fatalities tell a different story. At least two of Blake's closest aides, his flag captain and his secretary, fell at his side and Blake himself was hit in the thigh by a flying iron bar causing a severe laceration to his thigh. In true Blake fashion, he did not allow the wound to hinder him in his role; he considered it essential that all around knew he remained in complete control. Indeed his injury was neglected for the next two days whilst the fighting continued.

The following day, Blake's fleet caught up with the Dutch merchant fleet shortly after midday. The rest of the day was spent harassing the Dutch vessels with one or two being captured. The day after that was more of the same but by now the Dutch men-of-war had been reduced to some thirty five vessels. Tromp headed for the coast of Normandy; for some unknown reason Blake backed off and failed to finish the job. Perhaps the wound he had received was sufficient reason. For Blake, what was left of his life, was to be plagued by long periods of ill health.

Premature obituaries

By the end of February 1653, Blake was land based. His wound and the fever resultant from it gave great cause for concern. The press were reporting his condition as so bad that they were virtually writing his obituary and others indeed actually reported him as already dead. Despite premature obituaries, Blake was back at sea in June 1653 and was called upon by Richard Deane and George Monck to joined them in the battle that was already raging with the Dutch. Monck was very much a contemporary of Blake and was very much an army man rather than sailor. He is even reputed to have given his ships the order to "left wheel".

Blake's arrival was greeted with cheers by the English fleet whilst the Dutch preferred to turn tail and head for shallow and safer water. In a battle with no English losses, the Dutch had twenty ships captured or sunk, seventy four managed to survive.

Although no English ships were lost, casualties again were high on both sides. English losses included Deane. This must have particularly saddened Blake, the two men having served together in so many battles. Deane's end was swift if not gruesome. His head was taken off by a cannonball and Monke who was at his side swiftly covered his colleagues body to avoid disturbing the men.

The end of Tromp.

After the battle, Blake returned ashore, yet again too unwell to serve at sea. This time, after his recovery, he was to serve his time as a member of the new parliament. Another sea battle in Blake's absence saw one English loss for twenty three Dutch ships plus the loss of Blake's old adversary Tromp. This battle was in June 1653 and was the last fling for the Dutch who the following spring conceded defeat and a peace treaty was signed between the two nations.

It was time for the English to turn their attention to the Spanish.

The war with Spain

By August 1654, an unfit Blake was back at sea with a fleet of 24 ships. Many of these were new ships and Blake's influence on their choice of names appears fairly obvious. Three of them were the Bridgwater, the Langport and the Taunton. By late October Blake had arrived off Cadiz with a plan to engage the French first. They were at war with Spain. If Blake tackled them before the Spanish, he could expect to negotiate terms for a combined English and French assault on the Spanish. If time then permitted, he would turn his attentions to the Barbary pirates off the North African coast.

Blake spent the next few months patrolling the Mediterranean ports just missing the French fleet each time. There was a considerable period, unbeknown to Blake, when they sheltered in a harbour reluctant to come out, knowing that Blake was out there somewhere. He turned his attention to the North African coast where the Tunisians had captured an English ship. Blake was demanding its return.

Porto Farina, Tunisia.

The captured English vessel was in the harbour at Porto Farina, well protected under the harbour guns and in the midst of a small Tunisian fleet of men-of-war. Blake's attempts to negotiate back the ownership of the vessel were unsuccessful. A small party that Blake sent into the harbour were fired on by the Tunisians.

Blake's tactics were to retire from the area lulling the Tunisians into a false sense of security. Several days later he returned and just after daybreak sailed straight into the harbour. Half his force set to the destruction of every ship in the harbour whilst the remainder, including the Bridgwater, set about the destruction of the castle and its gunnery. After several hours, having ensured every ship present was adequately ablaze, including the one which caused the disagreement in the first place, Blake and his fleet sailed on. The whole thing had been so simple and yet on paper it should have been impossible to sail in to a fortified position under its own guns and fire every ship in a fleet of similar size. It was another measure of Blake's capability.

After Tunisia, its neighbour Algeria signed a peace treaty with Blake allowing English ships shelter in its harbours and giving them the right to replenish their supplies. Blake spent most of that autumn in the Mediterranean. Whilst little else happened in terms of real activity, he had gained allies, the French were now working with the English in the war against the Spanish and the English navy was respected throughout Europe.

When Blake returned to England for re-provisioning, the country was once again in a state of unrest. Against an unstable political background and again with problems of pay for those serving at sea, a number of ships' captains plus two other generals-at-sea resigned.

Mountagu joins Blake

In January 1656, Edward Mountagu was appointed to be General-at-Sea alongside Blake. We know from Blake's earlier experiences that when the going got tough, he preferred to share the burden and undoubtedly Mountagu's appointment had his blessing.

Blake and Mountagu sailed to the Mediterranean in search of the Spanish fleet. The intelligence they gathered there indicated that part of it was in the West Indies, part was not due back for several weeks and the rest were snugly tucked up in well protected Spanish ports. Meanwhile English shipping was being attacked in the Atlantic by Spanish ships which skirmished out of ports such as Dunkirk and Ostend, these being in Spanish possession. Cromwell wanted a victory, he desperately needed a significant win over the Spanish. Blake and Mountagu were frustrated by their inability to produce one.

The next few months were spent locating and destroying privateers and the harbours in which they sheltered. Whilst this made life easier for English merchant shipping, it did nothing to help Blake in his desire to locate and engage the Spanish fleet. All ships which could be remotely considered hostile stayed well clear of the area. The Spanish ships in Cadiz harbour stayed put. Blake decided to send part of his fleet to negotiate terms for the use of ports along the Barbary coast in the hope that apart from establishing another source of supply for much needed provisions, he could also convince the Spanish that the best part of the English fleet had given up and gone home.

Destruction of the Spanish Plate fleet.

To some extent he was successful. When the Spanish Plate fleet returned from South America they were convinced there were insufficient English men-of-war around to stop their safe arrival at their home port. To their surprise, the small fleet that Blake had left behind for just such an opportunity were ready and waiting. The English ships, including the Bridgwater, set to with great enthusiasm. The result of the battle was the total destruction of the Spanish Plate fleet, all ships being sunk except two which were wrecked on shore. The value of the Spanish loss was nine million pieces of eight.

Whilst this sounds a lot of money, Blake realised that it was only a small part of what was expected. He knew there must be more on its way. He also knew that the Admiral of the larger Plate fleet would probably hold up at Tenerife, one of the Canary Islands, which was very heavily defended and under Spanish rule. Blake's choice was to head for Tenerife, in which case the ships blockaded for so long in Cadiz harbour would be free to escape, or to stay close to Cadiz and hope that the second Plate fleet sailed into his hands.

The battle of Santa Cruz, Tenerife.

Some months went by with no action and no signs of any incoming fleet. When positive news finally arrived that the larger Plate fleet were definitely at Tenerife, Blake checked the state of the Spanish fleet in Cadiz harbour and determined that they were nowhere near ready to put to sea. He decided to run the risk and head for Tenerife. It was April 1657 when Blake reached his target at Santa Cruz. He selected twelve of the fleet to head the attack including once again the Bridgwater.

They moved into the harbour in the early morning. Sixteen Spanish ships were harboured there under the relative safety of a fort with forty guns overlooking the central position in the harbour. Another fort protected the coast a bit further south. Heavy trench work ran parallel with the coast giving additional defensive positions. The smaller ships of the Spanish fleet were moored up along the shore line. The larger

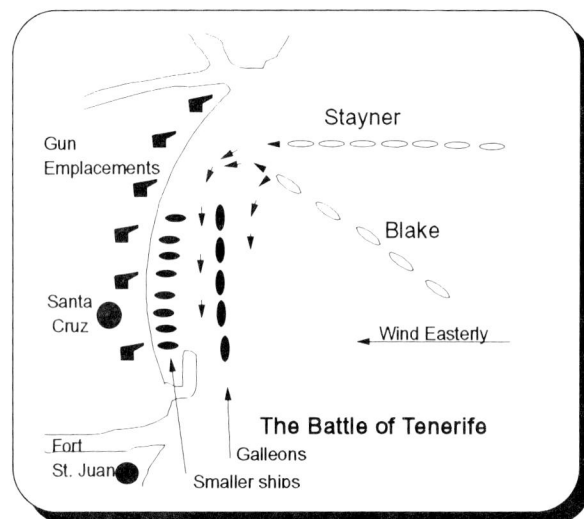

The Battle of Tenerife

galleons were anchored in a parallel line in deeper water.

The English ships positioned themselves by sailing between the two lines of Spanish ships, anchored up and allowed their ships to swing around for the best position. By putting themselves between the two line of Spanish ships they made it almost impossible for the guns ashore to fire on them without hitting their own ships on the way. When the bombardment began it was not long before the English guns had silenced the enemy. Superior gunnery and the shear power of the English guns paid dividends. The larger Spanish galleons took longer to finish off and needed Blake to send in his larger ships. The only task left was to withdraw with the minimum damage from the surviving guns on the surrounding hillside.

Now that the Spanish fleet was destroyed, there was no reason for the Spanish guns to hold back. Not without some difficulty, Blake's ships withdrew at what was the end one of England's finest naval victories at a port which was previously considered invulnerable.

The victory at Tenerife was a major stepping stone in the ultimate defeat of Spain. Not only had it destroyed a major part of Spain's fleet, it had deprived it of the gold and silver much needed to finance the army.

News reached Cromwell of the victory. Congratulations were sent to Blake with the message to return for a well earned rest, leaving part of the fleet for policing purposes. Blake received the message at Cadiz.

Blake's death at sea

On the journey home Blake was taken ill and his health deteriorated rapidly. Scurvy, dropsy and his old wound combined to overcome his failing body. His only wish now was to see England once more. Alas his wish was not to be fulfilled. Blake's death came at sea on August 7th, 1657, but not in the midst of a battle as one might expect. He passed away within two hours of Plymouth Sound, his body brought home on the St. George.

Blake's naval career as the Commonwealth's General-at-Sea lasted seven years but it was a seven year period into which he crammed more naval victories and victories of greater significance than Nelson in his much longer life at sea. Blake had no family life, the navy was it. His fellow Generals-at-sea all had wives. In Blake's childhood he had grown up in a family full of boys, bar for his young sister Bridget who was only two when he left for Oxford.

His Puritan upbringing and university life had kept him away from women. And perhaps having watched his mother produce what must have seemed an endless string of children, it can be understood if Blake was not inclined to take a wife. Thus when he entered into a venture, it was completely and utterly, unfettered by the ties and commitments of a home life.

He never lost his love of Bridgwater despite all the adventures he had away from it. It is said, no matter where he went in his career, he always had someone from Bridgwater close by with whom he could reminisce on the old town when the fancy took him.

He was considered a gentleman by friend and foe alike, and was respected for his chivalry. His death marked the end of seven glorious years when the English navy totally dominated the seas and made England a very significant European power.

His heart and bowels were removed and buried in St. Andrew's church in Plymouth. Gutted in a bombing raid. in World War ll, only the shell of the building now remains.

His body was taken to London where he was afforded a state funeral and buried in Westminster Abbey. His epitaph declared him to be "One who desires no greater worldly happiness than to be accounted honest and faithful in his employment".

To the shame of Charles ll, when he came to the throne he had Blake's body exhumed and buried in a pit in common ground within the Abbey's bounds in St. Margaret's Church.

Bridgwater never turned its back on Blake. The town museum and his statue remain as testament to the respect and admiration he still commands. The flag of the Commonwealth still flies over his house.

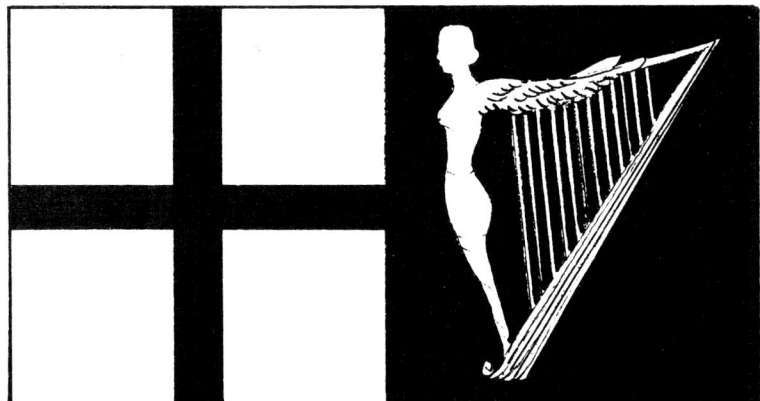

Commonwealth flag

The Monmouth Rebellion 1685

No event in the history of this country has left such lasting impression on the people of the West Country. Whilst the Monmouth Rebellion may be over 300 years old, West Country folk still speak of Monmouth with affection and Judge Jeffreys with contempt. Monmouth was a timely hero; handsome, charming, infectiously popular and above all a Protestant.

His mother and childhood

Lucy Walter was the mistress of Charles ll. Born of Welsh parents, raised in London, she lived in troubled times and fled with her Aunt, Margaret Gosfright, to Rotterdam in Holland.

During the same period, Charles ll, then only the Prince of Wales lived in Jersey and France, moving eventually to Holland. Here he took Lucy Walter as his mistress and only a few months after his father's death, Lucy gave birth to the illegitimate son of the now exiled Charles ll. It was April 9th, 1649. The young lad was named James after James l and spent most of his infancy on the continent.

In 1657 Charles ll moved his household to Bruges with a new mistress, Catherine Pegge. She also gave him a son. Meanwhile continuous ploys to remove the young James from Lucy eventually proved successful. Lucy died the following year in 1658.

The young James was looked after by members of Charles' court. Whilst they were mainly Roman Catholic in persuasion, James most influential tutor at this time was a Scottish Protestant, Thomas Ross. This man did much to convince James that his parents had actually been married and thus he was Charles' legitimate son.

James becomes Duke of Monmouth

1658 also saw the death of Oliver Cromwell. After a period without his influence, England was ready to receive a King and by 1662 Charles had returned to England and started to pour gifts and honours on the young James, by now thirteen years old. On St Valentines day, 1663 he honoured James with the title of Duke of Monmouth. Valentines day was appropriate. The young duke had inherited his mothers good looks and charm. It was these attributes that helped to make him so popular in the days before the rebellion.

On April 20th that same year, James was married to Anna Countess of Buccleuch, herself only 12 years old. In the period following the marriage, Charles ll took his son almost everywhere he went including state occasions, indeed treating him much as the heir to the throne, albeit Charles' brother, James, the Duke of York was recognised as the official and rightful heir. This proved a difficult time for the Duke of York who was suspicious of Charles' motives.

The young Duke

Charles ll ensured that his son was given public exposure at various social, sporting and state events. His good looks and charm soon won him many friends and the honours rolled in. By September 1663, he had been granted degrees by both Oxford and Cambridge universities.

James, Duke of Monmouth, was 16 when in 1665 England was involved in the second Dutch war. The Duke of York commanded part of the 98 strong English fleet and successfully defeated the Dutch, sinking 20 ships for the loss of one. Monmouth was present during the action and acquitted himself well, gaining much in experience and stature. The Duke of York took much credit from the victory and both men gained in popularity.

Monmouth continued his life in the court of Charles ll having many flirtatious relationships with ladies of the court, despite his marriage which had become little more than a business arrangement, the sole purpose of which was to produce heirs. One of his many affairs was with a Moll Kirke, an affair which ultimately led to a dramatic breakdown in the relationship between the Dukes of York and Monmouth.

Unbeknown to either of the Dukes, Moll Kirke was having an affair with both of them at the same time. The situation took a complicated turn when she become involved with a third lover, the Earl of Mulgrave. Monmouth discovered the relationship and arranged for the Earl to suffer accordingly. The Earl in turn, in order to exact his revenge, told York of Monmouth's affair with Moll. The relationship between the two Dukes was never the same again.

The French connection

In 1668 Charles sent Monmouth to stay in France with his aunt, the Duchess of Orleans, only 5 years older than the duke himself.

A strong bond soon developed between them. Relationships between the two nations improved to the point where a treaty was signed guaranteeing the never ending co-operation between them and they simultaneously declared war on the Dutch.

Monmouth was seconded to the King of France with a troop of 2000 men and was soon in the thick of the action, gaining many successes by his leadership from the front. His bravery and success were recognised and honoured by the French. The experience was

later to serve him well (but not so at the Battle of Sedgemoor).

York's growing unpopularity.

1672 and 1673 saw further honours bestowed on Monmouth including Lord High Chamberlain of Scotland and Chancellor of Cambridge University. In 1674 he took a new mistress, Eleanor Needham, who bore him 5 children, his first borne being called James.

James, Duke of Monmouth

Monmouth however, whilst unpopular with his wife, increased in popularity with the general public. Good looking and suave, he presented himself as a caring leader of those who served him ensuring that those who fell on hard times were well cared for.

In 1678, having gained significant experience in military matters, Monmouth was appointed Captain-General in charge of all the English forces. This greatly angered York who protested strongly to the King. He had already declared that such an appointment would not be acceptable and would cause the King and Monmouth to lose his friendship.

Meanwhile Monmouth was gaining more experience fighting on the continent at the side of William, Prince of Orange.

Rumours and religious unrest

Religious unrest approached a peak in 1678. Rumours were rife. Fears of a papist take over with plots to kill the King were taken seriously as were rumours that the country was to be cleared of Roman Catholics. The Earl of Shaftesbury worked hard to discredit the Catholic York and build on Monmouth's popularity. Eventually York had to succumb to public pressure and went into exile on the continent.

By 1679 unrest in Scotland had grown to a level where there was open revolt. A Scottish force of 6000 took Edinburgh and Monmouth was sent in to crush the rebellion. This he achieved at the Battle of Bothwell Bridge with a force half the size of the Scottish rebels. He showed significant mercy in putting down the rebellion by ensuring his men did not take advantage of the routed Scots.

Whilst this humane act won him respect across the nation, York did his best to present it as a weakness and an attempt to win the Scots over to Monmouth and inevitably his claim to the throne.

Monmouth in exile again

Shortly after this episode, the King was taken gravely ill and Monmouth found himself in exile once again. He had not been in Holland long before he was unsuccessfully trying to win over William, Prince of Orange. Frustrated by his failure and encouraged by an invitation from the Earl of Shaftesbury, Monmouth returned to England without the King's blessing. Word went round of his return; the bells rang, bonfires were lit to celebrate the return of the Protestant Prince as he was now popularly known. The King

James, Duke of York

however refused to admit him and he was ordered back into exile.

This time however he stayed in London. His presence was a continuous thorn in the side of Charles who now permitted his brother, York, to return to London and take up his place at the royal court.

The West Country tour

By 1680, Monmouth, now well and truly estranged from his wife, took yet another mistress, Lady Henrietta Wentworth. In July of that year, encouraged on by Henrietta, he set out on a tour of the West Country where he knew the Protestant support for himself would be strong.

Everywhere he went, the reception was exceptional with flowers strewn in the streets, church bells ringing and the local people chanting tributes to their Protestant Prince. At White Lackington, 2000 horsemen and 20,000 locals greeted him. 22,000 met him at Exeter. West Country folk were highly suspicious of Catholic intentions and were quite ready to demonstrate their support for Monmouth.

Monmouth's fall from grace

The following year Monmouth lost titles and honours as fast as they had previously been bestowed upon him. Charles even forbade all in his service to have any links with Monmouth. Later that year, Monmouth journeyed to the Midlands and the North to build on the support he had already developed in the South West.

Monmouth himself was generally well received but his presence led to much rioting. Charles had him arrested and returned to London. Despite this, he remained at large, working continuously to build his band of followers who plotted to bring about his return to grace and the throne.

Various plots to assassinate the King were planned, most being discovered and the perpetrators punished or executed. Monmouth's involvement in these schemes, including the famous Rye House Plot, was obvious to the King who issued a warrant for his arrest. For a period of nine months, Monmouth remained in hiding with friends at Toddington Manor.

He wrote frequently to the King pleading forgiveness and in time the King gave way and took him back into the family, but only after Monmouth had confessed his part in certain conspiracies, none of which threatened the King directly, only the Duke of York. In confessing he was obliged to name many of those involved, but on the understanding that no harm would come to them and that he would not be called upon to give evidence against them. This was agreed. The Duke of York, however was not prepared to let it go at that and Monmouth's confession was published. This was too much for Monmouth who then denied everything and immediately found himself once more out of favour.

The following weeks saw many of those 'betrayed' by Monmouth coming to trial and Monmouth himself being called to give evidence. Monmouth was not prepared to do so and in February 1684 he disappeared to Brussels. The King still kept in contact with him and kept him financially supported.

The final exile

From Brussels, Monmouth moved to Holland to be well received by William, Prince of Orange. The closeness of their friendship angered King Charles and even more so his brother, the Duke of York.

In the February 1685, Charles died. Monmouth never had chance to make his peace with his father and it was some while after his father's death before William broke the news. York, now having become James ll, was potentially a dangerous enemy for William, despite being his father-in-law. James as a staunch Roman Catholic was closely allied to France. The two Catholic powers posed a major threat to Protestant Holland. James wrote to his father-in-law stating that he was breaking off all relationships with Monmouth and assured him of his support in all things other than religious affairs.

Monmouth left William's household and spent his time avoiding capture. During his travels he linked up with many supporters who were now out of necessity living on the continent. They worked hard to persuade him to make an early attempt to take the throne. It had to happen before James became too well established.

In the end it was Monmouth's mistress, the Lady Henrietta Wentworth who convinced him that his destiny was to be the Protestant ruler of a republican England. The exiled conspirators were ready for Monmouth to swing into action.

Preparation for the rebellion

Monmouth worked in conjunction with the Earl of Argyle to produce two rebellions simultaneously. Argyle was to take control of Scotland and Monmouth, England. Monmouth sent messengers into the West Country and Cheshire to ensure his supporters were ready for his arrival.

Back in England, James was crowned in the April and consolidated his position as King against a background of gradually waning resentment of his Catholic practices. Argyle's attempt in June to take Scotland failed in all sorts of ways. It was a complete disaster, especially for Argyle himself who literally lost his head as a result. Monmouth was not to hear of this disaster until a considerable time after the events had taken place.

Monmouth, still in Holland cashed in all his assets which, along with sizeable donations from supporters, gave him enough to launch his expedition. After several days delay due to adverse weather, he sailed from Holland with 82 men including Nathaniel Wade, a lawyer by profession and one of those exiled to the continent.

Monmouth arrives back in the West Country

Monmouth landed at Lyme Regis on June 11th and after a stay of four days, had recruited nearly 3000 volunteers. Word soon reached the King and within days a force to counter Monmouth's intrusion had been raised.

Monmouth suffered from many broken promises of support. This concerned him greatly and to counteract it, he took the advice of those close to him and had himself declared King Monmouth at Chard and again

on June 18th when he marched into Taunton. His 'coronation' took place at the Market Cross where he was presented with a bible and a banner by the 'Maids of Taunton', in fact the maids of Miss Blake's school, Sarah Blake being the sister of Robert Blake. By the time he left Taunton on June 21st, a force of some 7,000 men had been assembled. Monmouth made a number of proclamations in Taunton which made his position irreversible including the declaration that King James was a traitor and as such had a bounty of £500 on his head, dead or alive. Another was that no one should pay taxes to James. It was an ill-equipped but enthusiastic force which marched to Bridgwater where Monmouth was given a civic reception and proclaimed King again in front of the market cross.

His men marched on through Westonzoyland to Glastonbury and by June 24th to Pensford,

The Blues Regiment

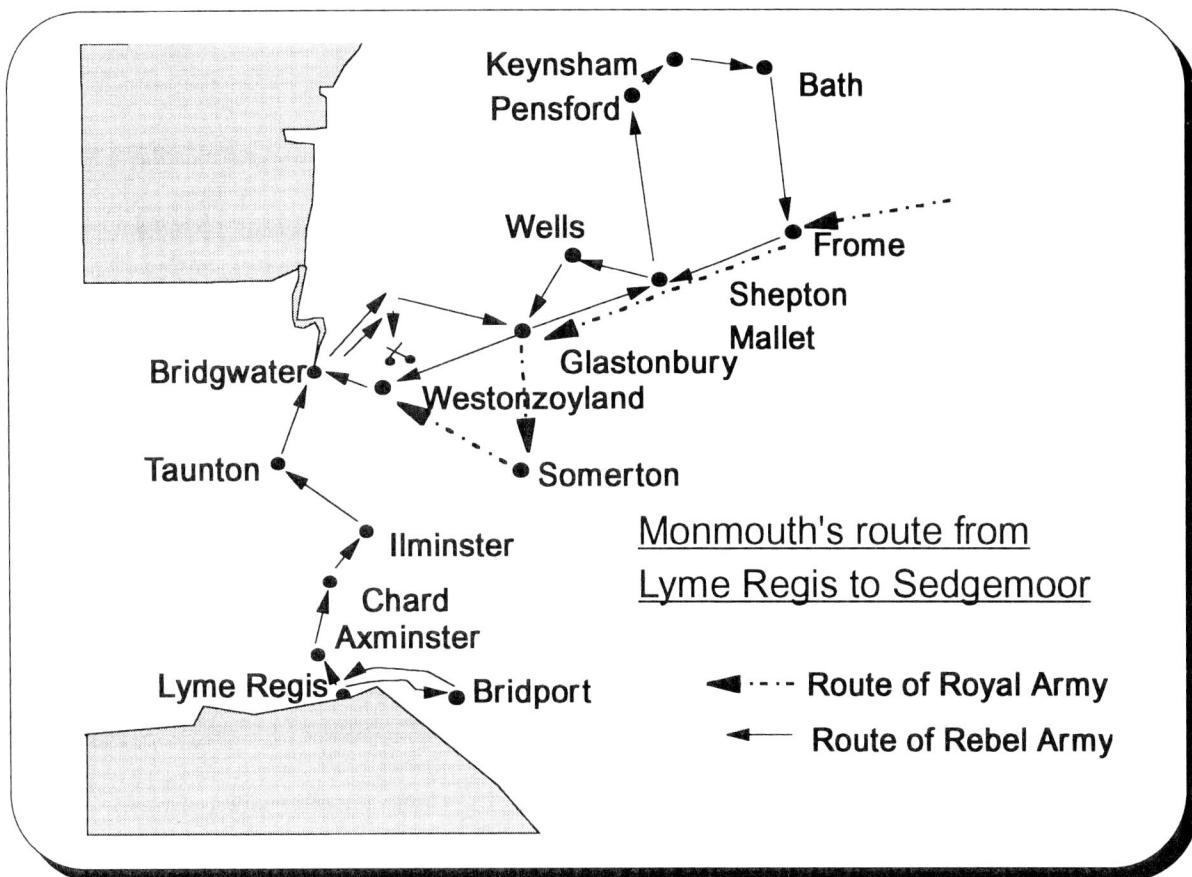

Monmouth's route from Lyme Regis to Sedgemoor

◄ ···· Route of Royal Army
◄── Route of Rebel Army

a few miles from Bristol, which would have been a major prize for Monmouth had he the capability of taking it.

A victory here could well have altered the outcome of the rebellion. Unfortunately for Monmouth, Royalist troops under the command of Lord Churchill were ready and waiting to ensure no such event would happen. They failed, however, to stop a small band of Monmouth's supporters from reaching the quayside at Bristol and setting fire to the ships, the Abraham and Mary. The purpose here was to create a diversion in order to attract the Duke of Beaufort's 4000 strong militia away from the city boundary. Churchill was not taken in by the ploy and declared that should Monmouth enter the city, he would have it razed to the ground rather than have it serve Monmouth's needs.

This message was taken seriously by Monmouth and by June 26th he had moved his forces to Norton St. Philip to the south of Bath. Here he stayed at the George Inn, but

not before encountering a troop of the King's Life Guard at Keynsham. The rebels troops were taken by surprise and suffered numerous casualties before the Guards withdrew.

Lord Feversham, a Frenchman by birth, was commander-in-chief of the King's forces and was already in the area with a significant force. Feversham decided to force the pace and sent his dragoons and 500 foot soldiers under the command of the Duke of Grafton against Monmouth . The battle which ensued just outside of Norton St. Philip was more successful for Monmouth. The King's troops walked straight in to an ambush. Monmouth had early warning of the dragoons moves and had positioned musketeers behind a hedge on a high banked lane. In the encounter the King's forces suffered 80 fatalities to Monmouth's 18 and Feversham withdrew into Wiltshire.

Monmouth's men marched on to Frome to another triumphant welcome. Despite their victory, morale was waning. Rain which had started when they left Bridgwater had continued in torrents. Monmouth needed the shelter of Frome for his men to recover. He also needed to increase his numbers by recruiting more locals. Unfortunately for Monmouth, the Earl of Pembroke had already visited Frome and disarmed the inhabitants. Not only though did Monmouth receive the news that arms and provisions had been captured by the royal forces but he also now learned of Argyle's defeat and capture in Scotland. He was on his own and events were not going to plan.

A despondent Monmouth, after resting his troops for a couple of days at Wells, returned his forces to Bridgwater on July 2nd.

The Pitchfork rebellion

King James chose his time well to offer a pardon to all those who had joined Monmouth's forces since his arrival at Lyme. A price had been put on Monmouth's head who discussed this development with his officers. The opinion of many was to cut their losses, retreat rapidly to a sea port from where they could effect their escape. The majority favoured a continuance of the venture.

The story of Mary Bridge

Lord Feversham, with his Royalist troops, had predicted Monmouth's movements with some accuracy. Anticipating the Duke's movements, he positioned his troops, apparently 6 regiments totalling 2000 foot soldiers and 700 horse, at Westonzoyland.

Whilst there, one of Feversham's officers assaulted a local woman and for his troubles was stabbed with his own sword by the woman's daughter, Mary Bridge. Apparently he had earlier visited her house with his men and had deliberately left his sword there in order that he could return and have his way with her. During the ensuing struggle, the young girl aged only twelve defended with courage her mother's honour. She grabbed the sword and stabbed him in the heart. She was taken to Feversham who praised her bravery, returned her to her mother and presented her with the sword. It can now be seen in Blake Museum. Also still to be seen today are the marks at the entrance to Westonzoyland church where the troops are said to have sharpened their swords prior to the battle.

Quite near Feversham's troops there was the Bussex Rhyne. This rhyne formed a defensive boundary effectively covering three sides of Feversham's encampment. The other side was covered by the artillery which had been positioned to guard against attack from the road between Bridgwater and Westonzoyland. In Somerset, rhynes are very wide, deep ditches which criss-cross the low lying moors allowing their drainage to be controlled. A fortune teller forewarned Monmouth to 'beware the rhyne'. It is believed that Monmouth paid no heed to this warning which he took as a reference to the River Rhine. Those who advised him on local issues unfortunately failed to see fit to warn him of the Sedgemoor rhynes.

A resident of Chedzoy using a telescope on the tower of Chedzoy church was able to see Feversham's troops camped at Westonzoyland. The size of the King's force was determined and the information fed to Monmouth, now in Bridgwater. It appears that the King's troops were in a fairly relaxed state and were drinking well. No one predicted an attack from Monmouth who was expected to be heading north.

Having received the news, Monmouth went up the tower of St. Mary's church in Bridgwater and saw for himself the position of Feversham's troops, in particular the artillery guarding the main road position. Monmouth knew and understood the quality of these troops, having served with them

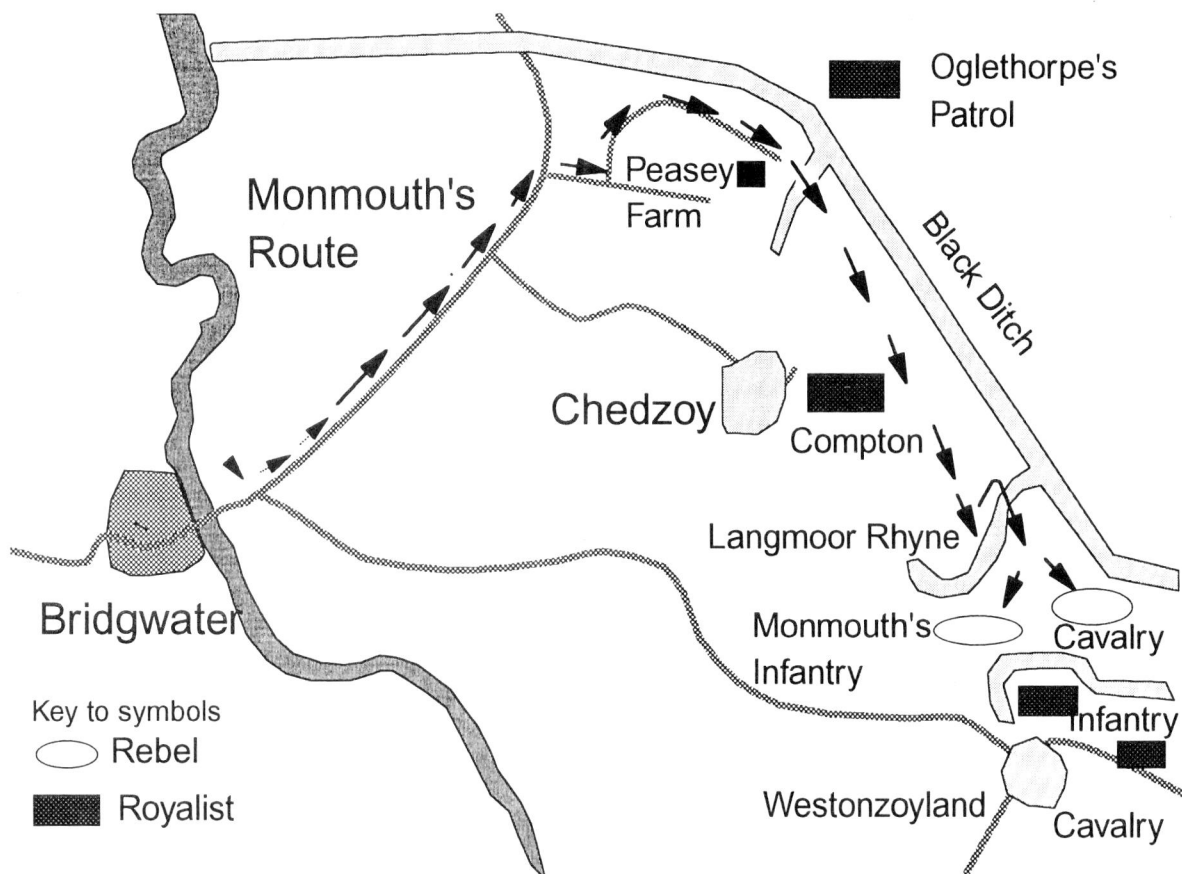

Key to symbols
⬭ Rebel
▨ Royalist

himself. He recognised that a surprise night attack was probably his only hope with a less disciplined peasant army. As enthusiastic as they may be, they would be no match for disciplined regulars. He also knew that any attack would have to be to the rear of the artillery, in other words, over the Bussex Rhyne.

Monmouth's troops were now down to 6000, mostly through desertion. They were split down into five regiments under their respective colonels; Nathaniel Wade's red, Matthew's yellow, Basset's blue, Foulkes' white and Holmes' green. With these colonels, Monmouth made the decision to effect a night attack.

The road to Sedgemoor

On the evening of Sunday, July 5th, Monmouth left Bridgwater Castle where he had been staying and an hour before midnight he led his troops out into the misty moonlit night. They silently moved out along what was then the road to Bristol but which is now the A39 to Glastonbury. A short distance outside the town, they turned right into Bradney Lane to Peasey Farm. Some heavy armaments were left on the way, to be picked up on the way back assuming the forthcoming battle was successful. More heavy equipment was left at Peasey Farm.

The troops moved on across the moor, around the village of Chedzoy towards Westonzoyland. The man with the local knowledge, Richard Godfrey led them successfully and silently over Black Ditch, the first major hazard and on towards Langmoor Rhyne. This was a much more significant obstacle and one that had to be crossed before approaching the final hurdle, Bussex Rhyne.

The warning shot

Only two of Monmouth's troops had successfully crossed one of the few fording places when someone fired a shot. As a deliberate act it was potentially suicidal. Monmouth had ordered that should anyone give away their position, those closest were to immediately put him to the death by the knife. As it happened it was a Captain Hucker who inadvertently fired the shot and he survived to fight gallantly until the end of the ensuing battle when he was taken prisoner and was later executed.

The damage was done. Churchill ordered his troops into position along the south bank of Bussex Rhyne while Feversham dressed himself at his lodgings in the village. Grey's cavalry advanced for Monmouth but suffered from lacking their guide. Misinterpreting their position Grey led his cavalry along the opposite bank of Bussex Rhyne. Challenged by the royal troops, they declared themselves as Monmouth's men and soon suffered the consequences as a barrage of shots ripped in to them. Their untrained and partly unbroken horses stampeded in all directions.

Monmouth and his troops saw Grey's horse retreating as bats out of hell. The effect on Monmouth's untrained men was predictable. There was a fairly rapid rate of desertion as the faint hearted had second thoughts about what was to come.

Predictably Monmouth fought bravely and actually had the regular troops retreating. But the rebels valiant efforts were insufficient with the regulars gradually regaining control. Eventually the artillery were turned to face the rebels. A barrage of artillery fire followed by a cavalry charge turned the table completely.

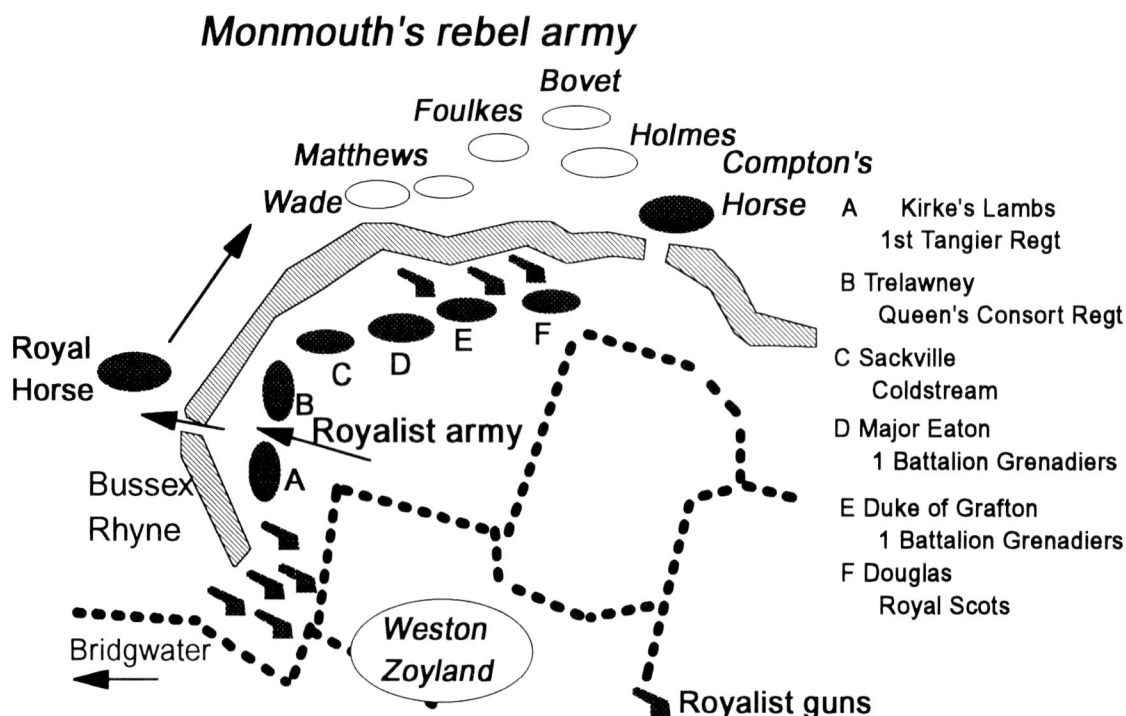

Monmouth's rebel army

62

Escape from the field of battle

Bitter fighting continued for some hours with many of Monmouth's men fighting only with the tools of their trades rather than conventional weapons. By the end of the day hundreds of rebels and Royalist troops alike had lain down their lives. Grey, realising all was lost, persuaded Monmouth to flee the field of battle, accompanied only by a small but close party. Together they fled through Chedzoy up onto the ridge of the Polden Hills where much fighting was still evident. Monmouth was advised by some in his party to head for Uphill on the coast in what is now a part of Avon. Lord Grey, however won the day with his advice to head for the south coast and from there to seek shelter on the continent.

That night, July 6th, they sheltered with a friend of Monmouth in Shepton Mallet and the following day travelled down through the more remote parts of Dorset eventually to the New Forest. Disguises were obtained and the exhausted horses released. All travel now

King's Life Guard

had to be on foot and at all times trying to avoid the numerous Royalist troops who were scouring the country for Monmouth and his faithful few. They all now carried high prices on their heads.

The following day, Lord Grey was captured and the Royalist forces knew that Monmouth would not be far. The next day, July 8th, Anthony Buyse, the last man left with Monmouth was also taken and not unsurprisingly Monmouth himself was discovered asleep from exhaustion just a few hours later. Buyse's life was spared which suggests that almost certainly he had betrayed Monmouth at the very end. Messages were despatched immediately to let the King know the outcome of the search.

After two days, Monmouth and his last two followers, Grey and Buyse, were taken from Ringwood to Winchester. Monmouth wrote to the King pleading for his life. His uncle's hatred of him was such that no amount of pleading was to win him over. By July 13th, the prisoners and their escorts had arrived in Whitehall. Monmouth was granted one last interview with the King at which he pleaded for his life and even promised to adopt the Catholic faith. James hatred and distrust for Monmouth were complete. Monmouth was sent to the Tower and his escorts told to stab him rather than let him escape. Grey wrote a full confession from the Tower and earned himself his freedom, but only after heavy financial penalties. He later served the court of William lll.

The end of Monmouth

On Monmouth's last day, four men of the church attended him and obtained a written acknowledgement of his illegitimacy. The document was signed under pressure and almost definitely written to protect his children. It is unlikely that Monmouth would reverse his own conviction of his parents marriage after believing it for all of his thirty six years.

On the morning of Wednesday, July 15th Monmouth was taken at 10 o'clock to the scaffold. The crowd was, in the main quiet. Many openly wept. Others taunted him for a confession or acceptance of the Catholic faith. Monmouth responded with dignity and calm.

At the block he paid Ketch the executioner six guineas with the request to do the job well. The executioner's poor reputation preceded him and indeed he faired no better on this occasion. The first blow was so ineffective as to leave Monmouth still able to turn his head; the second blow left him still able to move, he crossed his legs wracked in pain; even the third failed to complete the job and the executioner was obliged to complete his task by removing Monmouth's head with his knife. The executioner had to be rescued from the crowd who were unable to accept his incompetence. His body was laid to rest beneath the communion table of St. Peter's chapel in the grounds of the Tower of London.

The persecution of the rebels

Whilst Monmouth's fate was taking its course, his followers were suffering their own fate. The day after the battle, 500 prisoners were held in Westonzoyland church. 22 rebels never made it that far, all being hanged from the same tree close to the battlefield. Five died in the church and a further nineteen hanged the following day. Captain Adlam was the first to suffer this fate despite the fact that he was already dying when he was hung.

The roads to Bridgwater were lined with gallows; desperate rebels hiding in the corn fields were flushed out and shot for the sport. The toll of executed prisoners would have been even greater had it not been pointed out

1st Dragoons

to Feversham that perhaps they were entitled to a fair trial first.

Close to the battlefield, the rebel bodies were buried under a huge pile of sand. Buried alive, with the corpses, were some of the wounded. The grave was subsequently excavated but now has become quite indistinguishable. And perhaps it's best that their remains are left undisturbed.

Swayne's leap

A number of tales are still related of the round up of the rebels. The most popular local story is that of Jan Swayne. A rebel fighting Monmouth's cause, he managed to escape after the battle and found his way back to his Shapwick home. There the troopers tracked him down and dragged him from his bed. As the King's men dragged him towards Bridgwater, with his wife and children doing their best to keep up, Jan Swayne seized an opportunity to affect his escape.

As his last wish he pleaded with his captors for the opportunity to leave his children with

Kirke's Regiment

a lasting impression of his athletic prowess. He was known as the region's best long jumper. The officer in charge agreed and untied his hands. Jan Swayne took four giant leaps and disappeared into the dense undergrowth. With his life at stake, he had good reason to ignore the brambles which tore at him from head to toe. The troopers were unable to catch up with him as he took advantage of his better knowledge of Loxley Woods and the marshes below.

To commemorate the occasion the locals placed four stones to mark his leaps and these can still be seen today by following the sign posted footpath on the right hand side of the road as one drives from Bridgwater to Glastonbury through the area of the woods.

John Plomley's betrayal

A similar tale, though with a sadder ending, relates to John Plomley. He was the local

champion runner and being brought before Feversham, he was given the opportunity to literally run for his life. Feversham is claimed to have offered Plomley his freedom if he could outrun his fastest horse. Plomley seized the opportunity and ran like he'd never run before. Over the agreed distance he outpaced the horse beating him by a length with the horse closing fast. Exhausted he fell to the ground from where Feversham's men dragged him off to be hanged, the wager not being honoured.

Kirke's Lambs

Feversham, recalled to London, was replaced by Colonel Percy Kirke and his regiment, ironically known as Kirke's Lambs. Kirke and his regiment were the fiercest and cruellest in the English army. Kirke's first chore was to take the prisoners to Taunton for trial. Before embarking on that task, he had twenty or so prisoners executed. He was well known not only for his barbarism but also for his corruptness. It was his practice to take bribes in return for releasing those whose friends and families could afford it.

One story relates how Kirke was implored by a young local maiden to release her lover. All she had to offer was her honour. This he took with great pleasure. After having his wicked way, the poor disgraced girl was allowed to look out of the bedroom window only to see that her lover was already hanging from the gibbet with Kirke mockingly telling the girl that her lover was now free to go wherever she pleased to take him.

On arrival in Taunton, he immediately had a further thirteen hung, drawn and quartered. Their hearts were thrown on a fire and their quarters, after being dipped in pitch to help them last longer, were placed at various points around the town. Kirke was relieved of his position, not for his barbarism but for allowing the wealthier prisoners to purchase their freedom. He was replaced by the infamous Judge Jeffreys.

Judge Jeffreys and the Bloody Assize

Judge Jeffreys came to the West Country with a vicious reputation and immediately set about making it even worse. His first call was at Winchester where he tried an aged deaf lady accused of harbouring three rebel fugitives. The evidence against this lady was not particularly strong and the jury failed to return a guilty verdict. Jeffreys vented his wrath on the jury and intimidated them into returning a guilty verdict. That being achieved, he condemned her to be burned at the stake the same day. The local clergy appealed in the strongest possible way for clemency and Jeffreys reduced the punishment to beheading which took place a few days later. Only after it was too late was it realised that perhaps those she had been accused of harbouring needed first of all to be proven guilty as rebels, which they never were.

Judge Jeffreys

Jeffreys moved on to Dorchester and here rapidly found thirty guilty, many of them on the slimmest of evidence. Twenty nine of these were put to death. Jeffreys guaranteed that those pleading not guilty and then found guilty would be put to death. There was much reason for even the innocent to plead guilty once the finger of suspicion had been pointed.

The swiftness of his sentencing and execution of punishment was deliberate. Three hundred more awaited trial in Dorchester. Almost without exception, they pleaded guilty hoping for clemency. Eighty were swiftly put to death, their bodies quartered and hung at various points around the West Country. Those who avoided the death penalty were either flogged and released or transported into slavery, mostly to plantations in the West Indies.

At Exeter, the pattern followed a similar course, a quick trial of one pleading innocence, find him guilty, put him to death, so frightening the rest into confession. The swift action again had the desired effect. The remaining twenty nine pleaded guilty and were all sentenced to death albeit some survived to tell the tale.

At Taunton, over five hundred awaited his arrival. Bridgwater naturally did not escape his attention. He is reputed to have stayed at Marycourt in St. Mary Street whilst eleven were executed at the Cornhill being hung, drawn and quartered. One who escaped the death penalty was Roger Hoar who actually got as far as the gallows before a payment of £1000 ensured his release.

On to Wells and a further ninety seven executions and almost four hundred transported. In total, one hundred and forty four were executed around the towns and villages of Somerset with almost all the rest being transported. Hundreds died either on the battlefield or at the hands of Judge Jeffreys. Over two thousand were transported, with many not surviving the journey. The Judge had been instructed by

King James to be ruthless. No one could accuse him of failing in his duty.

It was not just the numbers involved that shocked the West Country folk, but the way the deed was carried out. Executions were deliberately arranged where possible at the home town or village of the convicted prisoner. Family and friends would be obliged to watch the execution. The bodies having been hung would be drawn and quartered and then hung in prominent places.

Few survived Jeffreys' ordeal. Those that did were in the main wealthy and able to buy their freedom. Jeffreys' financial gains were enormous and without doubt there were cases where innocents were accused just because of their ability to pay. Jeffreys' reward on his return to London was to be made Lord High Chancellor.

The following year, 1686, James actually paid Bridgwater a visit, presumably to see for himself that the people of the town were correctly toeing the line. The same town leaders who led Monmouth to his coronation now led the King through the town. They must been living on their nerves right through his stay. What was the real purpose of his visit? Would they survive the next few days? Were the bloody days of Judge Jeffreys a thing of the past or was the King about to revisit those gruesome days?

He came and went and no more was said, that is until the following year when a letter arrived instructing the mayor and the aldermen to stand down from their office. A further letter a few days later told the townsfolk who they were to elect in their place. These included Roger Hoar who, not long before, managed to escape the gallows. He recovered sufficiently from that ordeal to become the Mayor of Bridgwater and is now buried in St. Mary's churchyard.

Monmouth's revenge

Whilst Monmouth insurgence may be viewed as a disastrous folly, in the end it achieved in failure what Monmouth had set out to do, to remove the Catholic dominance from England and put a Protestant monarch on the throne.

The barbarity of Jeffreys and the subsequent over confidence of James turned the English people so against James that he had to go. Confident after Monmouth's defeat and Jeffreys retribution, James introduced new laws governing religion which proved unpalatable to the majority. The peoples' hatred reached a peak and parliament called on him to go. He had no choice and Mary, the daughter of James ll, was invited to take the throne with William of Orange as joint sovereigns. Monmouth's endeavours were not completely in vain.

Battlefield memorial

A visit to the battlefield today, well signposted from Westonzoyland, will take you to the memorial. The wording on the memorial pays respect to 'those who fell doing the right as they gave it'. What a nice inoffensive way to honour the fallen who on the one hand had won the hearts and minds of the Somerset people and on the other hand were all guilty of treason.

> TO THE GLORY OF GOD
>
> AND IN MEMORY OF ALL THOSE WHO
>
> DOING THE RIGHT AS THEY GAVE IT
>
> FELL IN THE BATTLE OF SEDGEMOOR
>
> 6th JVLY 1685
>
> AND LIE BURIED IN THIS FIELD
>
> OR WHO FOR THEIR SHARE IN THE FIGHT
>
> SVFFERED DEATH
>
> PVNISHMENT OR TRANSPORTATION
>
> PRO PATRIA

The Eighteenth Century

The days of stage coach travel

Up to the start of the eighteenth century most transportation of goods was carried out by pack animals, either horse or mule. Travelling long distances was a risky business and so it was normal for those moving goods around the country to travel in convoys of 40 or more pack animals. The horses needed to be of a particularly robust type to cater for the heavy loads that had to be balanced just right.

The start of the eighteenth century heralded the advent of coach travel increasing from almost nothing to become a significant alternative form of transportation. Coaches would normally be pulled by 4 or 6 horses travelling at no more than 4 miles an hour. Express services existed, known as the Flyers, and these reached up to 5 miles an hour. A journey to London would therefore take typically 3 or 4 days.

Night travel in the early days of coaching was far too dangerous except on rare occasions when perhaps the moonlight would be good enough, but this only really lengthened the travelling time by another hour or two. More frequently travel would finish late in the afternoon, all those involved having had a long enough day without the need to suffer any more stress. This may seem a rather early time to finish especially in the summer months but not so when one realises that they frequently started at 3 o'clock in the morning.

London in just one day

By the start of the next century, the state of the roads and the standard of the coaches had improved to the extent that the journey time to London was down to a full day's travel. The London coach used to leave each evening from outside the old post office on the East Quay. On arrival in London, the first thing our weary traveller would do, if he were wealthy enough to own a watch, was to reset the time. Until 1843, Greenwich Mean Time was not in use. Therefore midday, wherever you were, was when the sun was directly overhead. Thus on arrival in London, where sunrise and sunset are ten minutes earlier, all watches were moved forward ten minutes.

On its return, the coach would bring the previous day's papers from the capital. These would be paid for in advance by those with an interest in current affairs. They would not take kindly therefore to anyone else reading them first but that was what Mr. Holloway, the Post Master, used to do. This malpractice combined with his inability to avoid almost daily blunders led to his dismissal.

This was not the first complaint against the Post Office. There had been another back in 1675 when it appears a complaint was raised that the Bridgwater Post Master could neither read nor write. This caused severe problems in distributing the mail but at least there was no danger of him reading the London papers first!

To travel to the capital in those days was for most people literally the trip of a lifetime. The traveller would, as a matter of course, consult his solicitor to update his will before embarking on such an adventure.

By the mid 1800's, there was a considerable choice of travel and now at much greater speeds; some of the coach companies boasted 11 miles per hour as their average speed for the journey. With fourteen changes of horses on the way, this brought the journey time to London down to 12 hours. The "Swiftsure" coach went by the Bath Road to the Piper's Inn, Glastonbury, Wells, Shepton Mallet, Frome, Andover and on to London.

Giles and Hooper Waggons, Brown and Brice Waggons and Whitmarsh Waggons all offered the trip to London, covering the whole week between them. Journeys between Bristol and Exeter were covered by Snell's who stopped on alternate days at The Ship Aground, formerly in Market Street, Chadwell's Waggons, which stopped in George Street, and Brice's Waggons who used the Rose and Crown in St. Mary's Street. Also from the Rose and Crown, one could get a Martin's Waggon on its journey between Bath and Taunton.

The Three Crowns in St. Mary's Street served the needs of Webber's Waggons on their trips to Honiton. The skittle alley of the Three Crowns still shows the old metal rings along the walls where the coach horses were tied up between journeys. In addition there were Nation's Waggons between Bristol and Minehead, Granfield's Waggons from Bath to Minehead, Slocombe's between Bristol and Stogumber and Lavin's between Bristol and Wiveliscombe.

St. Mary's Street riot.

At the time of writing, trouble in St. Mary's Street is a topical issue and regarded as a relatively new phenomenon. However, nothing since 1717 has been seen to match the riot that occurred one hot July's evening.

A troop of dragoons travelling from Bristol to Exeter had stopped for a few days just outside the town. On Sunday, 20 July, a group of officers went to the Swan Inn on the Cornhill and commenced a drinking session which went on until the following morning. Early on the Monday morning, Thomas

Dowsett, William Freeman and Jonathan Cockram were ready to leave.

As they went to depart, one took a bag from a barrel and was observed to do so by a passing landlord who entered the Swan and notified his colleague of what he had just witnessed. Ensign Dowsett took offence, words and insults were exchanged and Dowsett pulled a loaded pistol from its holder and let loose a shot at the visiting landlord's head. The bullet missed by a fraction of an inch and lodged itself in the bar wall.

The mayor was summoned and in turn he called out the town's two bailiffs to arrest the dragoons. Dowsett and his fellow dragoon Freeman proved less than willing and the mayor was obliged to call out the constables, one an ironmonger, the other a maltster. On arriving at the Swan with a warrant for the arrest of the offenders, the soldiers closed ranks around their colleagues, drew their swords and sounded the call to arms on a drum.

In no time at all, forty or so dragoons had rallied to the call with weapons drawn. The culprits escaped from the back of the Swan Inn into St. Mary's Street. There the riot act was read and eventually the commanding officer of the dragoons arrived with a force strong enough to bring his errant men under control after what was a minor skirmish by military standards.

Shortly after the incident, the dragoons appeared before Taunton magistrates where justice was seen to be done and Bridgwater returned to its usual quiet ways.

Reverend George Whitefield

Another skirmish followed in 1739, but this time provoked by a member of the clergy. The Reverend George Whitefield had been invited by the parish vicar to preach in the town. He was an extravagant and extrovert non-conformist, noted for his provocative sermons. His visit to Bridgwater was no exception. The congregation were so offended that they had the town fire brigade bring out the pump and hosed him down whilst he continued to preach his sermon.

Castle Street

Without doubt Bridgwater's finest legacy of the Eighteenth Century is Castle Street, built in 1720-23 on the instructions of the Duke of Chandos and designed by local builders.

After the civil war, the castle had been destroyed on Cromwell's instructions. Thus the area of the castle was a sorry site and deemed to be a problem. A royal commission was set up to arrange its disposal. The Console General of Queen Anne's army, James Brydges the Duke of Chandos, was charged with the task. He arranged for Castle Street to be constructed, the architect

being Benjamin Holloway who also built The Lions building in West Quay for his own use.

The whole of Castle Street is Early Georgian in style being of a uniform nature at first sight. On looking more closely it will be seen that each dwelling place has a different style of door, porch and window. The street managed to maintain its cobbled road until relatively recently. Possibly the finest Georgian street in the West of England, it was chosen as one of the locations for the film Tom Jones starring Albert Finney.

The Duke of Chandos Glass Kiln

Another legacy of the eighteenth century is the Duke of Chandos' glass kiln. The duke attempted to introduce a number of new industries to the area. A soap works failed in 1725 and a distillery in Eastover failed soon after. The Duke mistakenly saw a glass kiln as a worthwhile investment emulating the success of others elsewhere. The materials

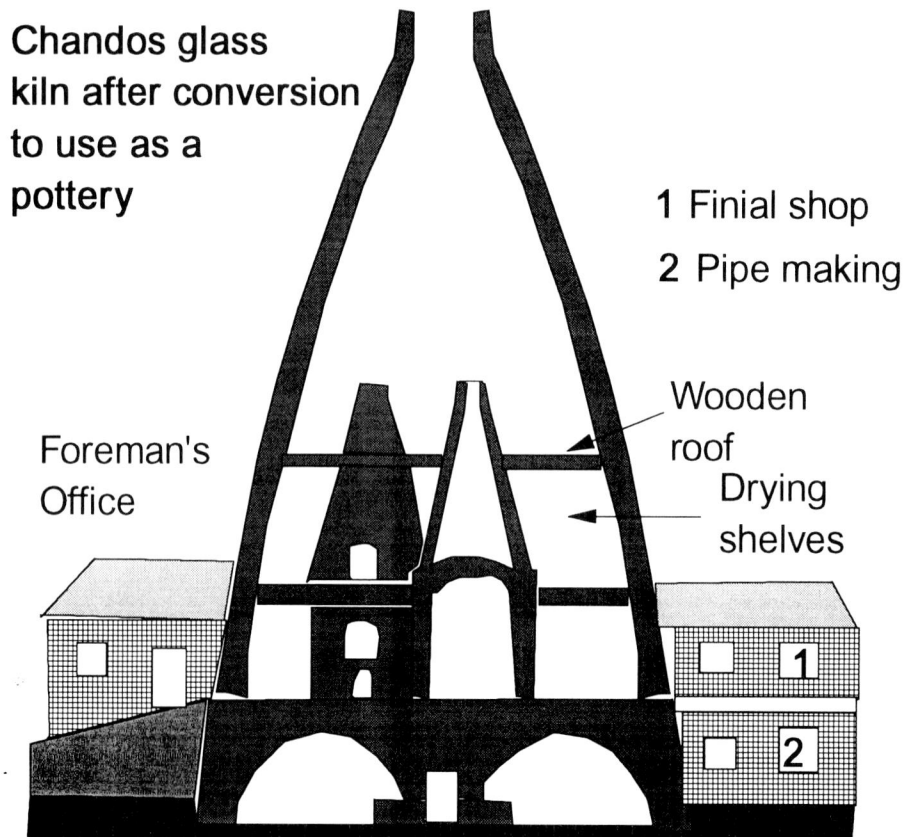

Chandos glass kiln after conversion to use as a pottery

Foreman's Office

1 Finial shop
2 Pipe making

Wooden roof
Drying shelves

and workers for this were brought in from Stourbridge. Unfortunately the venture failed and the kiln having been built in 1726 was abandoned in 1733.

It continued to prove useful for many years serving both as a pottery kiln until 1943 and a prison for French captives during the Napoleonic Wars. On September 20, 1977 the glass kiln was classed as an ancient monument.

Bridgwater bell foundries

The Eighteenth Century appears to have been a successful time for the bell foundry industry. Many bells cast in Bridgwater during this period can be found around the county and even further afield. Numerous businesses appeared to exist although none at the same time. This would suggest that only one foundry existed and passed through different ownership. It was probably somewhere in the Colley Lane area which was favoured for engineering enterprises. Apart from bells, cannon and agricultural items were also cast.

One of the earliest foundry businesses was Thomas Bayley, Street and Company (1738 to 1773). Their bells can be found in Charlynch (1743), Enmore (1739 and 1752) - albeit these were recast by George and Thomas Davis (1796), - Hinton St. George (1756) where Thomas Bayley also made the weather cock, Lopen (1765), Northover church at Tintinhull (1765), St. Bartholomew's at Crewkerne (1767) and five bells at All Saints Church, Langport (1772). St. Andrew's church at Old Cleeve used to boast a Thomas Bayley brass Candelabrum (1770) which was removed as unsightly in 1870 and put in the schoolroom.

Thomas Pyke appears to have taken over in 1776 until 1781 with just one bell traced to St. Margaret's in Tintinhull (1779).

Then George and Thomas Davis put in seventeen years from 1782 with bells in Hinton St. George (1783), St. Margaret's at Tintinhull (1787) and Stoke sub Hambdon (1787).

1798 to 1829 saw J. Kingston producing with Isaac Kingston joining in 1801. Thomas Kingston joined them from 1808 to 1832 and Edmund Kingston made an appearance in 1831. Their bells can be found in Shepton Beauchamp (1798), two at St. Bartholomew's in Crewkerne (1820) and one each at Huish Episcopi (1822) and Hinton St. George (1828).

Bells were being made earlier than this in Bridgwater. We know that Charlynch church had five bells from Bridgwater around 1538 and one made in the 14th century is now in a church in Reykjavik, Iceland. I have no idea how it got there!

Corrupt voting - the first recorded incident

During the eighteenth century there were only a limited number of people entitled to vote in parliamentary elections. Bridgwater appears to have a particularly bad record of corruption in these elections. The worst instances came later in the nineteenth century but certainly there was already something rotten as early as 1741.

In that year there were three candidates, Vere Poulett, George Bubbs Dodington and Sir Charles Wyndham. The voters went to the High Cross on polling day, where the Cornhill is now sited, and registered their votes. There was no secrecy in the ballot box in those days. All votes were recorded including who voted and for whom. Thus the whole affair was very open to scrutiny and, if there were any accusations of corruption, it was very easy to check the facts after the event.

In the year concerned, Wyndham came bottom of the poll and he published an article stating how the results as declared could not have been correct. He was convinced he knew he had received more votes than were actually declared in his favour. Feelings were running high. The town clerk in particular felt that his professional integrity had been called into question thus making it necessary for him to publish the results. He even detailed how the votes had been cast. As it turned out, the results had been declared honestly and correctly. Where things had gone wrong was in Wyndham's expectations of his support.

It appears that Wyndham's supporters had gone beyond the bounds of that which was reasonable. For example, his supporters in the country had come into the town and declared to the town's traders that in the future they would only supply provisions to those who promised to vote for their man Wyndham. With this threat hanging over them, many made their pledge but then failed to fulfil it. The town clerk felt it was not only important to clear his own name but also to let the Wyndham's people know who had genuinely voted for their candidate. He included in his statement his opinion of Wyndham's agents who were described as behaving more like bullies and also criticised the other candidates' agents for their unprofessional practices.

There is little doubt that with the intimidation and bullying, bribery would also have been rife. The town clerk's statement was supported by a list of all voters and against these names the town clerk actually indicated those who had voted other than as previously they had promised.

Bridgwater Races

By the end of the eighteenth century, one of Bridgwater's most popular distractions was Bridgwater horse races. The course was on Chilton Common, which oddly enough was across the river from Chilton Trinity, between Castle Fields and Hawkers Farm, roughly at the junction of Bristol Road and Wylds Road.

The reason for this side of the river being known as Chilton Common dates back to the time before the river altered its meandering course to its present position.

The race course was of fine grass and over a mile around its circular route. In the centre was a natural grandstand sufficient to hold 3,000 spectators. The races, which were certainly being held by 1780, were almost daily events and a poster of 1794 gives an idea to the number of races and type of entrants involved. On the 25th August of that year the following races were scheduled:-

Novice (not yet having won £20 in one day) hunters owned by Somerset men, the best of three four mile heats.

Novice hacks not yet having won £50, entrance fee half a guinea (52.5 p).

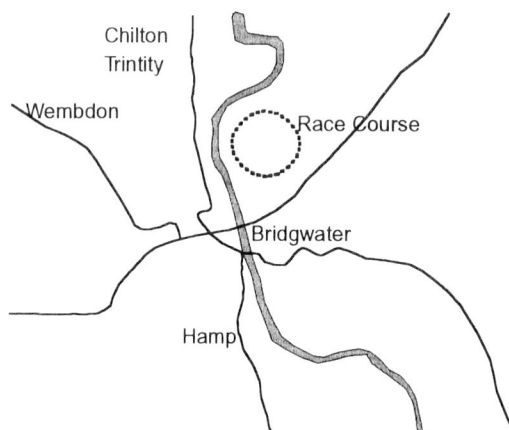

At various times the races waned and ceased, only to be later revived as they were in 1813 when Taunton Races were transferred to Bridgwater, and again in 1854. These races were still going in 1860 and a map of 1822 has the course clearly being shown. The horses had to be registered at the Crown Inn before the races started and were subject to the "Newmarket" rules which were recognised nationally.

In 1898 the Bridgwater Steeplechase and Hurdle Race was established under National Hunt rules and run in September. But in 1905 this race and all others on the course were abandoned. Attempts to revive them in 1926, this time at Durleigh, met with limited success and the last race there was run in 1929.

Bull baiting

Another 'sporting' activity which may well have taken place in the 18th century was bull baiting. Although there are no records as such, one of the fields next to Castle Fields used to be known as Bull Baiting Acre.

John Walford's gibbet

There was an air of expectancy in Bridgwater on 17 August, 1789. John Walford, a charcoal burner from Nether Stowey had been brought in to the town to be tried for the murder of his wife. In the eighteenth century, hangings were very public affairs and the source of much merriment. If Walford was found guilty, then a large number of Bridgwater people would make the journey out to Nether Stowey where the hanging would surely take place. It was the tradition for hangings to take place near the site of the crime.

Walford's case was put to the court. Born in Over Stowey, he followed the trade of charcoal burning on the hills behind Nether Stowey towards Crowcombe. It was a lonely existence but suited the quiet, industrious fellow. He was a handsome lad who was popular in the village especially with Ann Rich, the miller's daughter, to whom he was betrothed. His stepmother, however, objected to any marriage and in those days that was enough to delay the happy occasion indefinitely.

Against this background, Jane Thorney, the daughter of another charcoal burner, turned her attentions to young John. Jane, although not blessed with a great deal of intelligence, wormed her way into John's life. Under cover of darkness, she would visit his lonely hut on the hills offering him comfort. Inevitably she became pregnant and John Walford followed the honourable but fatal path and at the age of twenty four married Miss Thorney. The date was 18 June, 1789.

Almost at once life became intolerable for John. His newly wedded wife taunted him over the recent events, how he had been betrothed to the prettiest girl in the village but now had to make do with her. She kept on at him incessantly, life became impossible. Then on the fateful night of July 5th, only a few weeks after the wedding, walking back to their hut after a heavy drinking session at the Castle of Comfort Inn, she provoked him once too often. In a rage he took her by the throat and squeezed the life from her body. Seeing that no one was around, he carried her body on up the hill towards their home and disposed of her in a shallow ditch alongside the road. He scraped out a shallow grave in the remains of a prehistoric ditch, placed her body within and covered the area with the windblown leaves.

Jane Thorney's body discovered

Jane's father eventually became suspicious having not seen her for some days. The villagers were alerted. They were all well aware of Walford's hatred for his wife and a search was organised. Her body was not too difficult to find and Walford made no attempt to hide his guilt.

And thus it was that at the trial in Bridgwater, a trial which lasted only three hours, Walford was condemned to death with his body to go to medical science. The jury however had other ideas. Had there not been three other murders in the same area all within living memory? Was it not time an example was set that would leave a more lasting impression on those likely to stray from the straight and narrow? The judge conceded and agreed that the body should be left on the gibbet until nature took its course.

Execution day

On the day of the execution hundreds went from Bridgwater out to Nether Stowey to witness the hanging. It was a fine late summer day and picnics were organised and plenty of drinks made available. Hangings were always good sport, the victim being booed and insulted as if being hanged was not humiliation enough. The horse and cart with Walford on the back made its way up the hill. The gibbet was already in place.

Walford, for his last request asked to speak briefly to Ann, his first and only true love. She was helped onto the platform. The couple looked into each other's eyes, a few words passed between them and as they moved forward for the farewell kiss, the attendants pulled her away and lifted her off the platform. The moment had been so touching that the crowd to a man fell silent. All were moved by the tender scene they had witnessed and their hearts went out to poor John Walford.

The cart was pulled away, his body swung and jerked for a while and, once pronounced dead, he was cut down from the gibbet. His body was then placed in a cage and once more hung from the gibbet for the crows to do their worst. The crowd, some few thousand strong, silently made their way home.

The body remained in the cage for a full year before the continuous twisting in the wind brought it crashing to the ground. John Walford's bones were buried beneath the gibbet. For a hundred and twenty years or more the gibbet remained in place and even today the spot is known as Walford's Gibbet.

A short distance further up the road is a square of grass bordered by a hedge where the Quantock Staghound's occasionally meet before a hunt. The spot is known as Dead Woman's Ditch and is the very spot that Jane Thorney's body was discovered. Bridgwater people still visit the area for summer picnics and most of them have no idea of the events they predecessors went there to witness.

The river and shipping

The River Parrett

As we move from the 18th to the 19th century, the River Parrett increases in importance. This was the century in which it became most significant in terms of trade and its influence on the development of the town.

The source of the Parrett is near South Perrot on the Dorset border. On its way to the sea, it is joined by the Isle, the Yeo, the Tone and the Carey. It is tidal as far as Langport, well over 20 miles from the sea and on its tributary, the Tone, up to Creech St. Michael. This inland reach of the tidal effect emphasises the overall flatness of the Parrett basin.

The Parrett meanders far and wide over the flat expanse around the Bridgwater area. At one time in the last century it actually changed course. The river wound around a long sweeping bend almost meeting itself in a complete circle. Apparently a number of unknown people, one night cut a channel of forty yards across the isthmus without being discovered. This left an island surrounded on all sides by the river and known as Dunball Island.

The river from then on followed the shortest route and gradually the old river course silted up and disappeared. This left a parcel of land on one side of the river which used to be on the other and explains how "Chilton Levels" came to be on the Dunball side of the river.

The tidal bore

The tidal bore, which reaches as far as Langport, is the phenomenon caused by the strong tidal pull combined with the rapidly narrowing channels of the Severn and the Parrett. This results in a rush of water to be pulled into a rapidly narrowing funnel shape thus causing the gradually increasing wave at the front, called the bore, to be formed. A much older name for it, but no longer in use is the "Eagar". The effect is maintained well inland until either lockgates or an increase in land height puts paid to its power.

At its full strength on the spring and equinox tides, the bore can reach several feet in height. A ten foot high bore in 1875 had disastrous consequences, flooding virtually the whole of Sedgemoor. On lesser tides it can be almost imperceptible but between one and two feet is quite normal. The bore travels at about six miles an hour. This effect is not unique to the Parrett but there are few other places it can be witnessed. Certainly the River Severn and the Amazon share the experience; in fact the Severn and the Parrett have a tidal rise and fall second only to the Amazon. The Parrett in extreme cases will experience a rise of thirty six feet on spring tides.

The Caerleon jammed under the Town Bridge

On one occasion, the Newport based ketch Caerleon broke away from her moorings under the force of the bore and became jammed under the bridge. As the waters rose, which it does just like in a canal lock, the ship looked doomed, either through having her back broken or simply being submerged as the waters rose. As it turned out, all was well when the waters subsided as the tide turned and spared her for more journeys on the treacherous river.

The danger of this river should never be underestimated and it can be blamed for the loss of many lives. There is an unpleasant and haunting character to the river. Having claimed a victim, it will wash the body up and down the river for weeks at a time before its final surrender.

Bert Iley, who lived at Riverview Terrace and knew the river well, apparently fell in one night. It was a month before his body was spotted at Dunball having spent all those weeks going up and down the river. A local man, Ivor Binding, was a worker employed on the preparation of the new bridge on Broadway who met a similar fate and took a similar length of time to be recovered.

In more recent years there was the case of a young lad who tragically disappeared and met the same fate. Again the river kept its secret for a cruel and punishing length of time, as if to wring the maximum grief and pain from the bereaved.

Perhaps the longest the river kept her secret was when Henry James of York Road fell in the river in May 1940. His body was not recovered until the November.

The big freeze

There was one occasion in 1895 when the tide made no impact at all on the river. During the hard February of that year the river froze to such an extent that not only was there a great gathering on the solid ice, but also a bonfire and ox roast was organised just under the town bridge.

In similar fashion the villagers at Somerset Bridge held a tea party whilst those at Moorland held a pancake frying session, both of course on the frozen river. On the gloomy side to this tale, the severe conditions of that winter put a stop to all river traffic, clay extraction and any agricultural work. The town was devastated and a distress fund and soup kitchen were set up to help those unable to work through the difficult times.

River traffic

Depending on the state of the tides, the Parrett is capable of taking ships up to 300 tons, as far as Bridgwater, a distance of 14 miles from the sea. In practice, most ships which used the river were around the 50 to 70 ton capacity. If you consider that the loads carried by the lorries of today are around the 30-40 ton mark, then you can assume that a fully laden ship held the equivalent of about two lorry loads. River traffic declined rapidly with the advent of the railways. This was particularly the case when the Severn Tunnel railway link was opened, a problem which was exaggerated by the fact that the railway company also owned the dock.

Early days of shipping

Amongst the earliest records of river traffic is a complaint from Langport that the lord of Aller was stopping the free flow of river traffic between Langport and Bridgwater.

Accounts from 1300 show Sir Simon de Montacute as the owner of two galleys and a barge at Bridgwater all of which were called into service by King Edward. The following year Bridgwater sent no ships into the service of the nation although one was requested. This did not please the King who sent two clerks the next year with power to punish as they saw fit if ships were not forthcoming.

In 1306 the Sauneye of Bridgwater mastered by William de Wyght is recorded carrying lead to Gascony. In 1314 and 1317 Bridgwater supplied ships for the Scottish wars and was still supplying them in 1330 when hostilities with the French necessitated ships from Somerset and Dorset to congregate at Bridgwater ready to do active service at His Majesty's command.

The 1350's and 1360's saw a decline in English supremacy in the Channel with numerous ships being lost. In 1375 alone 39

Binford Place and the Langport Slip Way

ships were sunk by the French in Bourneuf Bay including Bridgwater's Saint Marie, a 170 ton vessel valued at £180. Ten years later in 1385, a 120 ton Bridgwater ship joined the fleet of the Duke of Lancaster in the attempt to obtain possession of the Kingdom of Castille.

The 14th century saw Bridgwater traders importing wine from Bordeaux and herrings from the channel. Exports included wool and agricultural products to France, Spain, Ireland and Wales. Corn it seems could be exported to Wales but not to the continent. Wheat and pulses could be exported to Ireland, France and Spain.

The fourteenth and fifteenth centuries saw a significant trade in the export of wool products. The increase was sufficient enough for a slipway to be built in 1488 to assist the barges taking goods upstream to Langport. This is the Langport slipway between the town bridge and the library. The stone for this enterprise was quarried at Pidsbury, a part of Langport, and was floated down the

river on barges from a small quay at Pidsbury down to the town bridge.

Customs and harbour dues

Customs duty had to be paid on wool and hide that was loaded at the quayside. In order to avoid this, the traders would take their wares onto the river in small boats and load up in the middle of the river. Another way of raising money was through moorage charges, hiring planks, cranes and ropes, and the skids on which to drag the wine barrels.

Much later in 1565 a report by the Exchequer Special Commission recorded that *"Bridgwater is comonly ffrequentyd and hawntyd wt trafyque of machauntes and marchandyzes to the inward and outward and ys eete to be contynued ffor that purpose. Ther are no places or sellers, ware houses or store houses nere unto the seyd porte where ladying or unladyng ys or hathe byn usyd whereby the Quenes Majestie ys defraudyd off her custome as ffar as we know."*

77

Five years later we had the 'Jhesus' owned by John Boyce recorded as available for duty with Queen Elizabeth's navy with the following nine Bridgwater seamen:-

James Dockett	Richard Cogen
Robert Stephens	John Prewett
Richard Hardricke	George Hoe
Robert Mayo	William Cooke
Thomas Phillips	

The voyage of the Emanuel

In 1578 we have the well documented voyage of Frobisher on his search for the North West passage to China. On that voyage one of the vessels in the fleet of fifteen was Bridgwater's 'Emanuel'. She was also known as the 'Busse' and was a deep sea fishing vessel or small trader, well suited to the heavy seas she was to endure on her epic journey. During a particularly violent storm she became separated from the rest of the fleet. During that period the crew discovered a previously unknown island which they called the "Sunken Land of Busse". For some years this appeared on maritime charts until an inability to rediscover it led to its removal.

And that wasn't the only Emanuel with a Bridgwater connection. Centuries later, a Bridgwater man Commander R. D. Graham, having suffered an illness brought on by the pressures of business, decided to sail to Newfoundland single handed. On May 19, 1934 the Emanuel, a 30 foot cutter, sailed from Falmouth to Newfoundland, down to the Bahamas and back the following June.

By the seventeenth century, the import of coal was perhaps the most significant single item. Records of 1616 show coal, grain, salt and herring being carried up to Langport in considerable quantities. Nine years later Langport suffered badly through lack of supplies due to an outbreak of the plague in Bridgwater. This led to the movement of boatmen being forbidden.

Coal coming in through the port of Bridgwater continued well into this century and only really breathed its last in 1969, when the local Courtaulds factory turned to oil and gas as the fuel source for its generators, and the dock closed virtually over night.

Over the years, imports covered coal, timber, twine, hemp, linseed, esparto grass, grain, hides and valonia (a product made from

East and West Quays

acorns and used in dyeing). Exports included timber, pit wood, cement, plaster of Paris, gypsum, bricks, tiles, pipes and cloths including the Bridgwater serges and kerseys.

Vice Consuls for Germany and Scandinavia

Bridgwater's trade covered the globe, predominantly the United States, Canada, South America, the Mediterranean, France, Spain, Norway, Sweden, Russia, the Baltic and the West Indies. There was even sufficient trade for Germany to have a vice consul on West Quay, being George Bryant Sully. Norway and Sweden shared John Charles Hunt in Castle Street as their Vice Consul. The Custom House was also on West Quay with hours of opening from 10 a.m. to 4 p.m. The Excise Office was based in the Lamb Inn in the High Street.

19th century major businesses

During the 19th century, four local companies very much dominated the market. The small vessels of the Haviland fleet traded in coal, culm and limestone. The Axford's faster schooners were used for coastal trading. Stuckey and Bagehot had even larger ships which were unable to come higher up stream than Combwich until the opening of the docks. Sully, one of the names still well remembered in the town, traded in coal and culm around the UK and with France.

Until just before the start of the World War ll, both sides of the river were used as quaysides. Vessels moored up trading their

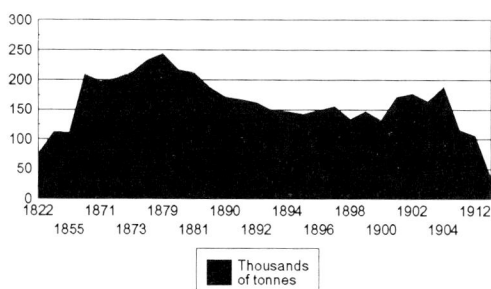

Port of Bridgwater shipping tonnages

wares with up to 4000 ships per year navigating the river channel. They turned over as much as a quarter of a million tons of coal, timber, grain, hides and wines each year.

The last visitors to East Quay

After a gap of some eleven years, the steamer 'Parrett' used the East Quay several times between 1947 and 1949 to offload cargoes of flour. The last sailing craft to use the quay was probably the Trio which visited in 1934 and was owned by the Warren family of Kendale Road. In the ports heyday as many as twelve vessels would be moored up at the same time along the quays.

The Parrett, the Enid (skippered by Warpy May) and the 'Crowpill' (skippered by Jibo Searle) were all familiar sights long after the war bringing coal up the river for use at the Cellophane factory.

Until the opening of the dock, most shipping coming up the Parrett moored up on the East Quay or West Quay, the prime positions being those nearest the town bridge.

This bridge acted as a barrier to any movement further upstream, thus on one side of the bridge we had the seagoing vessels including many coal carrying trows and on the other the flat bottom barges or 'lighters' which took coal and timber along the Parrett and its tributaries into the deeper parts of Somerset. From there it was carried by pack horse to more distant lying areas on higher ground unsuited to river barge navigation.

The lighters had the advantage of being able to pass under the bridge in order to collect and deliver their loads. I remember as a child playing in the old abandoned barges that could be found along the river bank particularly around the brickyard areas. These not only satisfied the needs of a young lad with a vivid imagination, conjuring up long trips along the river to unknown places, but they also served the needs of various forms of wildlife especially lizards and slow worms which are so seldom seen today.

Port status

A charter of May 26th, 1200 refers to the right of the Lord of Bridgwater to collect 'lastage', being a tax on cargo or ballast of a ship. Bridgwater has been classified as a port since at least 1348 and in 1402 became a port in its own right with no links with Bristol as had previously been the case. There is a significant difference between being a port and being just a harbour. The additional status that goes with the port authority allows the port concerned to collect dues from the whole of its catchment area and to control the shipping in that area. For Bridgwater this authority extended along virtually the whole of the Somerset coast, from the mouth of the River Axe to the Somerset / Devon border, the next nearest port being Bristol.

Much later, in 1845, the borough was also given the responsibility for maintaining the effective navigation along the course of the river and ensuring all the appropriate safety aids were adequately maintained. I remember as a borough councillor in the late 1960's being a member of the Port and Harbour committee. One of our more enjoyable tasks was to visit the river navigation light at Burnham and another at Combwich. Having satisfied ourselves that all was well and both lights were flashing at the correct pace, we would then retire to the Ship Inn at Combwich where a pleasant evening was always guaranteed. This annual inspection had its origins in the changes of 1845.

Ship building

Towards the end of the eighteenth century, there was a significant increase in river traffic. Problems with the tides meant that many vessels had to moor up at Combwich and then have their loads transferred upstream to Bridgwater on smaller vessels. The difficulty was not just a case of getting to Bridgwater but where did you moor when you got there? And could you moor up before the river level dropped too low and could you safely offload once the tide had gone out? The early nineteenth century saw an increase in the export of bricks and tiles destined for Wales, Liverpool, Ireland and Cornwall. A ship building industry developed, partly to deal with local shipping problems by building vessels which were suited to the river.

The first big ship known to be built in Bridgwater was the Nancy, a brigantine, in 1766 albeit in 1671 the Admiralty approved the town as suitable for the job. Other smaller vessels were built before but there is no evidence of anything more significant.

Certainly ships were recorded as Bridgwater vessels long before the 17th century and the town had at least one shipwright as early as 1593. John Trott is recorded as having built the 'Friendship' around 1697 for William Alloway, a merchant. The Trott family were quite influential around the river. John Trott had a graving and repair dock built on the east bank which later became a dry dock.

During the second half of the 18th century, ships were being produced one a year on average supporting a significant number of dependent businesses such as rope and sail makers. By 1810 there were two shipyards, one on the East Quay owned by the Trott family and the other at Crowpill, both building brigantines. Other yards opened up and built mostly ketches, sloops and smacks. Carvers Yard was one of the most productive building ships up to 200 tons whilst Gough and Nation on the other side of the river produced larger vessels up to 350 tons.

During the first half of the nineteenth century, 7 shipyards turned out 51 vessels. The next fifty years saw a further 88 vessels taking us up to the end of the nineteenth century. One of these was the Britannia, launched on September 24, 1831.

The Brittania which was built at Bridgwater and was launched on Saturday, September 24, 1831.

The launching of the Britannia

The newspaper, the 'Bridgwater Alfred', for September 26, 1831 gave a detailed report of the launching of the Bridgwater built Britannia.

"At an early hour the quays and banks of the river presented an interesting sight. All the vessels in the harbour were decorated with their colours and the banks were lined with crowds of people of all ages and conditions mingled in one close mass, presenting to the eye a living scene of interesting variety. Precisely at eight o'clock, the sound of the hammer striking away the blocks was heard and immediately the majestic fabric glided into the water, amidst the deafening cheers of the surrounding thousands. We never saw a finer launch and not the slightest accident occurred.

To the bulk of the spectators, the launching of a ship is nothing more than a pageant, a spectacle which they rush on to enjoy without any knowledge of, or even any desire of knowing, the means by which the operation is performed."

Records show at least 167 ships having been built and registered in the town, so we can assume there were probably a good few more than that. In the main they were sloops and schooners built for coastal traffic but included ketches and even square riggers for the more distant ocean travels. Bridgwater smacks were built with full and deep lines, straight stem and square sterns. Up until 1908 Quantock oak was used to construct the vessels which needed to be robust to deal with the heavy cargoes of brick and tile and the pounding of the sea and the Parrett's bore.

The Matilda, a smack built in 1830, came to a tragic end exactly a hundred years later when she was wrecked in the Bristol Channel just above Aust in 1930. She was the last of all the Bristol Channel trading smacks.

Two years after the Matilda was built, the Norah, a Bridgwater trow was bought by Captain Len who hauled her up to the Uphill wharf just to use her as a house boat. A 190 ton sailing vessel of 100 feet in length was launched from John Gough's yard in 1857 and was named the Admiral Blake. By 1864, Gough's ships were clearly getting larger with the launch of the 400 ton barque Cesarea.

The Irene

The last boat to be launched from a Bridgwater boatyard was the ketch, the Irene, on May 27th, 1907 from Carver's Yard. Built for the Bridgwater brick and tile firm, Colthurst Symons & Co. she is still operational and well cared for. This was well documented in a recently produced television programme "the Channel Traders" which had her as the main feature in two episodes of the series. Built of pine and oak, she was made to work out of the Somerset coastal ports. Journeys west included Watchet and Minehead and those to the north and east covered Cardiff, Avonmouth, Bristol and up the Avon as far as Gloucester and beyond.

The last vessel to enter Carver's Yard was The Crowpill which many Bridgwater folk still remember with affection. Her skipper was Jibo Searle, a man afraid of nothing, certainly not fog. He mainly carried coal from South Wales for Sully's and was known to navigate the river in worse conditions than many would attempt.

Purpose built ships were not enough to deal with the demand for river transported goods. They may have facilitated the journey up the river but did not address the tidal rise and fall once they arrived. There was only a small window of opportunity each day to travel the river. The tide comes in for two hours, stands still for half an hour and then runs out for the next ten. The town was in need of a floating harbour, a dock, a safe haven where vessels could load and unload untroubled by the effects of the tide.

Bridgwater's last ketch, The Irene

82

The docks and canal

Canal and dock development

Schemes for canals and floating harbours were popular talking points from 1811 right through to the 1840's, most of them coming to nothing. In 1820 a scheme was put forward for the development of a canal between Taunton and Bridgwater. It required an Act of Parliament for the scheme to go ahead. The plan was part of a much larger vision including a canal from the River Avon at Bristol right down to Taunton.

There had always been a regular trade between Bridgwater and Taunton using the Rivers Tone and Parrett. Problems occurred though during long dry spells when there was insufficient water for the traffic required. By 1827, thanks to the skill of the engineer James Hollingsworth, the canal was opened from Firepool in Taunton terminating at Huntworth at the Bridgwater end. The canal owners went into competition with the conservators of the Tone navigation rights, a battle which saw many disputes and court cases over a period of five years. The two sides went into a damaging price war, tolls dropped from 1s 4d to 6d per ton.

It became necessary for the canal company to apply to Parliament for the right to buy out its competitor, albeit a condition was imposed upon them to maintain the navigability of the Tone. Despite this condition, and despite the prices returning to their previous levels, maintenance on the river was almost non-existent. Control was returned to the Tone River Conservators who in turn deprived the canal of its water supply.

Canal extended to Bridgwater

In 1837 the royal assent was given to a proposal to extend the Bridgwater to Taunton canal from its Huntworth terminus down into the town and on to its present terminus at the docks. Work on excavating the dock began soon after with several hundred navvies being employed at the peak of the activity. The engineer in charge was Thomas Maddicks, a Devon man whose work was already to be seen in the nearby town of Taunton.

The heavy alluvial clay removed in the excavation was used as far as possible to create bricks for use in the buildings that were to spring up around the dock. The remainder was dumped on a spoil heap which became known as The Mump and was only recently removed with the more modern dockside development.

Canal, road and rail infrastructure

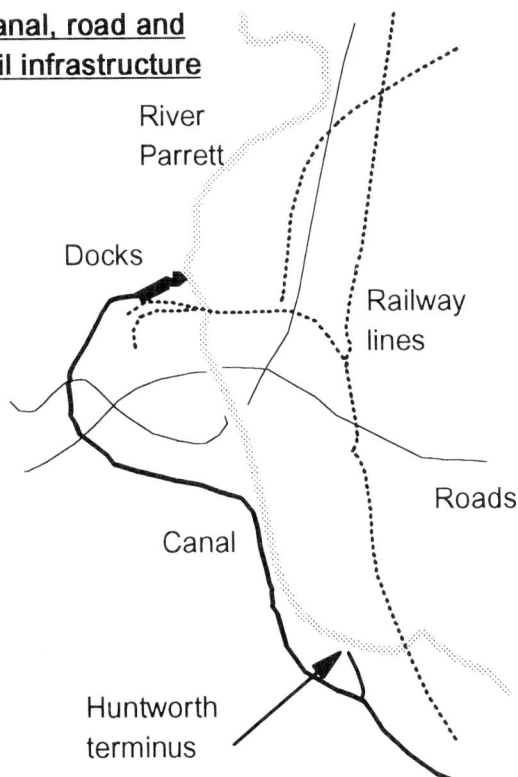

River Parrett

Docks

Railway lines

Roads

Canal

Huntworth terminus

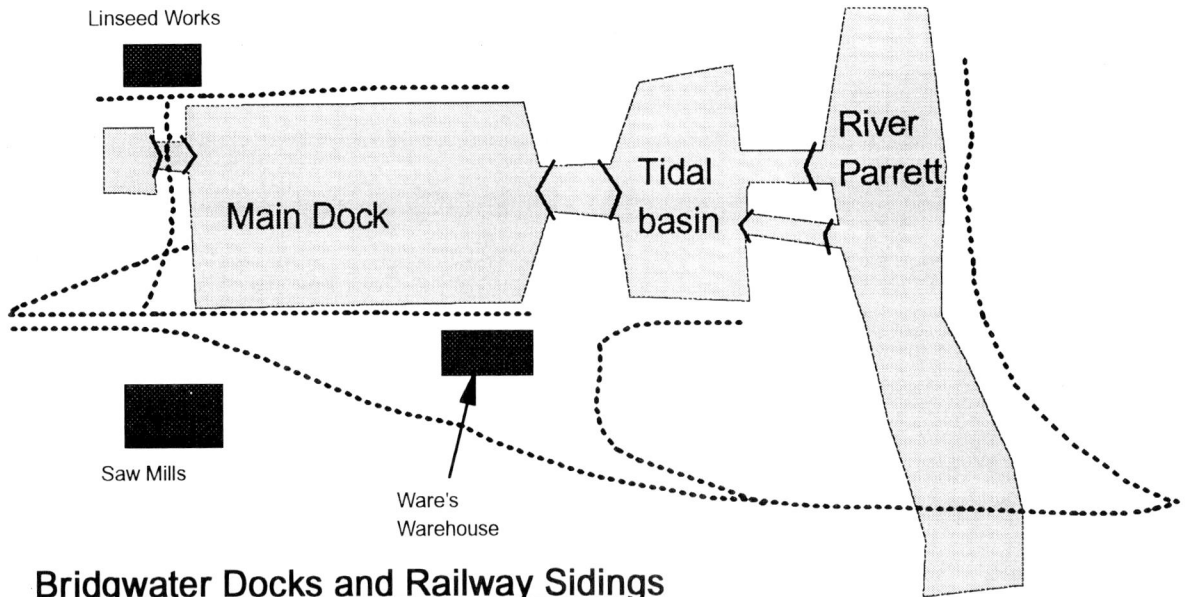

Bridgwater Docks and Railway Sidings

A major feat of engineering was required where the canal passed through the area from Albert Street to the Victoria Road Bridge. The Albert Street area in particular is of interest, this section requiring a deep cut to be made in the red sandstone earning it the name of the Canyon. Walking this section today, shored up as it is with massive timbers, leaves one wondering how long the job will last. Thomas Maddicks, having completed his project retired into obscurity and died in the workhouse in Taunton at the age of 84.

By 1838 the Grand Western Canal was linked to the Bridgwater to Taunton canal at Firepool at the Taunton end of the canal. This made navigation possible all the way from Bridgwater to Tiverton.

The opening of the docks

1841 saw the opening of the docks and floating harbour, including the best part of what is now called Wares Warehouse and the Bascule Bridge which allowed for both road and river traffic to live in harmony. This bridge was closed for many years after the war but was reopened for public use in 1983.

The Canyon, Albert Street

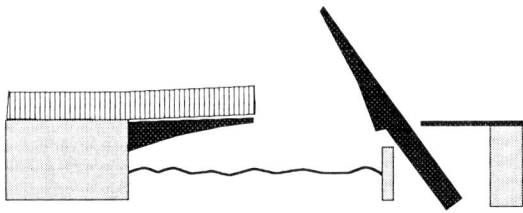

Bascule bridge in partly open position

Amazingly the whole exercise of constructing the dock saw only one fatality and that was actually nowhere near the dock itself. A local man was delivering a 6 ton stone to the dock when a thunderclap caused his horses to bolt, overturning his wagon and killing him in the process.

The very first vessel to enter the dock, on Thursday 25th March, 1841 was the Bridgwater built sloop "The Henry" with her captain Giles Billing at the helm. She was brought into the dock by the port's first steam tug, the Endeavour, which had sailed down the Parrett to meet her with a band playing and a party of dignitaries on board. It was a great occasion justifying the declaration of a local Bank Holiday which meant thousands turned up for the occasion.

Cannons were fired and the church bells rang, bands played and the national anthem was sung. Civic dinnes were held at the George Hotel and the Royal Clarence; no expense was spared. This was the start of a new era and the end of a period of heavy toil for those involved in the excavation and engineering. The three year exercise had resulted in a floating harbour 190 metres by 65, with 105,000 cubic metres of soil being removed. It had two entrances from the river, one for ships and the other for the much smaller barges. It was capable of taking any ship up to 180 feet in length and 31 feet across the beam.

Wares Warehouse was built in three phases. The three western bays (at the canal end) were bonded warehouses for the Canal Company; the rest was added by the Bristol and Exeter Railway Company. The whole development has recently been converted into flats and a dockside bar with the whole dock area being carefully and tastefully developed into a residential area around what hopefully will one day be a successful marina.

Apart from Ware's Warehouse, Bowering's animal feed mill still survives alongside the Newton Lock which links the canal with the dock. Also surviving are the stables, now converted to housing, close to the river itself.

The Black Bridge

The docks were eventually bought by the Great Western Railway company which in 1870 constructed the telescopic bridge across the river known as the Black Bridge and this was originally used as a horse drawn railway link to the main line. A similar horse drawn link existed to the Bristol and Exeter Railway at Dunball wharf which was opened for Bridgwater coal merchants in 1844.

The bridge was supported by two large piers, one on each side of the river. When ships came up to dock alongside East or West Quay, the two telescopic sections of the bridge would be slid back into their well on the Eastover side of the river allowing ships to pass between the pillars. There were only two bridges of this type ever built.

Unfortunately after its closure in 1957, British Railways, who then were the owners, allowed it to be officially vandalised. Whilst one section of BR was working on a plan for its preservation, another section was breaking it down for scrap. Its transverser and engine house were removed although parts of the gearing mechanism still remain. The boiler at least has been preserved and can now be found at the Westonzoyland Engine Trust. Just before its closure, the bridge was re-opened after some years of disuse. Unfortunately war time defence work had

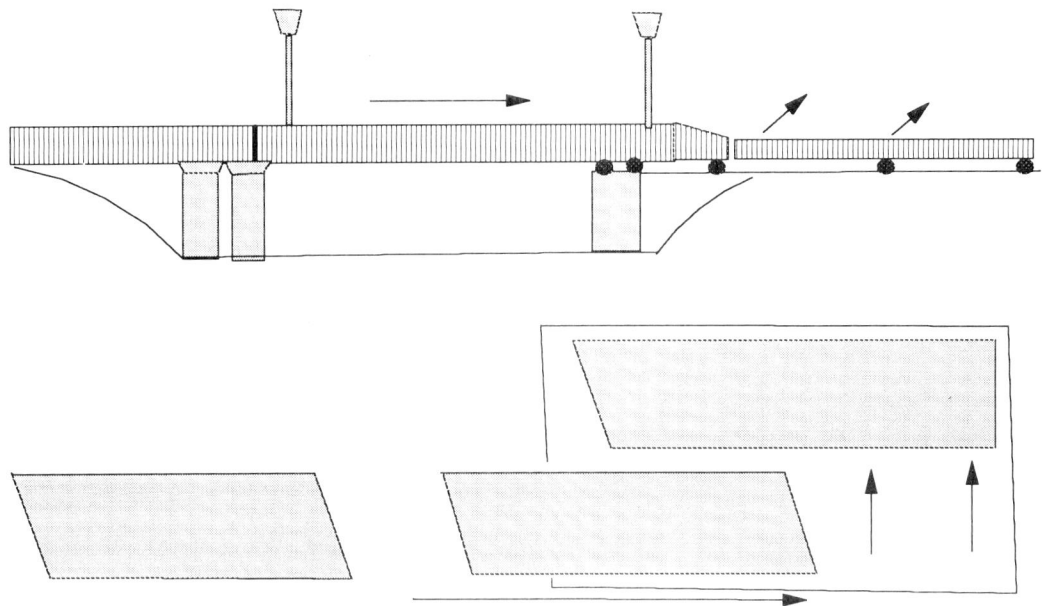

Telescopic bridge showing how end section on bank rolled across
sideways creating space for central river section to roll into vacated space

produced some damage and one of the traversing wheels suffered a breakage.

Introducing Bertha

The first major problem to be encountered at the dock was that of silting. The problem had been anticipated but its effects under estimated. In reality the silt deposits were accumulating at about a foot in depth each month. Within a few months of opening the docks, Bertha was brought in.

She was a steam driven dredger designed by Brunel. Her role was to scrape the base of the dock, as she dragged herself from one quay to the other on chains installed for the purpose, dislodging and stirring up the silt. This would then be flushed out by the fresh water supplied from the canal. The idea worked well and kept the dock operational for many years. Bertha was eventually retired and now has a home at the Exeter Maritime Museum. At the time of her retirement, she was the oldest piece of British Rail equipment still in active service.

Pilots and hobblers

Years of prosperity and change followed the opening of the dock. Tugs increased in numbers and hobblers reduced. The hobblers were the rough and ready band of men whose job was to haul the ships up the river. The pilots, and there were over twenty in Bridgwater, would sail out in clippers to meet the ships in the channel, often racing each other to claim the responsibility and the five shilling payment.

The pilots having guided the ship into the river, the hobblers would either row the ships along its course or manually haul the ships up the river using ropes produced in the town. On reaching the quayside, they would 'hobble' the ropes around a bollard, haul the ship along until the next bollard could be reached, and so on until the ship was finally hauled into its mooring position. The hobblers would often walk from Bridgwater down the river bank to Combwich or Highbridge to pick up an incoming ship. If none arrived

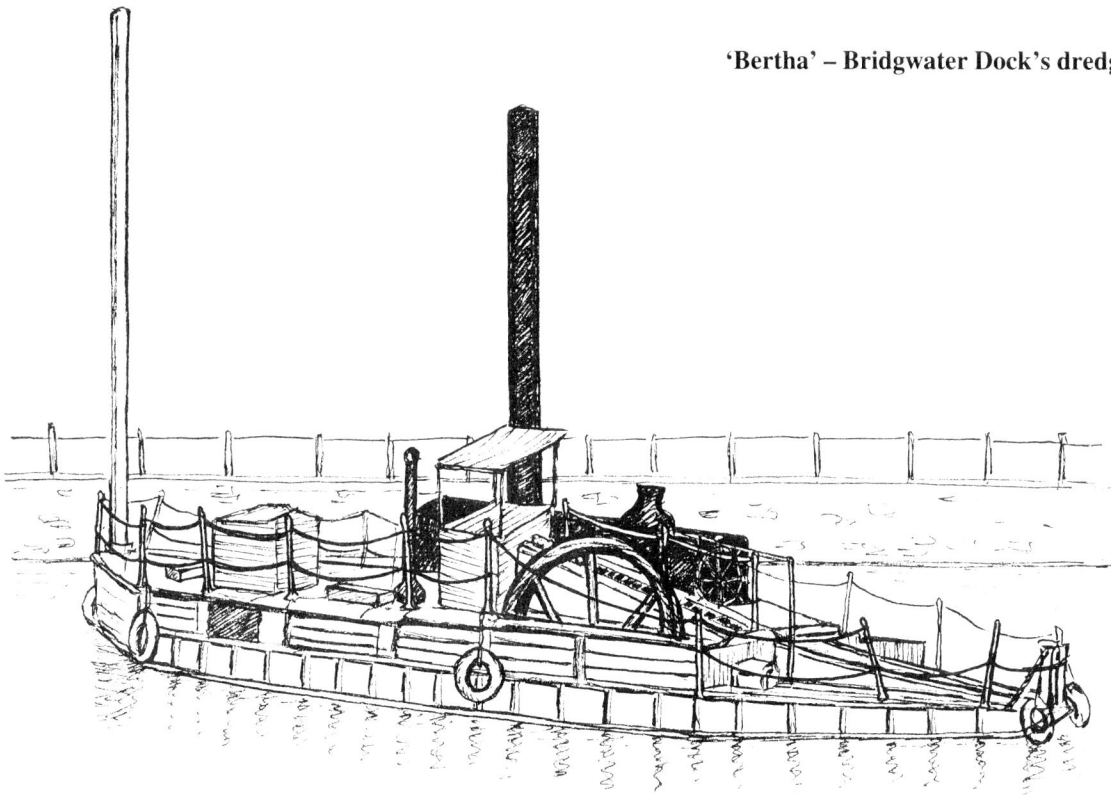

that day, they'd turn round and walk back with no wages for their troubles.

Apart from the decline of the hobblers, other manual labour was replaced by cranes and dockside paraphernalia. Jobs lost in one area were balanced by new ones in others.

Pubs and chapels

The increase in the number of licensed houses served as one example. The names of inns of today and those of yesteryear reflect the local association with the sea. The British Flag and the North Pole still survive, those that have gone included the Anchor, the Dolphin by the Town Bridge, the Ship Aground and the Ship Afloat, the Hope and Anchor by the Black Bridge, the Steam Packet in St. John's Street, the Sailors Return and the Sailors Home, The Salmon (now the River Parrett) and the Shipwright's Arms.

Then of course the number of Temperance houses also had to increase. One of these was on the East Quay, the building occupied at the time of writing by Connell's, the estate agents. The seamen even had their own chapel, the Mariner's Congregational in St. John's Street. Built in 1837 for the use of seamen, it seated 350 people, had its own school and survived until the 1960's.

Trade reached such a level that at times it was possible to walk from one side of the dock to the other, or indeed across the river, by walking across the decks of the ships, such was the level of activity in the middle to late nineteenth century.

Decline of river and canal trade

But the prosperity was not to last. Having peaked in 1861 at between 160,000 and 200,000 tons of traffic, there was a marked decline, from 1878 to 1900 dropping from its high position to half that volume. The growth of the railways and the move from sail to larger steam driven ships made the Parrett a less attractive and more expensive route for local imports and exports. The opening of the Severn rail tunnel in 1886 was particularly disastrous for the town's river traffic.

The decline was paralleled on the canal and by the turn of the century the canal traffic had

87

effectively stopped. The last commercial barge to run the length of the canal was in 1907.

It was never easy getting into the docks and potentially disastrous incidents were not uncommon. In 1928 a German timber boat, the S.S. Masuren, hit the river bank at the turn of the tide. She came very close to capsizing and her captain was obliged to cut free the timber on her decks when she had listed to an angle of 45 degrees. Its load of timber spilt into the river and eventually found itself travelling upstream. Inexplicably dozens of chicken coops sprang up along the banks of the River Parrett all the way from Bridgwater to Langport!

Reclamation of the canal

The dock continued to operate trading mostly in coal and timber until its closure by Act of Parliament in 1971. The last coal came in during 1966. By that time the canal had been a redundant feature for many years and was rapidly falling into a state of dereliction. In the mid-1960's, the potential to develop the canal as a recreational amenity was recognised. 1966 saw the inauguration of the Somerset Inland Waterways Society with the objective of returning the canal to its former state as a navigable waterway. Thanks to their efforts and the support of local authorities and the British Waterways Board, the canal is once more navigable along its whole length. It now serves the need of boaters as well as anglers, ramblers and naturalists.

Road, rail and other utilities

The Turnpike Trusts

It wasn't always necessary to maintain roads as we know it today. Traffic, before wheeled transport, was fairly light and not enough to cause wear and tear. Records show that as early as 1501, local merchants were paying the cost of maintaining the road from Bridgwater to Taunton.

The introduction of wheeled traffic led to a dramatic decline in the state of the roads across the nation. Roads which had lasted hundreds of years rapidly deteriorated and a national solution was required. In the early eighteenth century the Turnpike Act was introduced. This allowed tolls to be charged for the use of roads, the revenue being used to ensure they were maintained to a reasonable standard.

In Somerset, Bristol and Bath were the first to react with Bridgwater taking third place in 1730. The members of the Bridgwater Turnpike Trust (1730 - 1870) fixed tolls as they saw fit. The Act repealed previous ones which had restricted the size of vehicles that could use the roads. It was, therefore, up to the Trusts to keep pace with the now increasing size of traffic.

Roads in the area were improved at a fairly rapid rate. Roads from Bridgwater to Thurloxton, East Brent, Nether Stowey, the Piper's Inn, Langport Bridge, Bishop's Lydeard and Spaxton were all covered. Along these roads you can still see the mile stones and notices indicating the end of the turnpike roads.

In general existing roads were used. They were acquired, widened and generally improved. Only a limited number of roads were introduced, the Bristol Road as we now know it, being one of them.

The Trusts eventually disappeared in 1870 with the introduction of the Motor Car Act. The Red Flag Act of 1865 which required all vehicles to be preceded by a red flag was repealed in 1896.

The laying down of Bristol Road

Until 1822 the route from Bridgwater to Bristol was along the present A39 road to Glastonbury as far as the Crandon Bridge, or Silver Fish corner as it is still popularly known, where the road forked left up over Puriton Hill and down towards Pawlett. During 1822 to 1823 the new road was laid much improving and shortening the travelling distance between Highbridge and Bristol.

The need for this improvement was, no doubt, a great benefit to the coach companies. At that time there were 9 carriers on 14 routes with 11 coaches between them. The following years saw an increase in carriers and routes until the arrival of the railway in 1841. The pattern of road traffic then changed with a reduction in long distance travel by road but an increase in the short distance local traffic from the railway station to the villages and towns further west.

New town bridge of 1797

In 1793, the old bridge over the river was in a very poor state of decay, as were the quaysides in the town. It was decided that a new bridge was required and that it should be an iron one.

This was shortly after the time that the first iron bridge was developed by Andrew Darby at Coalbrookdale. Indeed, the famous "Iron

Bridge" was being built at the same time as the new one for Bridgwater. The various parts required were cast at Ironbridge in 1795 by Thomas Gregory, sailed down the River Severn and up the Parrett to Bridgwater. Completion seems to have been a long time coming. It was not until 1797 that the cast iron bridge with its elliptical arch was opened.

An Act of Parliament was necessary in order to build a new bridge and repair the quay sides, also in a bad state of repair. The act, which can be found in full in our local library, refers to the old bridge as being 'narrow, incommodious and dangerous to passengers, carriages and cattle, passing over the same and the said bridge is very ancient in want of repair and so constructed that the navigation of the said river is rendered very inconvenient and dangerous'. All sorts of conditions were attached to the Act. No goods could be left on the quay side for more than 7 days. Vessels staying one month were to pay one shilling a week for the privilege.

The bridge did not open until 1797, but the commemorative plaque, still visible today, clearly states 1795. This reflects the time gap between casting and erection. The 24 foot wide bridge costing £4000 was paid for by raising tolls on the roads into the town.

The bridge was to last for nearly ninety years when it was decided to replace it due to the changing demands of local traffic. It was proving too narrow and too steep. Heavy loads, which must have increased dramatically with the introduction of the docks and railway, frequently required additional horse power to cross from one side of the town to the other. To understand the problem, its well worth a visit to Ironbridge to see the bridge spanning the Severn there. From a distance, the gradient looks very gradual but on walking across the bridge one realises that the bridge does not flatten off at its crown but the two approaches meet at quite a sharp angle, certainly for heavily loaded horse drawn carriages. The design of Bridgwater's bridge was similar.

Town Bridge and Fore Street

New bridge of 1883

And so in 1883 the new 75 foot span bridge, designed by R. C. Else and G. B. Laffan, and made by George Moss of Liverpool, was opened on November 5th with the carnival procession using it for the first time.

The story is still told in Bridgwater of how the Mayor unexpectedly was unable to fulfil his duties at the opening ceremony due to an unexpected attack of the gout. The lady mayoress fulfilled his duties in his absence. However at the "no expenses spared" celebration at the Town Hall, the Mayoress having fulfilled her civic function, decided to leave the celebrations early and tend to her sick husband. Apparently on arriving home, the Mayor was found not to be suffering from gout at all but from an afternoon with his mistress! The accuracy of this story is not known.

Souvenirs from the old bridge were sold to help pay for the new. One relic survives today being the town coat of arms still displayed over the portico of what used to be the Royal Clarence Hotel and now Royal Clarence House. The initials RC on the plaque stand for Robert Codrington, the

Borough Seal

Mayor in 1797 when the previous bridge was opened.

The new bridge was to remain the only road bridge over the Parrett until 1957 when the Blake Bridge was opened on the site of the old wooden Lime Bridge which served as an alternative but minor crossing point during the middle ages. In 1983, to celebrate the town bridge's first one hundred years, lanterns - replicas of the originals - were added to the bridge by the local Civic Society returning much of its earlier character.

The advent of the railway

1841, as well as seeing the opening of the dock, also saw the arrival of the railway line from Bristol. On June 1 the engine 'Fireball' took 8 carriages and 400 passengers from Bristol Temple Meads to Bridgwater in one and three quarter hours. At Bridgwater they stopped for a champagne lunch before returning to Bristol. Its importance was well recognised and the occasion was a big affair with the large crowd well entertained by the band of the West Somerset Yeomanry. The official opening was actually on June 14, 1841.

Owned by the Bristol & Exeter Railway Company, the railway reached down to Taunton the following year. The line traversed the river at Somerset Bridge and it was a young and not yet fully appreciated Isambard Kingdom Brunel who was responsible for the design and construction. The stone supports either side of the river were of Blue Lias and were floated down the Parrett on barges. Brunel's bridge remained more or less unaltered until 1904 when a steel girder bridge was placed on the same foundations created by Brunel more than sixty years before.

The expansion of Eastover

At the time that the railway came through, the town extended no further than the end of what is now Eastover at one end of the town and the Malt Shovel Inn in North Street at the other. The area which is now St. John's Street soon developed with the growth of the railway activity close to the site of the old St. John's hospital, with the other streets of terraced houses in that area following close behind.

Horse drawn coaches provided a service from the station linking it to the villages and the towns further west. One of these, the 'Exquisite', was serving passengers to Exeter in 1841 when the driver decided to argue the right of way with a railway engine. This was more or less at the site of the present Westonzoyland Road bridge. At that time there was a level crossing and no bridge. The coach overturned, the train came off the rails and one passenger received a broken ankle. A lucky escape perhaps but enough to trigger the idea of a road bridge.

Bridgwater Carriage Works

The development of the railways and the need for extra rolling stock increased significantly. In 1849 a railway carriage manufacturing works opened in Colley Lane. During its time it produced rolling stock for both gauge railways that existed at the time, even producing narrow carriages on wide bases in readiness for standardisation.

Great Western take over.

The Bristol and Exeter Railway was eventually taken over in 1876 by the Great Western Railway Company. Their riverside wharves were in regular use up to World War I and then used as sidings until World War II when their metal was commandeered as part of the war effort. These wharves were opened in 1845 and were originally horse drawn, being replaced by steam in 1867.

Somerset and Dorset Joint Railway

In 1854 the Somerset and Dorset Joint Railway Company opened a line between Highbridge, which at one time had as many as five platforms, and Glastonbury. The line was extended to Burnham-on-Sea in 1858. The terminal at Burnham was meant to serve as a link to South Wales thus allowing passengers from Wales to travel via Burnham to Poole in Dorset and from there to the continent. The scheme never took off and soon had its first disaster. The steamer Ruby was used for the channel crossing and early in its career was moored up at Burnham when the tide went out leaving her high and dry. The episode resulted in her back being broke albeit she was recovered and eventually went to the United States where she served in the Civil War.

More than 30 years later, in 1890, a direct line was opened between Bridgwater and Edington Junction. By that time the Burnham to Glastonbury line had been extended through Wincanton and Templecombe right down to the south coast at Poole.

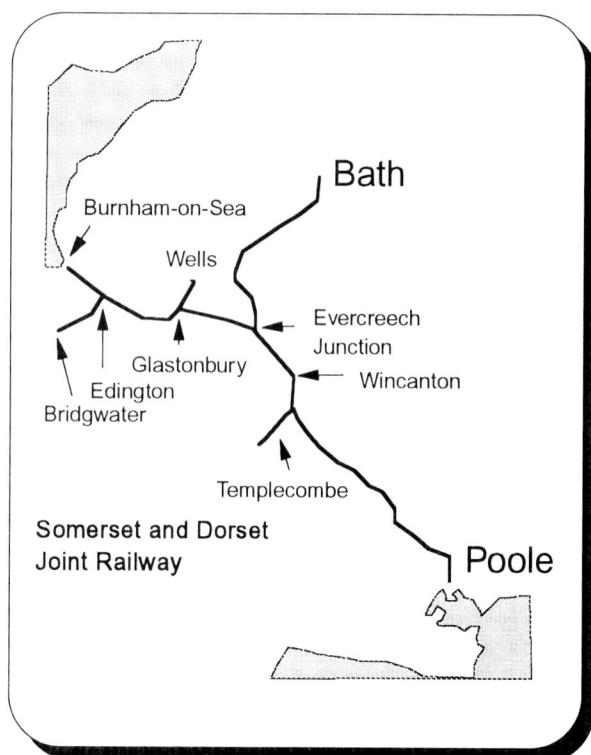

Somerset and Dorset Joint Railway

Day trips were now possible from Bridgwater to the beaches of the north and south coast. I remember as a child going to the S & D station where the Sainsbury supermarket is now sited. It was a summer treat for us to go via Edington Junction to Burnham-on-Sea taking a picnic lunch. The fare was 9d for adults and 6d for children. As many as two or three hundred children would board the nine o'clock train when the Sunday School annual outings took place. After a day on the beach, teas were taken at the Lifeboat Cafe in Burnham, once all the children had been rounded up from the beach.

The link to Edington crossed the Bristol Road at the junction with Wylds Road, closing to passenger traffic in 1952 and to goods in 1954. The line of the track crossed the road over a bridge at this point and can still be determined along a piece of land acquired by the Bridgwater carnival committee to serve as a permanent site on which carnival clubs can build their spectacular floats.

Inevitably the railway had its impact on the canal trade. Rail was becoming a cheaper and faster form of transport and the days of the canal were numbered.

The Bridgwater Railway Company

We know that the link line between Bridgwater and Edington Junction opened in 1890 but there was an even earlier attempt that failed. Perhaps it was never a serious attempt but more of a financial scam. In 1875 there was a serious campaign to form the Bridgwater Railway which would run from Bridgwater to Edington joining with the S & D line. At a public meeting of over 4,000 people, only four people objected, two of those only because they thought the route should pass closer to their villages of Chedzoy and Moorlinch.

The main thrust of the campaign for the new line was the poor quality of service on the Bristol and Exeter line with, it was claimed, nine out of ten trains running late. It was claimed that to go to London it was quicker to go by horse and cart to Highbridge and from there take the S & D to Waterloo than to get the B & E train to Paddington.

Goods regularly took several days just to get out of the Bridgwater sidings and a further two to three weeks to arrive at their final destination. Customers would specifically ask the B & E to route their goods over the S & D line, a facility which was available to the customer by Act of Parliament. The B & E however had their own way of deciding the best route, and that was basically the one which did the most to line their own pockets. Bridgwater's own link to the S & D line was the only acceptable solution.

On March 17th, 1875 Parliament approved the Bridgwater Railway bill. The solicitor acting for the Bridgwater Railway Company happened also to be the solicitor for the S & D Railway Company, a gentleman called Toogood.

The B & E board never believed that the proposed line would pay off. However if it opened it could do untold damage to their own trade. They approached Mr. Toogood and suggested that rather than go to the expense of seeing the bill through the House of Lords only to open an unprofitable line, it would be better to stop the scheme immediately. This Toogood agreed to do, as long as the B & E paid all his expenses to date plus the savings the B & E would make by not going through the House of Lords, plus an element of profit for himself on top. This was accepted and whilst Bridgwater for the time being lost its railway, Mr. Toogood was a wealthier man.

Perhaps Toogood's plan all along was no more than a scam. His professional status suggests he was no fool. His position with the S & D Railway speaks sufficiently for his understanding of railways and the way they

River
Parrett

Wharf

S & D line

Quantock
Terrace

Castle
Fields

Bristol
Road

Docks

GWR line

Telescopic
bridge

S & D Railway
station

Hospital

Isolation
hospital

Workhouse

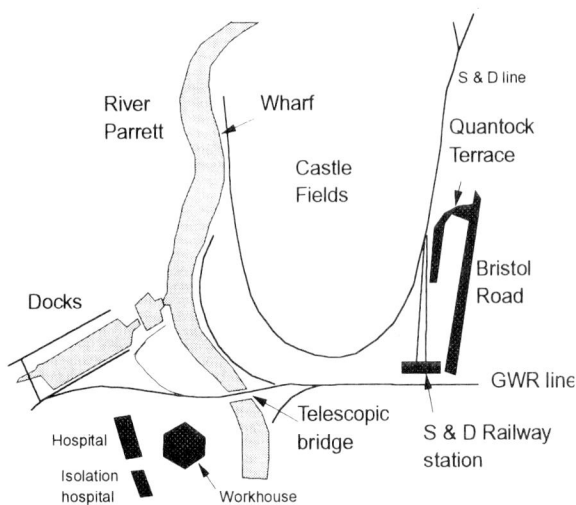

ran and made profits or losses. It can be assumed that he realised the financial risks and the probable reaction from the B & E Railway Company.

The second and successful attempt

In 1882 another attempt was made to set up the Bridgwater Railway Company. Toogood was once again involved and the same arguments applied. Despite a very sound case regarding the uncertainty of the financial viability of the scheme by the objectors, namely the B & E , Parliament and the Lords passed the act. This time Toogood received no bribes or offers from the B & E who presumably now lacked belief that the scheme was a serious threat, perhaps just a repeat of the previously successful scam.

There then followed eight years of bribery and corruption and plenty of problems leading nowhere except to create business for the company's solicitor. The only activity seemed to be in raising the funds for a scheme where no effort was being made for its actual development.

Inevitably the shareholders had enough. They sacked the board all bar one and brought in fresh faces with a greater commitment to the railway's development. Work finally started

in 1888 with the line opening on July 17th, 1890. A grand opening ceremony was planned but alas it rained all day. It poured down. The celebrations were a washout but at last the line was operational.

Prosperous days for the Bridgwater Railway Company.

The first decade saw a great deal of activity with cattle pens, toilets, stables and plate layers huts being constructed along the route and at the stations at Bridgwater, Cossington and Edington with Bawdrip being a later addition. A limestone quarry was opened at Cossington taking advantage of the railway link and the Bear Creek Oil Company opened a depot by Bridgwater station. A riverside wharf was constructed being 400 feet in length. A steam crane built by Thomas Smith near Leeds was used to transfer loads between ships and railway trucks alongside the wharf.

By 1892 there were nine trains in each direction each day offering links to London and Southampton. There were even twelve sidings, a station master and four porters.

The runaway train!

The station was not far from the Cross Rifles Hotel which must have fared well in the days when the station was open. At least one railway worker was a regular there. He was a goods guard and on one night managed to miss the train he was supposedly guarding. He left it to the last minute to leave the pub and return to his duties. Meanwhile, unbeknown to him, his train was already leaving. A friendly porter on the station platform waved goodnight to the engine driver. He in turn interpreted this gesture as the all clear to leave and pulled out of the station with his erstwhile partner still in the Cross Rifles wondering why he could apparently hear an engine leaving the station!

Good profits were made from the day the line opened right up to the First World War. During the war years the nation's railways came under government control and rail traffic was co-ordinated by a central committee. This resulted in many railway companies merging once the hostilities were over and the Bridgwater Railway Company became part of the London South Western Railway in 1921 after thirty years of theoretical independence.

The next thirty years saw it in decline and a financial drain on the resources of a succession of owners until British Railways put it out of its misery in 1952.

The depression years of the twenties and early thirties brought it close to closure in 1933. It just escaped again in 1939 thanks to the increased activity when the Second World War began. The post-war decline led to its closure to passenger traffic, the last passenger train leaving on November 29th, 1952. It rained torrentially all day. Start as you mean to finish! On October 1st, 1954 the last goods train pulled out. The premises were used for several years after that by British Rail whose dock branch line ran alongside the old S & D premises.

Apart from the Bristol and Exeter, and the Somerset and Dorset, other lines were also considered but abandoned. Amongst these were rail links to Stolford and Stogursey.

Gas lighting 1834

By an act of parliament in 1834, Bridgwater was permitted the introduction of gas lighting in the streets of the town which previously had only been lit by oil lamps. The introduction of gas for the streets was an important advancement for the townsfolk who were now able to use it in their mostly rented accommodation. When the gas lights were introduced, a lamp lighter was also required. His role was to do the rounds of the gas lights each morning and evening, and

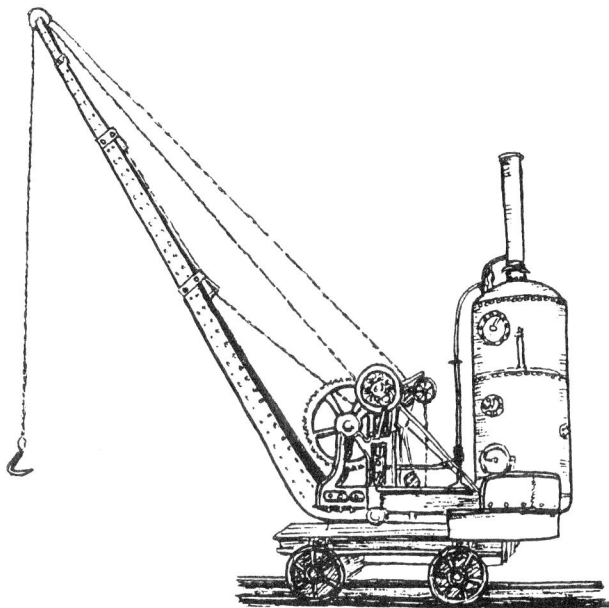

Wharfside crane

with the aid of his bicycle and a long pole would switch them on or off as appropriate.

The gas works were erected in what is now Old Taunton Road. One major by product of the gas works was tar. The use of this product for road surfacing began in Somerset in 1908 but it was not until 1921 that the first serious trial was conducted between Bridgwater and North Petherton. Needless to say the trial was a success and 1925 saw Trinidad Lake Asphalt being laid in the town and the death of the Cornhill Bonfire with it.

Ashford Reservoir water supply.

In December 1879, the Bridgwater Corporation Waterworks were opened at Ashford Reservoir near Cannington. At the time this was a major enhancement to the town which had not yet grown to the size which would demand the later Durleigh and Hawkridge reservoirs. Until the opening of this reservoir the town had been almost entirely dependent on locally bored wells for its supply. The Ashford reservoir was used to hold water which was pumped up to an underground holding tank at the top of Wembdon hill from where there was a good enough head of water to meet the town's demands.

Bricks, tiles and other industries

Brick and tile trade

Although the brick and tile industry didn't really take off until the nineteenth century, the production of these items started much earlier. From Bridgwater's medieval beginnings until the seventeenth century, local clay had been used to fashion pottery and similar items. Towards the end of the 17th century, the potential for local clay as a building material was being recognised. Early developers like the First Duke of Chandos who built Castle Street were among the original exponents of Bridgwater clay as a fashionable and practical material for building farm and manor houses. The practice in those days when building a house was to extract the clay from nearby. If it didn't exist nearby, another material was used.

The present day Police Station would appear to be the site of the first commercial brickyard followed by the one at Crowpill. The bricks here were hand made and examples can still be seen in Friarn Street, Dampiet Street and St. Mary's Street.

More yards sprang up along the river as the demand increased. As the end of the eighteenth century approached, a more organised industry was forming. Brick yards were now permanent sites with purpose built updraught kilns. The closeness of the building site was no longer a particular issue, anything up to ten miles was considered reasonable. This industrialisation led to a higher quality brick of a more predictable appearance and it was from these beginnings that the brick and tile industry was to flourish.

During the nineteenth century there developed a major brick and tile industry with yards from Burnham-on-Sea up as far as Burrow Bridge. Thousands of years of flooding of this low lying area had caused large deposits of alluvial clay to be laid down. The quality varies across the area but in general was found to be well suited to the manufacture of bricks and tiles. The Chilton Trinity area, for example favoured tiled manufacture.

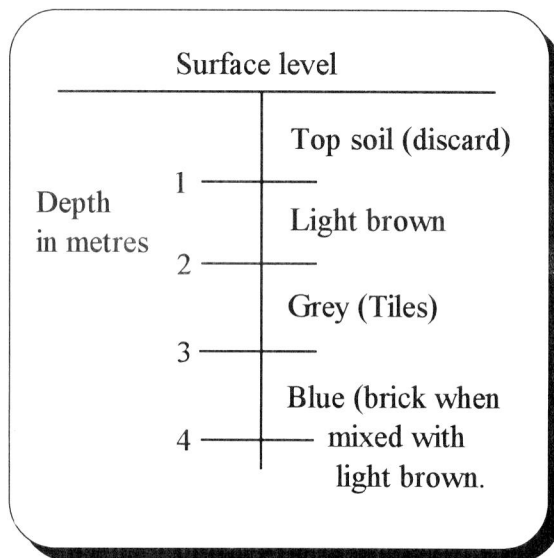

The big company names in the Bridgwater area were:-

Colthurst Symons - Castle Fields, Burnham, Somerset Bridge, Somerset Yard, Screech Owl, Puriton and Combwich.

John Browne - Chilton Tile Factory, Old Taunton Road, Dunwear, Chilton Old Yard and Pawlett.

John Symons - Saltlands.

William Maidment - Parrett Works in Bristol Road.

John Board - Wylds Road.

Barham Brothers - East Quay

H. J. and C. Major - Salmon Parade, Taunton Road and Colley Lane.

W. Robins - Parrett Way.

The main products were the red bricks which feature predominantly around the town and the popular Double Roman roof tiles for which William Symons can take the credit. These were so called because they resembled the original roman style of tile which was formed by moulding the tile over the knee.

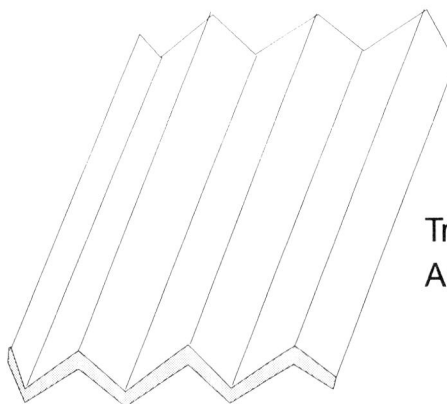

Triple Angular

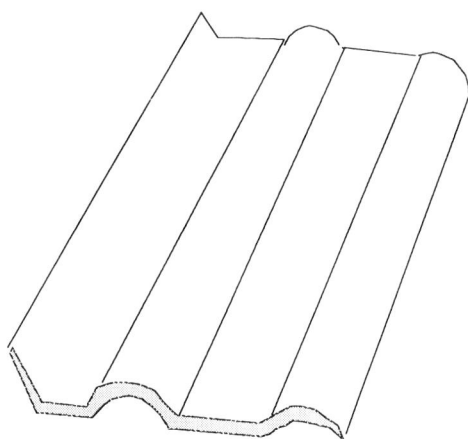

Double Roman roof tile

The kilns were capable of firing up to 5,000 tiles at a time. The firers knew every trick in the book when it came to the best way to use the flues and draught holes. The secret was to fire the tiles at just the right temperature for just the right length of time. Any mistake would lead to split tiles being recovered from the kiln at the end of the firing.

The kiln would be loaded with faggots, but latterly with nine to ten tons of coal. Once lit the flues would be used to control the draught and the speed at which the coal burned. At the end of four days the kiln would be sealed to extinguish the fire and then left for four days to cool.

Before firing, the tiles would be shaped in a two part mould. The top part of the mould

had a handle attached and this was used to slide the tiles carefully into the kiln as a baker slides the uncooked loaves into the oven.

In addition to the standard products, fancy gable end ridge tiles were also a speciality and it is well worth looking at the roof ends in St. Johns Street and areas of a similar age to spot the various patterns involved.

The Bridgwater bricks and tiles were taken all over the country and far and wide around the world. They can be found as far apart as the Bronx in New York, China, Canada, Australia and New Zealand. The volume of exports in 1903 made it necessary to construct a new quay for loading the outgoing ships.

After the North African campaign in World War II, when some allied troops there were still waiting for the invasion of Italy, many were given the task of clearing up the war damage. Imagine the surprise for the Bridgwater contingent to find the name of a Bridgwater brick and tile company on so many of the tiles in that far flung land. It may seem peculiar that local products of such a weighty nature should have travelled so far and in surprisingly large quantities. Perhaps it is less surprising when one considers the amount of shipping travelling between the Mediterranean and Bridgwater bringing wine into this country. That ensured a full load one way but left an empty ship going the other. Why not tiles to fill the load?

Life in the brickyards

Life in the brickyards was very hard. Half the male workforce of the town at one time worked in the yards. During the winter months, when the clay could not be dug, half of them were laid off until the weather improved. The pay was poor and the hours long and hard. Families struggled on the pay and it was normal for children to work to supplement the family income. A by-law had to be introduced to protect children under the age of thirteen and it was as late as 1947 before this was raised to fifteen. Even the thirteen year age limit was objected to by many, especially those who benefited from the child labour.

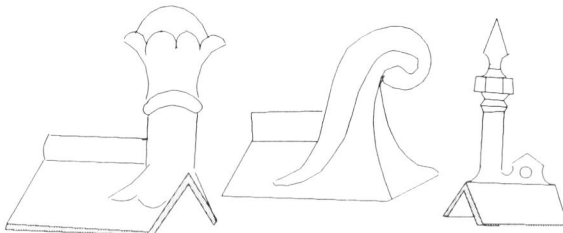

Finials for gable ends

The seasonal nature of the work, and the high level of winter unemployment associated with it, made it necessary in 1838 to establish a workhouse in Northgate. The records of the vice chairman of the workhouse in 1843 show the local women as working in the fields at a wage of 4 shillings per week plus 3 pints of cider a day. They must have been a fairly hardy lot what with the combined effects of labouring in the fields plus 2 or 3 gallons of cider a week.

Trade unions

In 1840 there were about 1300 workers in the brick and tile industry which by 1850 had expanded to 16 sites within 2 miles of the town bridge.

Towards the end of the nineteenth century, conditions were right for trade unionism to take a necessary foothold. From 1870 to 1890, trade union membership jumped from 4% to 25% of the work force. Whilst the brickyard owners argued that low wages were a prerequisite for the prosperity of the town, the work force were pushed to the point where a strike was inevitable.

In 1886 an unsuccessful strike ended after a period of eight weeks. The employers refused to negotiate and eventually hunger drove the work force back into the yards, no better off than before the dispute began.

1890 saw a repeat of the industrial action but this time on a much wider scale with 600 workers withdrawing their labour. Once again the hardship proved to bring no benefit but it did show the workers, both union members and not, that strength came in numbers and union membership grew significantly in the years that followed.

Another unsuccessful strike in 1893 saw Tom Mann, a charismatic union leader, come to the town and during the next two years most of the brickyard workers became members of the Dock, Wharf, Riverside and General Labourer's Union.

The brickyard strike of 1896

The next strike came in 1896 with a complete withdrawal by the entire work force. Feelings rose high. The strike dragged on and disorder broke out to the point that the King's troops had to be brought in from Plymouth to put down the 'uprising'. The mayor, Henry W. Pollard, read the Riot Act on the steps of the Town Hall.

The presence of the troops was not popular and requests for billets in the local inns and hotels led to their doors being locked. This time the strike action paid off and rates of pay were increased. Mr. Pollard's action did little to effect his popularity. He still holds the record for being mayor of the borough on no fewer than 6 occasions and is of course the son of the founder of the local building firm which survives today having been established in 1860.

The troubles leading to the strike began on May 19, 1896 when the union leader handed the workers claim for an extra six pence per day to Henry James Major. He completely refused to negotiate, an intransigent position which he upheld throughout the troubles. On May 25, the notice to strike was issued. The brickyards lay idle, bar the pickets at their gates, and the Bridgwater Mercury headline declared '800 hands idle'.

On June 8, the strikers rallied at the Cranleigh Gardens recreation ground, still known as the 'rec'. A promise of nine shillings a week strike pay was coupled with the demand that all strike action was to be kept completely within the law. That same month saw a number of marches through the town. It also saw several unsuccessful attempts by the mayor to get the two sides around the negotiating table. Major would not budge.

On June 23, a mass picket at Barham's yard led to Inspector Barnett leading his officers into the fray where three were arrested and charged with intimidation. Found guilty, they received fines of a particularly heavy nature. Clearly examples were being set.

During the days that followed, additional police reinforcements were brought in and various unions across the country declared their support for the cause. At the end of June, Ben Tillett, another union leader of some renown was called in to add weight to the union case.

Police activity increases

On the last day of June, following an unsuccessful attempt the previous day to get the two sides together at the Town Hall, the workers rallied once more at the 'rec'. Police

East Quay updraught kiln

numbers were seen to be increasing rapidly and tempers were stretched to the limit. The next day, tile carts apparently on their way to the hospital with the unions blessing, were seized and held by the strikers.

The owners of the seized carts requested and obtained a police escort to recover the load which had been on its way from Dunwear to Wembdon. Strikers intervened once again and recaptured the carts after overpowering the police. Twenty six strikers appeared in court shortly after.

The following day, July 2, the town was full of strikers and police, who had now been increased by an extra hundred or more. "Harris and Tapscott", the owners of the cart, demanded action from the borough council, the controlling authority for the borough police force. Outside the Town Hall, the crowd grew increasingly hostile.

During the day, rumours ran rife regarding the possible arrival of troops from Plymouth where the Gloucestershire regiment were waiting to sail for South Africa. At 7 p.m.

they arrived at the railway station and marched from there to the Town Hall, with reversed bayonets, to be billeted with the extra police who had been brought in.

At nine o'clock the real action started. Police charged the crowd with night sticks in order to recover the captured tile carts. The carts were overturned to form barricades and the tiles were used as missiles. The police were forced back and were besieged along with the troops and councillors in the Town Hall.

Reading of the Riot Act

The siege lasted until 3 a.m. when the mayor went to the Town Hall entrance and read the Riot Act. Out rushed the soldiers, bayonets fixed, forcing their way into the strikers through the use of their rifle butts. The police followed and through the combination of surprise and force, dispersed the crowd. The not surprisingly high numbers of resultant injuries included that of a young female reporter who simply failed to get out of the way in time.

Thus Bridgwater came under military rule for the first time since Cromwell. Two full days later, after a period of cleaning up both personal injuries and damage to property, a union ballot was held on whether or not to continue the strike. To the amazement of the brickyard bosses, the strike continued with further marches and rallies being organised.

The strike inevitably took its financial toll. The cost of policing was enormous. Strike pay had dwindled to five shillings per week and was close to running out. On July 5, the strikers resolve buckled under the severe hardship they were suffering and they voted for a return to work.

In defeat, there was some glory. The next year's pay round saw wages increased from twelve to fifteen shillings and hours reduced to twelve per day.

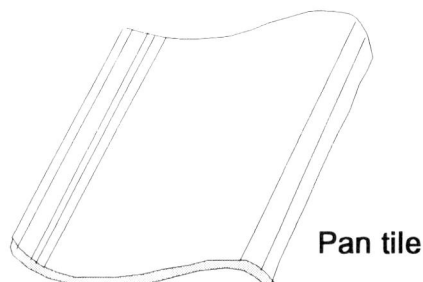

Pan tile

The decline

General industrialisation that took place throughout the nineteenth century inevitably led to the decline of Bridgwater's labour intensive brickyards. The First World War almost brought production to a stand still. The period after World War ll saw Europe rebuilding and alternative products coming to the market. Many of these weathered better in severe frost conditions than the Bridgwater clay products.

Alternative products such as concrete blocks and competition from the London Brick Company finally saw off the brickyards in 1965 when Barham Brothers 'fired' for the last time and in 1970 when Colthurst Symons closed their Castle Fields works.

The brickyard legacy

Within the old town borough, fifty five acres had been excavated leaving large deep pits to be used in some other way. Sixteen brick yards existed within two miles of the town and around it a further two hundred and fifty acres had been utilised. The output from these was as high as seventeen million bricks per year plus a large number of tiles.

Many of these pits now serve a recreational purpose as fishing waters. Others within the town, have been filled in with waste and returned to normal usage. The Bridgwater College and Wylds Road industrial estate serve as examples of land reclaimed in this way. A town plan of forty years ago would show the way the very shape of the town had been determined by the presence and position of the clay pits.

Bath Brick

The tidal nature of the Parrett was behind the development of a significant industry which started around 1820, close to the town bridge, manufacturing Bath Brick. This was a domestic cleansing and scouring product and Bridgwater was the only place in the world that was able to produce them.

The river carries a heavy burden of silt which accounts for its continuous murky brown colour. It also carries an algae which grows in the freshwater streams and rivers which feed the Parrett. This algae is deposited at the river mouth as the tide runs out and is then swept back up the river as the incoming tide takes control. As the tide turns and slowly goes out, a layer of slimy yellow deposit is left on the banks. The area around the town bridge area it was just right for the making of Bath Bricks. A mile downstream, the deposit is to sandy, upstream too clayish.

To help collect the silt, brick pens were constructed along the river. As the silt laden tides ran over the pens, so the slimy deposit built up. After two or three months, the batches of silt would be harvested by digging out the pens. The harvesting was an all year round job although the winter gathering was stock piled for later use. The clay formed this way was ground by a crude horse drawn mechanism, then moulded and eventually kilned.

These bricks, measuring about two by three inches, were patented as an idea in 1827 by John Browne and were used world-wide as a scouring or cleansing agent. They were called Bath Bricks because at one stage the plan was to produce building bricks from this material by firing the raw material in such a way that the final colour would closely resemble that of Bath stone.

Something like 24 million bricks were manufactured annually by firing the clayish slime in a kiln until the colour was just right. A failure to get the right colour led to rejects being produced and thousands of these are still evident in the area. Whilst the excavation of the clay was work for the men, it was predominantly the ladies and their children who carried out the moulding and finishing work. The First World War saw these bricks being carried far and wide with the British forces using them as a part of their standard kit. The demand was so high that ten different companies were all producing them locally. Indeed there was nowhere else they could be made.

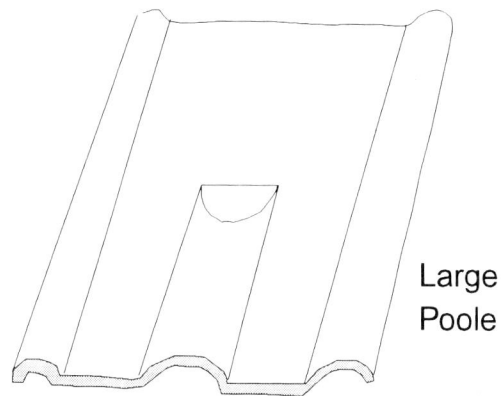

Large
Poole

The introduction of household detergents and scouring powders in convenient containers with perforated lids resulted in the loss of the Bath Brick market and production ceased just before the Second World War.

Castle House

Apart from the conventional clay bricks, cement blocks were also recognised and developed as a building material. Portland Castle House in Queen Street was built in 1851 as an example of how pre-cast concrete could be used as a building material.

A company called Acremans acquired the local franchise to make Portland Cement. The Great Exhibition was imminent and the opportunity was seized to promote Portland

Cement products to visitors from around the world.

People came from all over the country to view what was effectively a building trade catalogue of new ideas. They came by the hundred and yet the product was not to really take off until almost a hundred years later. The ideas were, if you like, ahead of their time. It was, in fact, the world's first example of pre-cast concrete, the building being partly built on the old castle wall and attached to it by iron bars. Regrettably, the building has been allowed to fall into a poor state of repair and a serious fire in recent times gutted the building, leaving a question mark over its future. Meanwhile, it remains a listed building and, unfortunately, an eyesore.

Pottery, drain pipes, flower pots and the like continued as a flourishing industry almost until the Second World War when alternative materials took their place. The derelict buildings left in the wake of the dying industry were in some cases dismantled and taken to Westonzoyland where they were used as hard-core in the construction of the airfield. This was the unfortunate fate of the Chandos glass kiln.

Wicker products

The local withy growing fields producing willow for basket weaving was the source of the raw materials for a fairly active wicker industry throughout the 19th and well into the 20th centuries. There were many small basket making cottage industries in the area based mainly in private homes. World War ll created an increase in demand for wicker baskets which were particularly well suited for dropping essential supplies into war zones by parachute. The resilience and flexibility of the baskets made them ideal for the ungraceful landings to which they were subjected.

Laundry baskets, bicycle baskets, fishing baskets, picnic hampers, lobster pots, garden and household furniture, all were made in the town with the local willow which was guaranteed to give a long lasting product, capable of enduring no end of punishment. The willow is a particularly resilient plant; it is almost impossible to snap a willow sapling in two. In addition it is quite easy to grow and to convert after harvesting.

Popular varieties are the Black Mole and Champion. These can be grown simply by making short cuttings and pushing them a couple of inches into the soil. They root very easily. Once they take a hold, they are pruned close to the ground in their first autumn and will then grow at about an inch a day and soon reach six or seven feet high ready for harvesting. They are cut close to the base of the single shoot from which will grow several more lengths the following season. Once harvested in this way, the bark is easily removed by flailing the withies.

The withy branches do not suffer from side shoots in the first year of growth which makes the removal of the bark a fairly simple process. If this makes it all sound very easy, then before embarking on a new career, take a look at the withy growers typical working day. It's long hard back breaking work. The plants grow easily enough but much stooping and bending in damp wet conditions makes it a job for the men and not the boys and rheumatism is an occupational hazard.

Life was easier for the basket weavers. Not for them the long hours in damp conditions. Instead their lot was to sit for long periods on the floor propped up with a wall behind them whilst forming their baskets between their knees. Industrialised businesses flourished around the town manufacturing wicker products. There were the Squibb's premises in Mount Street, Kraft Products in Cornboro Place, Betalls in West Street and Slocombe's in New Road.

Social aspects of the nineteenth century

Bridgwater's own regiment

During the Napoleonic period, there was great concern across the nation of a possible French invasion. The fort at the end of Brean Down remains as a testament to the concern felt. Napoleon himself had stated that he would be glad to sacrifice 100,000 men to invade England. Against this background, the government requested the formation of a number of volunteer units around the country. In 1803, twenty thousand enrolled in Yeomanry or Volunteer Corps in Somerset from a population just below ninety thousand.

In 1794, a corps of two companies of Volunteer Infantry was raised in Bridgwater. The Bridgwater Volunteers started with sixty privates in each company and by 1795 had their own quartermaster and surgeon. Their Adjutant, whose only military experience was a short spell in the Somerset Provisional Cavalry, was John Crosse who was paid eight shillings a day including two shillings for his horse. Their commandant was Lieutenant Colonel Jeffreys Allen, M.P. for the borough.

That same year, on September 4th, Lady Poulett presented the Volunteers with their own colours following a procession of local ladies from the Town Hall to the Cornhill. The Bridgwater Volunteer Infantry had now grown to five companies of seventy privates each. Although they were confined mainly to the town, their duties outside included taking French prisoners from Plymouth to Bristol prison.

Eventually, in 1807 along with many other local units, the Bridgwater regiment agreed to transfer to the "Local Militia" accepting militiamen status.

In 1865 we have the first mention of the Bridgwater Troop of the West Somerset Yeomanry commanded by Lieutenant Colonel C. K. K. Tynte. In 1868 there is a record of national honours being won by Lieutenant Carslake, a Bridgwater man of the Somerset Yeomanry. He had won a national rifle shooting contest and was given a hero's reception. Escorted by the Yeomanry Cavalry, he was carried through the town on a carriage with the bands playing and his Bridgwater and Stowey troops proudly bearing drawn swords.

Bridgwater Borough Police Force 1834 - 1940

The old police station and gaol were in Fore Street until 1875. The gaol with separate accommodation for men and women was kept by James Bussell. The town had its own borough police force with a chief constable, two sergeants and ten constables. They were governed by a watch committee.

In 1875 they moved to the High Street until 1911 when they settled in their current spot in Northgate. This was seen as a very sensible move because it put the police station smack between the brewery and the workhouse.

On October 1, 1940 the borough police force was amalgamated into the County Constabulary. The present station was opened in 1966 but not without some embarrassment. When the main structure was complete, it collapsed in a heap and work had to start again.

Life was very different in the Fore Street days. The old fashioned style of Bobbying applied and no doubt to good effect. Bobbies walked the beat, knew the people and had the ability to spot anything out of character for the town. The officers were allowed to carry canes with which to inflict instant punishment on petty offenders. Perhaps we're too soft these days.

The cannon, 1857

A cannon captured in the Russian War was presented to the town and put on display near the Town Bridge where it stayed until 1886. It was later decided to re-site it at the junction of Bristol Road and Bath Road. It survived in that position until the Second World War when it was removed to provide scrap metal for the war effort. The area is still known as The Cannon to many locals.

Nineteenth century newspapers and libraries.

The nineteenth century appears to have been a good time for newspapers and libraries. There were three reading rooms, one situated in Taunton Road and opened in 1856. The other two, which both had libraries, were in St. John's Street (1860) and West Street (1861). There was also the Literary and Scientific Institution in George Street with over 1,500 volumes and a museum. In 1894, there was also a Free Library and Reading Rooms in part of the Town Hall with over 2,500 volumes of standard works.

The first purely Bridgwater paper and the first published in the town was *The Bridgwater and Somersetshire Herald*. It was published every Wednesday by George Aubrey in Fore Street and survived from 1825 until its last copy on 3 August 1831.

The first newspaper to bear Bridgwater's name was the *Taunton and Bridgwater Journal*. Its first edition was published on 30 March 1811. Lasting five years until 1816 it was published by James Savage and was financed by the local Conservatives.

The *Journal* was succeeded by the *Alfred* published on Mondays which ran from 10 August 1831 to 30 December 1833. Its full title was *The Alfred, London Weekly Journal and Bridgwater and Somerset General Advertiser*. Printed in St. Mary's Street it was owned by John Bowen and edited by Harry Clement Heard until its incorporation into the *Dorset County Chronicle and Somersetshire Gazette* which was published in Dorchester.

The *Bridgwater Times* started on 1 January 1846 and was printed in Fore Street until its final edition in September 1861. It was owned by Samuel Bowditch West and edited by George Thomas Donisthorpe. The first issue showed a map of the local rail network and referred to its reporter being denied admission to a meeting of the town council.

Bridgwater Mercury

The oldest surviving newspaper serving the town is the *Bridgwater Mercury*. It was originally run by W. A. Woodley, a clergyman's son, who was petitioned by the numerous prominent townspeople to get it started. This happened on 25 June 1857 in Ball's Lane, now George Street, before moving to King Street. During 1859 and 1860 it was subjected to various name changes but always had the Mercury in there somewhere. Mr. J. T. Dunsford joined the paper as its editor in 1865 and was the victim of a cruel tragedy in which he lost his wife and three children.

Mercury office fire, 1883

The paper's premises suffered a fire on 25 July, 1883. His three daughters perished in the flames and his wife died from the fall as she leapt from the upstairs window unsuccessfully attempting to land on a neighbours bed. The fire also destroyed all of the papers historic records. The Mercury of course is the only one that survives today.

The *Bridgwater Gazette, Somerset and Devon Chronicle and West of England*

Advertiser (yes, that was its full name) started in Tiverton in 1871 under the control of George Rookes. It was bought out by James Bulgin for the Liberal cause and became the *Bridgwater Independent* on 4 July, 1885. Published in George Street on Fridays, it survived until 10 June 1933 when it was bought out by the Mercury.

Records for 1861 show the *Bridgwater Standard* being published by Conrad Stokes in St. John's Street. It lasted from 16 October 1861 to 26 March 1870.

1885 saw the very short lived *Bridgwater Guardian*, published in the old Gazette office in Fore Street as a voice for the Conservatives.

Although they belong to the 20th century, two other publications are mentioned here for completeness sake. A short term venture was the *Bridgwater Echo* from 1902 to 1904 which took over from the *Highbridge Echo* and vanished with its resurrection. And the *Slave Market News* ran from October 1924 to July 1936 being published in Bridgwater.

Riots after the general election of 1832

At the time of the general election of 1832, there were three Bridgwater newspapers, The *Bridgwater Alfred*, the *Bridgwater and Somersetshire General Advertiser* and the *London Weekly Journal*. The *Advertiser* had in fact been brought out the year before presumably in preparation for the forthcoming election.

For many voters, the bias of the *Advertiser* was so blatant that they felt it justified to invade the editor's house, smash the windows and raid his cellar. On hearing what was happening, the editor sped home only to be beaten by the mob. The fighting which followed this incident led to the Riot Act being read and a number of people arrested and charged.

Some of these were tried at Taunton and amazingly released on a technicality despite a rock solid case against them. The remainder were taken to Wells where a prolonged trial took place. The trial lasted long enough in fact that it was necessary for all concerned to stay overnight in an hotel. They had a great time, both accused and jury enjoying themselves together, some actually ending up in the same bed!

Not surprisingly, knowing what went on the night before, the previously implausible verdict of not guilty was announced. Once again the prosecution were completely at a loss to know what they had to do to secure a conviction.

More corrupt voting and disenfranchisement

During the mid-nineteenth century, corrupt voting was common place. It was accepted as standard practice to take a bribe for the promise of vote, the going rate being £10. The practice was so rife that there were some who claimed that the only ones not taking bribes were those giving them.

In closely fought elections, the "ante" increased significantly even going as high as £50. Since the state of the poll was known as the day went on, the price for a vote would increase more rapidly as the close of polling approached. The really clever voters would time the sale of their vote to obtain the best price during the day. The blessing for those seeking election was that the actual number of inhabitants allowed to vote were relatively small, only 400 out of the 12,500 inhabitants. Even then, the high cost of bribes must have put the cost of an election in excess of today's costs.

Whilst bribery was widespread, it was never the less, a very covert affair. Various ways were found to cover up the illegal practice. Commodities would be sold for very round figures, £10 for a pig, £50 for a parrot, and then the purchaser would forget to collect the goods. Public drinking houses acted as trading centres for votes. These houses tended to be very partisan, supporting one party or another. To enter one of these houses was as good as pinning on a rosette. In their back rooms the transactions would take place with various terminology being used to hide the truth. Those providing the bribes would be referred to by such expressions as 'the man in the moon' or the 'mysterious stranger' and the bribe as a 'packet of tea'.

In May, 1837 a by-election was fought between the Conservative Henry Broadwood and the liberal Richard Sheridan. The Tories were successful with Broadwood winning by 279 votes to 221. The Liberals objected to the result and were able to prove 153 cases of bribery. Broadwood did not contest the action and was ready to resign his seat.

However the death of King William lV meant it was not necessary for Sheridan to take the seat which was rightfully his. The death of the King in those days necessitated the election of a new parliament and a further election took place in the July. The two Conservative candidates were returned with nearly 600 votes between them, the Liberals only achieving 7. So much for 'crime doesn't pay'.

What happened on this occasion appears to be a classic double cross. A number of Tory voters were bribed not only to vote Tory but also to convince the Liberal agent of their loyalty to the Liberals. So loyal were they, it was argued, and so many were they in numbers, that a Liberal victory was a foregone conclusion and bribes were not necessary on this occasion. The result of this double cross was that the Liberal candidates received a mere seven votes between them. This gives a very strong indication as to how many people were unaffected by the bribery system.

Further corruption was proven in the election of July, 1865. Henry Westropp, the Tory candidate, having successfully topped the poll, was proven to have carried out corrupt practices, in particular bribery. The November 1868 election returned two Liberal candidates who just pipped Westropp and a fellow Tory to the post. This time it was the turn of the Conservatives to complain and the Liberals, at the end of a four day enquiry in February 1869, were found guilty of corrupt practice. They were both unseated, despite the endeavours of the Liberals to cover up any evidence of their wrong doings.

Disenfranchisement

The time was right for a Royal Commission to investigate voting practice in the town. It was set up in the August of the same year. The enquiry took 47 days and a full report can still be found in the reference section of the local library. The report is massive. Containing the full proceedings of the 47 days, it fills 1,174 pages detailing 47,548 questions and answers. The enquiry concluded that bribery had taken place on a major scale. Corruption was so rife they had to conclude that there was no hope of a fair election ever again and Bridgwater was disenfranchised.

The enquiry tried to determine whether the corruption was a recent affair and as such would pass, or whether it was part of the very culture of the town and therefore unlikely to go away. They found that the numbers receiving payment for their votes exceeded three quarters of those voting and that this had been the case for as far back as they could determine - at least for all the elections in the preceding 40 years. They also found that where bribery had failed to succeed it was common practice for the voter concerned to be well looked after with drinks by the opposition in order to render him incapable of going to vote.

The people of the borough of Bridgwater had returned two members of parliament for the last time. Before they were allowed to vote again, the constituency had been enlarged to cover a greater geographical area and was to be represented by only one member.

The Workhouse

Bridgwater had two workhouses during the 19th century. The first was in Old Taunton Road, near the junction with St. Saviour's Avenue, and was the parish workhouse. Conditions were harsh, crowded and unhygienic. Within a period of only eight months, thirty nine of the one hundred and fifty five inmates died from small pox and dysentery.

A second workhouse was established in Bridgwater in 1837 covering forty parishes from Shapwick to Nether Stowey. This was a white brick, partly stuccoed building, holding 388 people and was controlled by a different body to the parish workhouse. The conditions, whilst still harsh, were far better than in the parish workhouse. It at least had heating and lighting and three meals a day.

The Northgate premises came in the wake of the Poor Law Amendment Act of 1834. Within two years of the Act being passed, seventeen Poor Law Unions had been set up in Somerset, each Union being run by a board of governors under the control of a commission. Thus the new workhouses were more influenced by 'government men' than local representatives.

The task these committees set themselves was to get the best value for money from the poor, reducing the burden on the taxpayer. Those in the Workhouse, therefore, were fed rations which were totally inadequate. Their diet was eight ounces of bread (six for the women) and a pint and a half of gruel per day.

From 1770 to 1833 there had been a continuous programme of improved drainage on the moors surrounding Bridgwater. Rivers such as the Cary which previously meandered were straightened to give a more rapid declining angle of slope. At the same time river banks were raised which gave the added benefit of improved navigation with deeper water.

Life in the Northgate Workhouse

During this period land prices increased four fold and enclosure became the practice. This had left a great many agricultural workers with no means of supporting their families. At the end of their tethers, they had no alternative but to enter the workhouse.

It was a bleak and cruel existence. Conditions were crowded, dirty and even frightening. Children slept six to a bed, fifty to a room just 27 feet by 15. It was the last place anyone would wish to go. For the elderly and infirm, there was the poor house. This had less of a stigma than the workhouse. The workhouse was for the able bodied. Of course not all of them wanted to work and thus the dregs of society would end up there. It was a real social humiliation to be placed in the workhouse.

The last place on earth

Some thirty years ago, my grandmother was aged and through ill health virtually bedridden. It was considered necessary for her to go into a hospital for the elderly. The one chosen was Blake Hospital at Northgate. It was well recommended and the care for the elderly was compassionate and professional. The problem was that it was on the site of what had previously been the workhouse which had been converted into a hospital in 1948. On hearing the news, my grandmother threw a tantrum. As weak as she was, there was no way she was willing to enter "Northgate". The old stigma remained. It was the last place on earth that you would go by choice and for many it was literally just that, their last place on earth.

In 1893 such was the demand on the workhouse that sixty one tramps were admitted in one week.

Those in the Northgate Workhouse faired better than those in the Parish Workhouse but a condition of the Poor Laws was that they should not be better off than those gainfully employed outside of the Workhouse.

Therefore they had to be fed less than the worst fed labourer outside. This was based on the principle of "less eligibility" as it was known.

Conditions were crowded. Families were separated. Men in one dormitory, women in another and children in a third. Children were expected to share six to a bed. With the adults, it was just two. The cramped conditions and unsuitable diet inevitably led to sickness and diarrhoea. Disease amongst the weakened inhabitants became endemic. It was not unknown for a dead body to be removed from a bed at night to create the space for a family coming in. The high deaths of 1837 and 1838 could have been predicted in such conditions. A simple change of diet would have helped a little, but the law did not permit it.

However the system brought benefits to the community. There was an annual saving of almost £5,000. Against this background, it was better not to draw attention to the impoverished conditions within! And so the Workhouse log book reported all being satisfactory 'under the circumstances'.

John Bowen, philanthropist.

John Bowen was a local man who travelled the world and worked in a number of roles including engineer, journalist and wine merchant. Following a period of ill health, he returned to Bridgwater and became involved in affairs of local interest. The Poor House system concerned him greatly and he openly expressed his dissatisfaction with its failure to achieve a humane offering for the unfortunate minority. His opinions brought him much criticism at both local and national level.

He joined the Board of Governors of the Bridgwater Parish Union and saw for himself at first hand the appalling conditions within. It could be questioned if other members of the board had shared the experience. It appears their obligations were to balancing the books and certainly not caring for the poor.

Inside Bowen found terrified, disease ridden occupants suffering intolerably with emaciated bodies. He resigned his position and set about publicising his findings. Letters to the Times and to Parliament listing details of twenty seven deaths in the previous six months brought him little but criticism.

One article he published was entitled "Is killing in an Union Workhouse criminal if sanctioned by the Poor Law Commissioner?". He also argued that the deaths of 94 from dysentery had been caused by the change of diet to a cheaper one which had been instigated against the advice of the workhouse surgeon. The workhouse chairman, however, congratulated the board on an annual saving of £4,843!

The minute book of the Bridgwater Board of Guardians for 1836-37 states that "*during 1837 the Board had to meet a sustained attack by a merchant of the town who served on the board for a period. His allegations were directed against the guardians not only on the score of cruelty and oppression but also on the failure to provide medical attention and food. Conditions, undoubtedly, were bad in this experimental stage, but improvements were forthcoming as new workhouses replaced the old parish houses which were not suited to the demands of a Union of parishes*".

Eventually an enquiry was held as a result of public awareness being raised but the board of enquiry was made up of the Poor Law commissioners. Needless to say they declared themselves innocent and Bowen to be an agitator. In fairness, he was politically motivated and inclined more toward negative argument than constructive criticism.

Bowen took his case to the House of Lords causing further embarrassment for the government and the commissioners. His statistics became public knowledge. He claimed that almost half the inmates had died in one winter, a death rate of 41% compared to 3% for convicts.

In the ensuing years, Bowen kept up his campaign. It's hard to tell if it did any good. Perhaps conditions would have been even worse. Who knows? It's hard to believe worse was possible.

In 1838 there were six such places in Somerset. The inmates would be hired out where possible to local farms and businesses. Those left behind were still obliged to work at the workhouse. Breaking rocks into gravel for use on the parish roads was a common form of justifying the inmates presence.

Life outside the workhouse was not much better for the working classes. Cottages were earth floored and many lacked even a ceiling. The lucky ones had stone floors. Families were crowded into small homes with one room up and one down. During the winter months they were cold, damp and poorly lit, perhaps with just a single candle. Rheumatism was rife in these conditions and to be expected in such a damp and low lying area.

Emigration to the New World and Australia.

Against this background of high unemployment and a poverty stricken workforce, it is understandable that there should be a period of sustained emigration from Bridgwater and the surrounding areas to the New World initially and latterly to Australia and New Zealand. Assisted passage was offered to encourage the fit and healthy to pioneer the relatively new colonies. Life aboard the emigrant's transport ships was as hard and fraught with danger as life in the workhouse, but at least there was a glimmer of hope for a better future on the other side of the globe.

Emigrants at dinner Illustrated London News, 13/4/1844

Although free passage was offered to Australia, the emigrant still needed to be able to afford a decent trunk in which to store the families clothes plus the cost of the fare to Plymouth or London from whence most emigrant ships departed. In many deserving cases it was the parish church which put up the necessary money.

From this period of emigration, we know that numerous other 'Bridgewaters' have been born. In all cases they are spelt with the extra 'e'. This does not disqualify them from being of Somerset origin since historic evidence exists to prove the connection and this is dealt with more fully in the later section on the 'Other Bridgewaters'.

Emigration certainly helped to relieve the problems of unemployment. The initial flow of agricultural workers was supplemented by tradesmen and other skilled workers when news came of the fortunes to be made in the goldfields. So successful was emigration as a cure to the West Country's problems, that the balance tipped the other way and labour shortages had become an issue by 1853 when the Bridgwater Times reported the increase in wages caused by demand outstripping supply.

Certainly large numbers emigrated to New York for example in 1852.

For those who wished to sail from Liverpool, now only a days travel away, the Somerset firm of W. Tapscott & Co. made the necessary arrangements. Their agent was W. Tiver who was based at the Lamb Inn in Bridgwater, since renamed and now called the Duke of Monmouth.

The Cholera outbreak

1841 saw the outbreak of a serious epidemic of cholera. Almost every street in the town was hit with more than two hundred lives being lost to the deadly disease. Strict controls on people moving around were introduced. Visitors to the town were sent away and even residents barred from leaving if they had been in a cholera infected home. Eighty eight people from Eastover were buried in a corner of St. John's churchyard

The Salvation Army

Against a background of poverty and need, the coming of the Salvation Army was almost inevitable. Their presence was first felt in the

110

town in 1880 and General Booth, the founder of the organisation, visited the town in 1884.

Witchcraft

Witchcraft was taken very seriously over a period of many centuries. The persecution of witches in the seventeenth century is well documented and has been the subject of numerous films such as 'The Witchfinder General'. It is easy to understand how witchcraft could be so popularly believed centuries ago against a background of ignorance, especially where scientific explanations are taken for granted today. What may be surprising is that the subject was still taken seriously as late as the nineteenth century. The following tales from Bridgwater were both from this period and reflect the depth of belief in witchcraft.

A cottager was having trouble with one of his pigs which was suffering from an unknown ailment. In cases such as this, it was considered pointless going to the vet. He could only help if the ailment was a recognised one. Thus the cottager took his pig to the local white witch who gave the appropriate instructions on how to cure the animal.

Following the witches advice, he lanced each trotter and both ears of the pig and caught the blood in a calico cloth. This, having had two long needles stuck through it from opposite directions, was taken into his cottage and having safely locked the door, the cloth was thrown on the fire and covered with turf. The ceremony which so far had been in complete silence, was now finished off with a reading from the bible until the cloth was totally consumed by the flames.

The ritual over, the cottager returned to the pigsty where needless to say the pig had returned to full fitness. Within minutes the old woman, suspected of having cursed the pig in the first place, turned up at the pigsty enquiring after the pigs well being.

Another story relating to the area of Witches Walk along the bottom of the Fairfield, tells of a mysterious white rabbit. This rabbit was regularly seen running up and down a lane and then disappearing into thin air. All attempts to catch it failed, indeed even dogs were unable to follow its scent. Presumably the animal was a witch in a different form.

The man who owned the pig cured by the white witch was able to confirm this . He regularly saw the white rabbit and without exception, whenever there was a sighting, the window of his old enemy, she who had cursed his pig, was open.

And so it was that, one evening, a group of local characters of an aggressive nature surrounded two cottages which shared a walled garden. The only way in or out was the narrow gap between the two buildings. The rabbit was in the garden and the gap was well defended by some of the locals, the remainder having entered the garden to catch the rabbit.

Inevitably the rabbit was caught by the ears and the mob set to dishing out their punishment. Before the rabbit could effect an escape, the owner of the pig let loose with a full blooded kick sending the poor rabbit flying. Before they could catch it again, it ran between their legs and escaped.

This in itself proved nothing. But if proof were needed, the woman suspected of being the witch was laid up in bed for several days suffering from bad bruising!

Founder of the YMCA

In 1821 George Williams was born in Dulverton, the son of a farmer. He was to become a Christian, philanthropist and

111

George Williams

businessman famed as the founder of the YMCA.

Born at Ashway Farm and educated at Tiverton, he was apprenticed in 1836 to Henry William Holmes, Bridgwater's leading draper with a staff of thirty. By 1837 he had been converted at the Zion Chapel in Friarn Street having become a devout Christian. The following year saw him on the committee of the nonconformist church pledging abstinence in 1839.

In 1841 he left the town for London with religion now his strongest influence and there developed the idea he first had in Bridgwater of a Young Mans Christian Association. He opened the first YMCA branch in 1844, the Bridgwater branch not opening until 1859.

The organisation grew to be one of the largest in the world. In 1887 the George Williams memorial hall was built for the YMCA on the corner of Eastover and Salmon Parade.

George Williams was knighted in 1894 following a recommendation from Lord Roseberry and died on November 6th, 1905.

Invention of the MacKintosh

John Clark (1785-1853), was a local Quaker born in Greinton but moved to Bridgwater with his parents in 1809. It was here, after an unsuccessful spell as a grocer and then a failed printer, that he developed a material which he considered to be particularly useful for the manufacture of waterproof raincoats. He sold the patent to a Mr. MacKintosh for the sum of £40 and we can all guess what happened next. Had things turned out differently it would be your Clark you put on in inclement weather.

He was a most unusual man. A cousin of the founders of the Clark's shoe business, he was an inventor of extraordinary talent.

One of his earliest inventions, which took him thirteen years to perfect, was a machine that made Latin hexameters. Now if that leaves you wandering what a Latin hexameter is, well it is clearly defined in any reasonable dictionary as a verse line of six metrical feet where the first four are usually dactyls or spondees, the fifth almost always a dactyl and the sixth a spondee or trochee. If that still leaves you confused, it was a style of writing used in Greek and Roman epic poetry using six words per line and the machine can apparently be viewed at Clark's premises in Street. The total combinations of phrases capable of being produced is over twenty eight million. The machine called the Eureka was exhibited by John Clark in London in 1845. The proceeds from the viewing charge of one shilling were sufficient for Clark to buy himself a house in Bridgwater.

The house was the first in Monmouth Street on the left hand side as you enter Bridgwater from the Glastonbury road, the one with church-like windows. It was whilst living there that he developed the waterproofing technique and earned himself the nickname of the "First mate of Noah's Ark" for his eccentric style of dress.

112

Victorian scandals

The coming of the Messiah

During the latter part of the nineteenth century, Bridgwater witnessed occasional visits from the self proclaimed 'Son of God'. These visits generated much interest and speculation in the town. The Reverend Henry Prince, or 'The Blessed' as he was known to his followers would visit the town in a grand open top carriage drawn by four large bay horses. He was protected on all sides by outriders wearing purple livery. Enormous bloodhounds ran before the carriage close on the heels of a vanguard who loudly proclaimed 'Blessed is he who cometh in the name of the Lord.'

The townsfolk generally considered the man and his followers to be harmless if not a little mad. They were however very wealthy and spent well in the town. A measure of their wealth can be judged when one knows that the Reverend Prince used a ceremonial carriage purchased from the Queen Mother. Clearly they should be encouraged and protected from any unjustified press criticism. And there was plenty of that to come!

The people of Spaxton generally felt the same. It was there that this strange community had set up their home, providing work for the locals and prompt payment for the tradesmen. All their dealings with the outside world were of such a nature that they would not attract a bad reaction from the people of Bridgwater and Spaxton. The church, however, held a very different view on the practices apparently happening up on the Quantocks and it was these which were to cause an international scandal.

The Reverend Henry Prince.

Henry Prince, born in Bath, set out to follow a career in medicine. He qualified at Guys Hospital but ill health interfered and he eventually followed a religious calling.

He took up instructions at Lampeter College in West Wales where he became such a zealot that his presence was an embarrassment. The problem for the vice-principal was that Prince had not actually done anything wrong, he had just become unbelievably pious and outspokenly critical. He had to go.

The curate of Charlynch

The vice-principal contacted the Bishop of Bath and Wells for help. Was it possible to find a small church at the back of beyond where Prince could be installed as a curate and do no serious damage to the church? And so he became the curate of Charlynch church near Spaxton.

While the regular vicar was away in 1846 on an indefinite holiday, Henry Prince had the opportunity to take the pulpit. He was a charismatic preacher and appealed to the lady members of the congregation. But it wasn't an easy beginning. The first few months saw virtually no one attending his services. No amount of threats of hell fire and damnation were going to wake up this sleepy congregation. Then he had a brainwave.

Declared the Son of God

At one of his services he stopped mid-sermon as if possessed. He threw himself about the church as the spirit took him. The congregation were enthralled. He had declared himself to be the son of God.

The following week, the congregation's friends turned up to see if the performance was to be repeated. And so the congregation grew with all and sundry arriving including many from Bridgwater and beyond. Some of those attending were less than savoury and there purely for the spectacle. For some of the hardened drinkers of Bridgwater it was good for a laugh. A few pints in town, out to the Lamb at Spaxton for a couple more and then off to the entertainment. The numbers attending increased so rapidly that separate services were held for the men and women.

The size of congregations grew with each sermon and numbers had to be controlled. Prince divided his flock into the righteous and the sinners. The sinners were told to stay away. The righteous were predominantly female, good looking and wealthy. Those who were refused admission as sinners were furious.

Defrocked

Families became divided, respected members of the community lost their status. The Bishop of Bath and Wells was once again called in to deal with the problem of Mr. Prince. This time the result was somewhat final. The Reverend Prince was defrocked.

He was already married before he moved to Spaxton. She was an elderly lady and very wealthy. This perhaps gives us a clue as to the character and motivation of the man. On the death of his wife, Prince inherited her fortune and with no delay married the parish priest's sister, Julia Starky. On being defrocked, they both moved to Suffolk.

Whilst there, he continued his preaching and found many converts. The pattern followed that at Spaxton. The congregation were whipped into a frenzy, numbers grew by the week, the sinners were weeded out and inevitably the Bishop of Ely was called in to move the man on.

The Nottidge sisters

Amongst his congregation were the five very wealthy and middle aged Nottidge sisters, each a spinster. Between them they had inherited £30,000. Three of them were sufficiently persuaded by Prince that they threw their lot in with him. A fourth joined later but was kidnapped by her family one night and committed to an asylum. The people of Spaxton heard the screams but preferred to ignore the event. It took about two years for Prince to discover her whereabouts. Prince convinced the courts that she was not mad and she was released into his care along with her inheritance. It was after this intrusion that the bloodhounds were introduced.

With the help of the inheritance, they were to move to Spaxton where the Agapemone was

built. But first there was a period in Brighton and then Weymouth where, preaching hellfire and damnation, hundreds were persuaded to part with their money to serve the needs of the Lord. When sufficient funds were available, two hundred acres of land were purchased at Spaxton.

The Abode of Love

And so it was that in the summer of 1846, a rather unusual group of people arrived at Spaxton. They were clearly well to do and rather grand in appearance. Soon the Agapemone (Greek for The Abode of Love) was being developed. Behind fifteen feet prison style walls, a twenty bedroom house, church, gazebo, cottages and conservatory were erected. Another feature was the chapel. Unlike any other, it was luxuriously furnished with velvet sofas and Turkish carpets. For the altar it had a billiard table

Those who dwelt within were very private and well protected. Apart from the surrounding wall maintaining their privacy, enormous bloodhounds patrolled within. Only the local tradesmen had any real contact. They would deliver their goods to a hand which appeared through a hole in the wall. Somewhat unusual maybe but who cares when the business is significant in value and the payments so prompt.

Prince recruited other young women into his care. In all cases the qualifications were based on looks and wealth. The looks were important since it was his duty inevitably to 'purify' these maidens. Within the community spiritual marriages were permitted, indeed they were dictated by Prince. The married couples however lived separately, the men and women having different cottages. The younger, better looking women lived in the main house with Prince.

The Great Manisfestation

He proclaimed that it was his responsibility to extend love from heaven to earth. A virgin had to be purified by the Holy Ghost, being of course himself. Nothing was left to the imagination, the act of purification was carried out with Prince and his spiritual bride performing naked in front of his followers, even his wife.

The act was known as the Great Manisfestation. Before it happened, the virgins came to the altar draped in white. Prince examined each one in turn and chose Miss Paterson who had grown up in the community since about five years old. She was no more than sixteen and a beautiful young girl. Her clothes were removed and on the billiard table (sorry, altar!) she was deprived of her virginity.

Not all followers found this practice acceptable. Many left the Agapemone and the news broke out regarding the happenings within. The press had a field day. The church was scandalised, the people of Spaxton kept quiet. The numbers leaving reduced and life was almost back to normal when another scandal arose.

The 'purified virgin' gave birth. This was not supposed to happen, indeed it almost suggested that Prince was the same as any lesser mortal. Clearly she had been impregnated by the devil and a demonic immaculate conception had occurred. Outside of the walls, most people had a different opinion on the cause of the pregnancy, one that had a more natural basis.

The immortal 'Beloved' passes on

In 1899, the 'immortal' Prince, at the age of eighty eight, passed on. His followers were devastated. For an immortal to die was the ultimate sin. He was buried in the front garden at midnight in the upright position

ready for the resurrection day. His grave, with others buried there, remains unmarked.

It was left to one of his disciples to identify a successor. The chosen one was the Reverend John Hugh Smyth-Pigott, a vicar in Clapton. And thus it was that unexpectedly at one of his Clapton services in September 1902, he declared himself before his congregation to be the reincarnated 'Son of God'. Many of those present were dumb struck. Others immediately proclaimed him as their God and very convincing they were too.

Word spread far and wide. The press turned out in force for his next sermon along with numerous objectors. Ugly scenes took place outside the church and a police escort was required to get him safely home. The press soon picked up that Smyth-Pigott was to retire to a Somerset refuge, the Agapemone.

Smyth-Pigott takes over the role

Established in his new role as the leader of the Agapemonites, Smyth-Pigott had an inventory produced of all of his followers showing their ages, interests and personal characteristics. Needless to say, it was announced that an intake of new and younger blood was required, female of course. They had to be attractive both physically and financially. The money would keep the place running and their physical beauty would satisfy the needs of Smyth-Pigott.

A second but spiritual wife

Although his wife was attractive enough, he felt the need to take a spiritual wife in addition. She was to be his Chief Soul Bride, Ruth Anne Price. It was she who bore him three children, two boys and a girl called Glory, Power and Hallelujah.

The scandal resulted in him also being defrocked by the Church of England and the sect remained withdrawn behind the walls of their Spaxton home. Visits by the Bishop of Bath and Wells in order to hand deliver the announcement were met with the news that the Messiah was away.

The press pushed hard to gather details. The Agapemonites stayed withdrawn in their shelter. The people of Spaxton remained tight lipped. Years of charitable acts from the sect towards the village people, including generous gifts at Christmas, left the villagers unlikely to give away any useful gossip.

The scandal and gossip died down and eventually Smyth-Pigott became a frequent and almost unnoticed visitor to Bridgwater. No longer the flamboyant horse drawn entry to the town, now just a discrete visit by motor car when necessary. He certainly lacked the flamboyant style of his predecessor. On one of his visits, two Bridgwater men tried to tar and feather him. The attempt landed them both in gaol.

Under Smyth-Pigott's leadership, the Agapemonites continued their comfortable if not unusual life style. As with Prince before him, he held the total respect and obedience of all within his walls. For decades the press came and went. Though lacking Prince's flair, he attracted public interest and amusement just as the Messiah before him. Bridgwater Carnival even had him featured in a tableau entry.

The end of the line

Smyth-Pigott's death came in March 1927 signalling the end of a community which lasted over a hundred years. At its peak, over two hundred people were members. Even in its more troubled days there had been at least sixty living there.

The last days of the Abode of Love

In 1958 Agapemone was sold to a private developer and split into flats. No more secrecy surrounds the place and surely the days of international scandal are over for this small Quantock village. The chapel where the virgins were purified was turned into a glove puppet studio by two men who worked in partnership producing educational and light entertainment films for the BBC. Spaxton quietly slipped back into its undisturbed way of life.

The Twentieth Century

The turn of the century

At the turn of the century, Bridgwater was still a relatively small town. Whilst the population had grown in numbers, the town had not spread itself geographically. Unlike many other towns, Bridgwater had faced inwards. The growth of housing developed in areas which were already populated.

Courtyard developments

This was achieved by the development of 'courts' which were accessed by archways between terraced houses. West Street had the highest density with seventeen courts in the one street. Friarn Street and St. John's Street had their own examples. Having walked through one of these archways, one entered a small circular courtyard with two-up two-down terraced housing right the way round the court. They were oppressive dwellings where light was at a premium.

By the 1950's they were effectively slums and were cleared not long after. A century earlier they had been the source of cholera with over two hundred lives being taken before the contagious disease abated. One reason it was so easy to set up these courts, and populate the town so densely, was the ready supply of water. Wells could be drilled almost anywhere producing effective supplies. Sanitation did not come so easily and hence the cholera outbreak.

1938 saw similar problems with an outbreak of typhoid. Schools and public meeting places were closed. The source of the outbreak remains unknown but the results were only too visible. There were many funerals in the town with the home of the deceased being stripped of bedding and mattresses which were taken away and burnt.

Thus the picture we have is of a town whose boundaries remained virtually unchanged during a period when the population had increased by a half compared with the day the railway came to town in 1841.

The first new estate

Until 1927 Bridgwater had not noticeably changed in size and shape. In that year the first new council houses were built in Kidsbury Road. Newtown Estate had started. One feature of these houses was the use of reject Bath Bricks in the construction of the front walls, a practice repeated in the building of Rhode Lane.

A few years before, in 1924, the Quantock Road was built in order to by pass Wembdon Hill, the steepness of which had led to more than one fatality.

The town fire brigade

The earliest reference to a fire engine was in 1725 when George Bubb Doddington donated one to the town. In 1830 the engine was kept near the south gate.

Before its move to Colley Lane in 1964, the town's fire brigade was sited around the back of the Town Hall in Clare Street. It had certainly been based there since 1880 and in 1906 enjoyed a newly opened station.

At the turn of the century, before Bridgwater began to spread itself beyond the old boundaries, it was possible to run to any fire in the town. Nowhere was more than about a mile away. The fire brigade, on hearing the bell sound, would leave their normal jobs, jump on their push bikes and cycle frantically to the fire station. The first two to arrive had the responsibility of dragging out the water pump and running with it to the fire. Those who arrived later would catch up on their bikes. Thus the fire brigade consisted of ten fit and fast athletes. On one occasion they were timed at eight minutes from the moment they arrived at the fire station to their time of arrival at the fire.

As the town grew, so the need for a motorised fire appliance became essential. Fortunately life became easier from 1935 onwards when the first petrol driven fire engine was trialled.

Introduction of electricity

In 1903, the Board of Trade granted a licence to the Bridgwater and District Electricity Supply and Traction Engine Company Limited. This permitted the supply to Bridgwater, Durleigh and Wembdon and allowed the company to dig up roads, railways and tramways where appropriate. The work had to be complete within two years. A generating station was built in Mount Street and power was on supply in 1904. The last area of the town to have its gas lighting replaced by electricity was St. Mary's Street.

The fuel supply to generate the power was actually gas. Direct current was the only sort available and retailed at 2 pence per unit or 7 pence if used for lighting. This latter charge was the maximum the company was allowed to make by the Board of Trade and even that had to reduce to 4 pence per unit after the first 91 hours of usage.

Eventually the National Grid came to town. This of course was the much safer and more useful alternating current. Unfortunately too many domestic appliances were already direct current and so it was many years before the change was made.

The advent of T.V.

Electricity led to television. I well remember the first time I saw T.V. I was five years old and my father was a postman. Very few families had T.V. then and it was to be some years before we were to get our first. However a fellow postman by the name of Aubrey Ryder already had one. He lived in Chamberlain Avenue on the Sydenham Estate. Our family of four had been invited to watch the coronation of Queen Elizabeth ll on Aubrey's set. It was June 2, 1953 and we walked out to the estate to join a room full of people. Crammed into the front room of a council house, it was a tremendous experience and exciting seeing an event live for the first time. The grown ups ooh'ed and aah'ed at the spectacle of the coronation and there was much discussion on whether or not this television thing would really catch on!

Another recollection of that visit was the colour of the street lighting along Bath Road. It was a peculiar purple colour. It was many years before I was to be aware of the significance of this lighting. It appears that there was uncertainty as to the best form of lighting for the town now that electricity was generally available. The local council therefore decided to try out two different types, the familiar orange and the less common mauve. The gas board felt put out by not being included in the trial. The authorities conceded and allowed them to join the trial. Thus the town was lit with three different forms and colours of lighting. Needless to say, gas had had its day and electricity prevailed.

Concern over a Suffragette visit

In the June of 1914, a young woman suspected of being a Suffragette visited the town. She stayed at accommodation in King Square where the local police kept a close eye on her. There was general concern throughout the country regarding the activities of these women who were suspected of planting bombs and starting fires to publicise their cause.

On one particular occasion, she paid a visit to St. Mary's church. There she sat amongst the congregation and was closely followed by Police Inspector Storey who sat right behind her. Everyone in the church was aware of her presence and the service was as tense as any could remember, sitting there waiting for the bomb to go off.

After the service, the young woman picked up her Dorothy bag, which all felt contained the explosive device, and walked out of the town never to return.

The depression years

The years of the First World War resulted in high levels of employment and the expectation of better things to come after the war. The 'land fit for heroes' that the returning soldiers had been led to expect was a long time coming. Unemployment in Bridgwater in those years after the war, when the economy was still trying to recover, reached over two thousand, a high number indeed for a total population of less than sixteen thousand. By 1933 almost a third of Bridgwater's labour force were unemployed.

These were depressing years indeed. Massive queues formed around King Square leading to the labour exchange. Children scavenged around waste bins seeking out scraps of food. Six elementary schools existed and each of these all witnessed the poverty with a good three quarters of the pupils in rags. Cardboard was stuffed into boots to squeeze out the last ounce of wear. Eastover was the largest of these schools and had the one-armed Mr. Hook as its headmaster. He was still there when I started my education. Along with other headmasters, he was treated with respect. It paid to behave in his presence in those days when the cane was part of the school's daily procedure.

Sunday schools were well attended institutions with three out of every four children being quite happy to attend. I'm sure the annual Sunday School outing to Burnham had much to do with it. If you were clever enough and brazen enough you could time your transfer from one Sunday School to another so that you could squeeze in as many as three trips in one season.

Child mortality rates were high and a child's coffin would be made of thin wood to keep down the costs and carried on a open top hand cart. Those who had jobs worked hard to keep them. The days in the brickyards were long with twelve back breaking hours being the norm.

Pawnbrokers and other bygone trades

The need for money was reflected in the presence of three pawnbrokers' shops in the centre of town. Best's pawnbrokers at the Cornhill and Paul's in Eastover served the two ends of the town. Fred Evis also had one in George Street complete with the pawnbroker's three balls over the doorway. It was 1955 before this one finally put up the shutters.

Friday was pay-day for the workforce. By Monday the money had run out and it was usually the mother of the family who would be obliged to take the family heir looms to the pawnbroker. The money offered against the articles saw them through until the next pay-day when the goods would be claimed back by refunding the money with a little interest.

Jewellery was the first to go along with any other non-essential luxuries. Next came the household goods, the larger items of furniture, followed by any clothes still decent enough to have any resale value.

Food for free

For those willing to risk the unpredictability of the Parrett and its tides, one source of food were the eels which ran in the river. I'm not talking here about the elvers which run up river on the spring tides but their full grown elders. Eels have a particular liking for worms, the bigger the better as any coarse fisherman can tell you. When eels are the last thing you want to catch, worms are the last bait you try.

One common way of capturing eels was by 'rayballing', sometimes called 'clatting' or 'worm balling'. This method entails the threading of a large number of worms onto a length of string or strong wool. The string is then tied into a large knot and optionally dangled from the end of a pole if fishing from the bank or held in the hand on a further length of string if fishing from a boat.

Either way, the technique is to dangle the ball of worms into the water until the eels can be felt tugging at the ball. The whole lot, worms and eels attached, are then smoothly raised to the surface and as they break the surface, swiftly but surely, they are lifted over a container such as an old galvanised bath. This needs to be floating in the water at the point where the eels will sense the air. The eels let go very quickly once they sense they are leaving the water and they have to be whipped over the edge of the bath before they drop back into the water.

This practice was quite common between the wars but little seen since. Having watched the local men in their dinghies near the town bridge, it was easy to pick up the technique.

I remember as a young teenager trying this out myself with a school friend at Combwich Pits. It really was quite easy to take a large number. The previous night had been thunderous, a condition which always meant the eels would be actively hunting out the worms washed into the ponds by the heavy rain. All those we caught, we placed in a convenient cattle trough. Unfortunately at the end of the day, when we went to recover our eels, all but a few had disappeared. We had forgotten about the eels' ability to travel overland, a practice essential to their breeding cycle.

Parrett salmon

Salmon were also taken from the river at one time, but only under licence costing ten shillings a year. Bill Pocock was a well known character who lived along Salmon Parade and used dip nets to catch the salmon. Bill used to trade in salmon, elvers, eels and mussels, albeit I believe the latter used to be brought up from Devon.

It was traditional never to fish for the salmon until after you'd planted your potatoes, with the best fish coming when the wheat was in flower. Unfortunately salmon no longer run the river, their decline started in the 1930's, but at one time there were sufficient to support twenty licensed fishermen.

It was the polluted and silted nature of the river which made the salmon possible to catch. Travelling upstream to spawn, the salmon would have to frequently rise. They were otherwise quite invisible in the dirty waters of the river. When they rose, fishermen like Bill Pocock would dip their massive nets under them and lift them out. This was normally done from a boat. The usual practice was to spot a salmon rise, throw a piece of wood at the spot, this would drift with the salmon and the salmon could be expected to rise somewhere upstream of that.

An old landlord of the River Parrett Inn, Harold Turner, was once found to have taken a salmon without a licence. The judge however let him off declaring it to be a sporting gesture. Taking salmon was not permitted on weekends for some reason. Perhaps that was Harold's problem.

Sturgeon, porpoises and snails

More obscure captures were made on the Parrett than just eels and salmon. On June 27, 1859 a one hundred and sixty pound sturgeon was caught and sold in the market at 6d. per pound. And then in 1913 a one hundred and sixty eight pound porpoise was foolish enough to be taken by Henry Laver in Bridgwater.

Another source of free food, before the last war, was the humble snail. These were considered a delicacy and were collected by old men, traditionally only when there was an 'r' in the month. This meant they were gathered in their dormant season when they were at their best. Once cleansed and scolded in brine, the open seal of the shell was cut off, they were boiled for twenty minutes, then removed from their shells and eaten with vinegar. They were particularly popular around the local pubs where they were also sold pickled. One local character who used to sell them was called Philly Baker and he would walk as far as Langport to pick his supplies.

The glory years of Bridgwater rugby

If the years from 1921 to 1935 did nothing else for Bridgwater, it provides the finest period of rugby. Among those playing for the Bridgwater and Albion who also took international honours were R. E. Prescott, T. E. S. Francis and Jim Barrington. Jim was a particularly fast and fluent half back who took his first cap in 1931. The Barrington family have had a long association with Bridgwater and sporting prowess runs in the family.

Rugby was strong enough in those days to support an alternative local club and the Old Morganians was founded in 1920 playing the matches at Durleigh. The club still survives today with its own ground at Chedzoy Lane.

Rugby actually started in Bridgwater in the nineteenth century. The first club was formed

in 1875 and the first game played against Taunton College School on November 22, 1876. Naturally Bridgwater won, by one try and one goal to nil. The Albion club formed in September 1891 and had similar success at their first game on October 31, 1891 convincingly beating Wiveliscombe Rovers.

Before this, however, rugby had developed sufficiently in the county for a Somerset Union of clubs to be formed. This happened on September 6th, 1882 at the Royal Clarence Hotel, reflecting how strong the sport was in the town.

Amongst the early stars were Sammy Woods who originated from New South Wales. He came to England to study at Cambridge and to Bridgwater to learn the art of brewing. He won his first international cap in 1893/94 against Ireland.

Bob Dibble first played in 1901 and remains, perhaps, the finest player the county has seen. On his return from the Boer War, still a teenager, he settled into the Bridgwater side and went on to gain 19 England caps including the honour of captaincy. He had an elder brother, James, who also played for the town and a younger brother, Frank, who was capped for Australia.

Then came World War 1 which took its toll of Bridgwater's finest and led to the Bridgwater club and the Albion merging into one. The club grew once again in strength and in the 1922/23 season many of its members, including Jim Jarvis, A. Spriggs, F. G. Spriggs, P. Lewis and J. Reed, represented Somerset in the side which took the honours in the county championships with Bridgwater's own Jim Jarvis as the captain.

Town centre shops

Probably the most noticeable change between the shops of the depression years and those of today is that of the general hygiene. For example butchers were always closed on

Mondays because that was the day they did their slaughtering. The pigs would arrive at the shop on the Monday morning and the butcher would spend the day out the back preparing them for the counter. Their was no town abattoir in those days.

Lucky was the lad who got a job with the butcher or indeed any other similar trade. The apprentice would start his career on deliveries, riding his bicycle with its enormous basket on the front. I remember from my own experience how difficult those bikes were to keep upright when fully loaded. I also well remember the extra bones that were essential to the survival of the butcher boys. These were the only currency stray dogs understood. They acted as the border guards on each housing estate in the town. However those that survived the delivery rounds could go on to be apprentice butchers with a job for life.

Bakers were much the same but needless to say the bikes were much easier. Queues outside the bakers at the end of the day were not uncommon. The practice was that any unsold items would be released at half price or less once half past six in the evening had arrived.

It wasn't just the delivery lad that could be seen on his bike during those depression years. Various tradesmen would ply their wares from bikes. The knife grinder was a regular visitor with his circular stone geared up to his bike. The muffin man toured the town ringing his bell for attention and French onion sellers were seen especially towards the end of the summer season.

Barber shops with their red and white poles offered another career opportunity. Here the apprentice's role was to learn how to prepare the lather, strap the cut-throat razors and learn how to hold a conversation on any subject under the sun. Their busiest periods were Saturday mornings when it was normal to queue for up to an hour and then ask for the regulation short back and sides.

Corner shops were a feature away from the town centre and offered almost everything at any time of the day. The advent of supermarkets brought about the rapid decline of these businesses.

Rope walks

Another bygone industry is that of rope making which was done in rope walks. These were long covered galleries under which the rope was twisted and formed into the finished product. At least two rope walks existed, one near the present bus station site and the other half way along Chilton Street.

Changes in transport

The 1920's and 1930's saw significant changes in transport. Horse drawn traffic declined in favour of motor powered vehicles. By 1925 it was necessary to introduce Tar macadam. This of course saw the demise of the Cornhill carnival bonfire but did much to improve conditions for the cars and lorries which were now increasing in number.

Amongst the earliest powered lorries were the old steam driven wagons. One of these was owned by Peace's of West Quay, the haulage company and two were owned by the Gas Company for hauling coke. One of these was driven by my wife's grandfather, Walter England, who lived in Kidsbury Road. Every where the wagon went, two bags of coal went with it. It was capable of hauling eight tons and under full steam was quite a noisy contraption.

The Bridgwater Haulage Company also possessed steam lorries and managed to catch the attention of the authorities in 1912 when one of their employees was fined ten shillings for breaking the speed limit for steam propelled vehicles, two miles an hour!

Brickyards decline is replaced by British Cellophane

The post war recovery in Europe worked against Bridgwater's principle industry. The devastation in France left them with the need to rebuild. It also forced them into introducing new technologies in order to match supply with the demand. Thus whilst in France, the brick and tile industry was moving rapidly forward with well mechanised businesses producing relatively low priced quality bricks, Bridgwater was suffering from an under capitalised labour intensive industry. The decline of the brickyards continued and unemployment worsened. The news of the opening of the British Cellophane plant in 1938 came like a shot in the arm and reduced unemployment to half its former level.

British Cellophane

British Cellophane, having opened its factory was soon to become the towns largest employer. Joining the company became an adventure for many of the local work force. The first thing Courtaulds did was to send its key workers for training at the company's headquarters. Fifty years on and the practice is still the same.

At its peak over 2500 were employed in the manufacture of cellulose film, mainly for packaging purposes, and a further 1,000 or so were employed by two other manufacturing units opened up by BCL on the same site. These were Bonded Fibre Fabrics (opened in 1951) and Plastic Films which have subsequently been sold off to Lamont Holdings and British Polythene Industries respectively. Cellophane, of course, was to become a world-wide household name and the BCL manufacturing base was increased to include a factory in Cornwall, Ontario in 1952 and another in Barrow-in-Furness in 1958.

The decline of the world market for cellulose film, resulting from substitution by polypropylene products has led to the closure of two of these plants. The original at Bridgwater has survived as the one most capable of serving the needs of the residual market which will become increasingly based on specialist requirements. At the time of writing, the numbers employed at the Cellophane plant are around 510 and whilst no longer the big employer that it was, the town still has a great dependence on its survival. In the grounds of this factory stands a 15th century manor house, but more of that elsewhere.

Durleigh Reservoir

The arrival of British Cellophane was not a matter of luck. The local authority some years before had decided in their wisdom that the town needed a more significant water supply. As a result Bridgwater was blessed not only with the now ageing Ashford Reservoir but in 1938 with Durleigh Reservoir as well. Thus there was an abundance of water readily available. If good luck did enter into it, then it came about because the opening of the new reservoir coincided with one of the worst droughts in living memory. At a time when the rest of the country was suffering, Bridgwater was boasting its success.

The publicity caught the eye of Courtaulds management up in Coventry and they decided to take a closer look. The ready supply of water, the tidal river to facilitate the disposal of effluent combined with a readily available workforce made the decision an easier one.

Other manufacturing units

Other post war manufacturing companies worthy of mention, albeit many are now closed, are the Sealed Motor Company, the Van Heusen collar factory, S. Leffman's foundation garments (now Bairdswear), Wellworthy Limited (now part of Amalgamated Engineering), Clarks Shoes and

Quantock Preserving Company (now Gerber Foods).

Accident or murder?

Before Durleigh Reservoir was built, there were a number of dwellings in the valley which were to be the subject of a compulsory purchase. One of these was the subject of a possible unsolved murder. If you visit the reservoir in a drought year when the water level is particularly low, then you see the remains of the old road to West Bower Farm and also that of a cottage.

This cottage, which was just opposite Durleigh Church, was the home of Ben and Betty Stoddard. Arriving from outside of the area and being a fairly private couple little was known of them except that they appeared to be devoted to each other, never being seen apart. In their employ was a gardener, Michael Abbotts and a maid, Grace Burton. After some years of apparent bliss, the couple drifted apart. No more were they seen walking together. He was to be seen hacking around on horse back and she taking walks on her own. The maid had also observed that loud aggressive arguments were increasingly taking place. The people of Durleigh drew their own conclusions. Perhaps there was an affair going on between the gardener and the mistress of the house.

Interest developed rapidly in what was going on. Then one morning, a local man discovered the body of Mrs. Stoddard. She lay at the base of an embankment, her head split open. Blood had spattered boulders nearby. Was it an accident or had some evil hand been involved in her demise? Whilst the coroner's verdict was accidental death, there were many who thought otherwise particularly when Mr. Stoddard disappeared after the verdict as rapidly as he and his wife had arrived some years before.

Home of the Queen of England

Also overlooking Durleigh Reservoir is West Bower Farm, reputed to be the birthplace of Jane Seymour. She was the third of Henry Vlll's six wives and died soon after giving birth to his much wanted son, the young Edward who was to become Edward Vl of England. Henry described her as the only wife with whom he could find no fault.

The farm once had a round dovecote with four foot thick walls, thirteen tiers of nests with sixty nest holes per tier. In this way over eight hundred birds were catered for in just one cote.

The Bath and West Show

Although we now all associate the West Country's grandest event of the agricultural calendar with the Royal Bath and West showground at Shepton Mallet, there was a time when Bridgwater was the venue.

I remember during the 1950's going to the showground at Huntworth to witness the "Bridgwater Show". Show jumping was one of the main attractions and big name riders were present on most days. Pat Smythe was perhaps the best known in the days after the war and she appeared on a number of occasions along with numerous other world class personalities. This show was the 'aftermath' of the Bath and West which was last held at Huntworth just before the war.

The Bridgwater Mercury for May 1939 reported on the "largest Bath and West show ever held". The event was held at Bridgwater, as it was on many previous occasions. That particular year, the population was expecting to go to war at any time. The importance of agriculture to sustain an island nation, isolated from imports by the dangers of enemy shipping, was well understood.

Apart from the obvious livestock and flowers, the ARP were present demonstrating what to do in the event of an enemy attack. PT displays provided by the complement of HMS Impregnable were mixed in with sheep dog trials and rodeo riders. This mixture of farming and militaria was a clear demonstration of the important part both were to play in the months to come.

Bridgwater population growth

The twentieth century may seem the wrong place to consider the growth of the town since its inception. However, it is during this period that the population tripled and so we deal with the complete picture in this section.

The first thousand years

If we assume that Bridgwater started around 800 A.D. with a population of perhaps 35, then it took about 600 years for it to grow to around 1,000. We know that the population in 1377 was 858 and that some thirty years earlier in 1348, roughly a third of the nations population died in the plague that swept the country with half the inhabitants of Bridgwater perishing as a result. The plague came in through our sea ports, albeit Bridgwater was unlikely to have been an original source since it is known that the plague progressed its way up from Weymouth.

Nineteenth century growth

Bridgwater's growth after the medieval period was gradual and steady and by the end of the 18th century the town's population was still below 4,000. The industrial growth in the nineteenth century, exaggerated by the impact of the arrival of canals and railways, saw a dramatic increase from 4,000 at the start of the century to 15,000 at the end. There is a slightly unnatural peak in the numbers in 1896 when the borough boundaries were extended and a dip in 1849 caused by the cholera epidemic and, to some extent, emigration.

The rapid growth gave rise to a need for additional churches. Thus St. John's was built in Eastover in 1846 and Holy Trinity was built in Taunton Road in 1840 to a design by Richard Carver. The Broadway dual carriageway now runs along one of its old boundaries and the church was demolished in 1958.

The twentieth century

The early twentieth century witnesses a less rapid increase. The chart below may suggest otherwise but the reader's attention is drawn to the scaling across the bottom.

Any increases which were gained in the first twenty years were wiped out with the effects of the First World War. A gradual increase between the wars was followed by the post World War ll baby boom years and a steady increase to the early 1990's.

Population chart for 800 to 1974

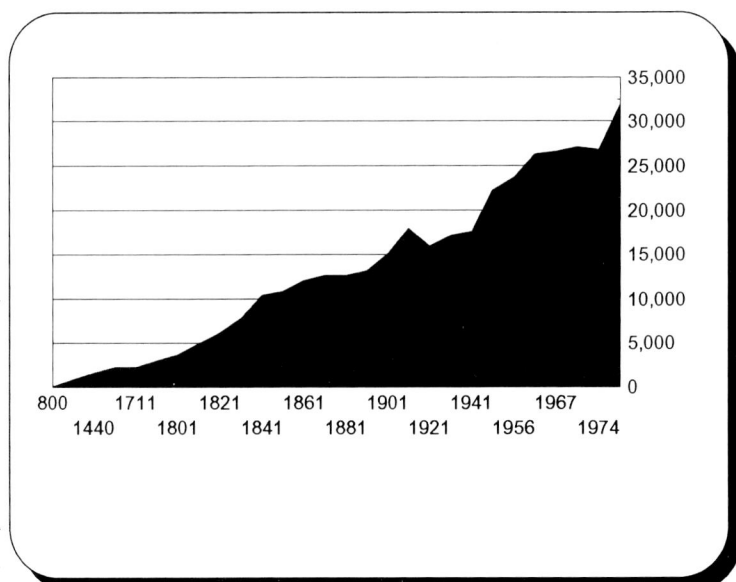

126

Bridgwater at war

Vernon Bartlett, Independent M.P.

Personally I don't remember Vernon Bartlett but many Bridgwater constituents spoke so highly of him for years after his term as our M.P. that it is easy to feel one had actually met the man. He was such a knowledgeable and respected individual who first made his mark just before war began.

In the September of 1938, Chamberlain was in Munich signing an agreement with Hitler and Mussolini. The various parties involved agreed that the Sudeten region of Czechoslovakia should be conceded to Hitler's Germany in return for "peace in our time". The Czechoslovakians had no say in the matter and Chamberlain returned a hero, convinced he could trust Hitler to stand by his word.

Vernon Bartlett had been on the continent as a journalist and had seen at first hand what was happening in Europe. He knew that the peace agreement Chamberlain had obtained wasn't worth the paper it was written on and he felt the nation should know. He was determined that Parliament should not be taken in by Hitler's deals.

On 27 October, 1938, there was a by-election in Oxford where Quintin Hogg stood successfully for the Conservatives against an Independent Progressive candidate opposed to any deals with Hitler. Supported by Labour and the Liberals, he also had behind him a number of Tory rebels including Churchill, Eden, Macmillan and Heath who campaigned under the slogan "A vote for Hogg is a vote for Hitler".

The following February, Bridgwater had its own by election with Vernon Bartlett taking the Independent Progressive platform against Patrick Heathcoat-Amory, the Conservative favourite. The Munich agreement was the main issue. Vernon Bartlett argued that Hitler could not be trusted and no more deals should be signed. The government preferred for Bartlett to keep quiet and not stir up trouble. They suggested to the Bridgwater electorate that Bartlett's statements were drawing Hitler's attention to Bridgwater itself. Even the German press joined in the criticism of the Bridgwater public for allowing such a provocative candidate to stand.

Despite the power of the Tory campaign machine and Hitler's propaganda, Bartlett won with a landslide victory and earned the respect of all parties during his time representing the people of his Somerset constituency.

ARP preparation

The nation knew that it was on the brink of war. All over the town preparations were under way. Conscription had meant that many men who had previously served in the armed forces and had remained reservists, had been called up and were back in active service.

The members of the ARP (Air Raid Precautions) brigade saw their first full scale practice run on July 12, 1939. It was a Saturday night and all street lights were extinguished. Shopkeepers, motorists and cyclists all honoured the request to respect the black out. With a clear sky but low moon, moving about the town was very difficult.

Shortly before midnight, all air raid wardens were at their posts. At the ARP headquarters at the west end of the High Street, two first aid parties, two immediate action parties and a decontamination unit set off in their lorries. The Auxiliary Fire Brigade stood at the ready and the Scouts acted as messenger boys. At midnight, the wardens in their outposts telephoned in their first reports on the previously arranged damage and casualties.

A fire at the Odeon gave the Auxiliary Fire Brigade its first task. The Immediate Action Squad were required to rescue people from demolished buildings, the first aiders took the wounded to the medical centre in Mount Street and the decontamination unit had to sort out the gas attack which had effected Castle Street. By one o'clock it was all over and by half past the ARP's had all gone home.

The day war broke out

"This country is now at war with Germany. We are ready". The nation heard the Prime Minister's words over their wireless sets on Sunday, September 3, 1939. Across the town, gas masks were distributed which were to be carried at all times.

On September 6th, the Bridgwater Mercury's headline read "At War with Germany with the King's message to his people." After the King's message was an article on "Somerset homes for mothers and children".

Arrival of the evacuees

Apart from the obvious impact of call up, perhaps the most visible sign that there was a war going on was the arrival of the evacuees from the big cities. Across the nation, three million women and children were to be evacuated. Bridgwater alone was to receive 6,400. By the end of the first week of the war, over a thousand had arrived for Bridgwater with a further thousand for the surrounding villages.

The first to arrive were the children from the East End of London. These unfortunate children, miles from home, in unfamiliar surroundings and frequently separated from their brothers and sisters, arrived at Bridgwater railway station, bringing with them a gas mask, a satchel and in some cases health problems.

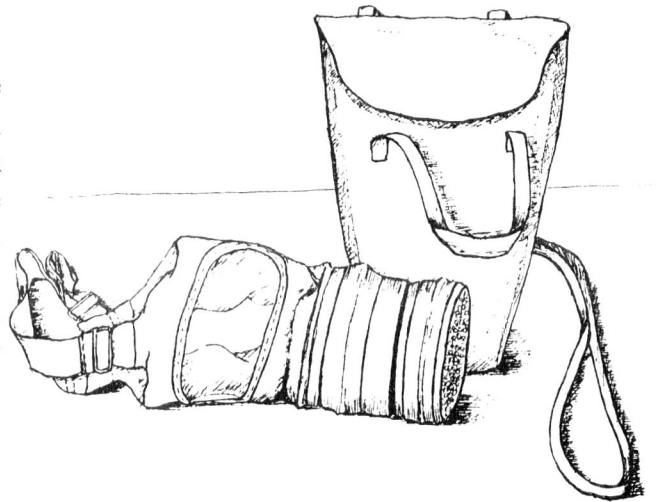

Scabies and ringworm were not uncommon in these children aged from five years to fourteen. Put on a train at Paddington with an identification label attached to their lapels, they were shipped off to Bridgwater.

On Friday September 8th, 1939 the first two train loads arrived. In the afternoon, 559 children arrived with their teachers. They were marched down to St. John's school, given biscuits, chocolate and a tin of meat before being allocated to a district or a family by the billeting officer, Mr P. H. Beckett. A fleet of 'motor buses' then took them to their villages.

In the evening of the same day, 800 children and their teachers arrived for Bridgwater itself. These were taken to Eastover School, suitably refreshed and distributed around the town.

On the Saturday and Sunday, yet more arrived for the village districts with several hundred arriving for Bridgwater late on the Monday evening. In fact, they were so late the billeting officer had given up on them for that evening. Their distribution was severely hampered by the lack of organisation and transport at such a late hour.

Problems for the parents

Their parents visited whenever they could but it wasn't that easy during war time. Not only was travel a problem, but when these city folk arrived in the Somerset countryside, looking for a particular home near a particular village, they had to manage without the help of directional signs or pub names. These had all been removed to make life difficult for the Germans, should they arrive.

These were difficult times for the evacuee children and their parents. Life in rural Somerset was culturally so different from London's East End. For those in the villages in particular, if they had difficulty settling in, it could be almost impossible for them to get hold of fellow evacuees with whom to share their problems and experiences. Recognising the need for these people to get together, the local Labour Party opened up 27 Friarn Street as a community centre specifically addressing the needs of the evacuees and their mothers.

Some children found severe difficulty in adapting to their new surroundings. To cater for their needs, a hostel was opened at Sunnybank off Rhode Lane. The arrival of the evacuees continued right through those late months of 1939 and into 1940. On June 19th a further 450 arrived for Bridgwater and a further 1,750 for the surrounding villages. Once again Eastover school was used as their first port of call. From there, following a medical and a bottle of Co-op milk, they were transferred to their new homes.

A large number of children ended up at Wembdon school and nearly didn't survive to tell the tale. The school and the nearby church were identified as the places to go in the event of an air raid. The windows in both buildings had wire mesh added to them to reduce the danger from flying glass. A hundred and thirty three children were to use the school with twenty five going to the church. September 27th, 1940 gave rise to an air raid alert. During the height of the Battle of Britain, a German Junkers 88 dropped its load of bombs over Wembdon with one exploding just a quarter of a mile from the school.

By the autumn of 1940, the rate at which evacuees was arriving had noticeably declined. On October 9, a mere 140 arrived and those the first for some while.

Social activities postponed for the duration

Clearly life could not go on as it had before. Food shortages, rationing, the menfolk away and the need to concentrate on the war effort led to numerous social events being cancelled. The first to suffer in the district was the Puriton Flower Show. All sport came to a stand still. The Bridgwater Harrier's Gymkhana was cancelled along with the Christy Band Fete due to be held in Blake Gardens.

Bridgwater's world famous carnival was abandoned and the annual St. Matthew's Fair was more or less limited to the trading side with virtually no funfair. Instead of Merry-go-rounds, circuses, boxing booths and numerous roundabouts, there was just one motor cycle show and one 'dodgems'. And by 7 p.m., the whole showground had to be in darkness.

The black outs

Failing to adequately 'black out' the town was a serious offence for anyone. One light exposed could be all an enemy aircraft would need to home in on its target, leaving death and destruction in its wake. And all because someone, somewhere had been less than vigilant. During September to December in that first year of the war, the Bridgwater Mercury had a regular column from the Police Courts reporting on prosecutions for black out offences.

LOCAL BLACK OUT TIMES

WEEK ENDING APRIL 22nd

		Begins p.m.	Ends a.m.
Tuesday	April 15	8.36	5.43
Wednesday	April 16	8.37	5.41
Thursday	April 17	8.39	5.39
Friday	April 18	8.41	5.37
Saturday	April 19	8.42	5.35
Sunday	April 20	8.44	5.33
Monday	April 21	8.46	5.31
Tuesday	April 22	8.47	5.29

The increase in accidents during the black out periods is very noticeable when one gleans the pages of the Mercurys during the war years. Road deaths, and drownings in particular, feature with almost weekly coroner's reports on unexpected deaths.

The black outs, as well as presenting problems, also presented opportunities. If you sold heavy black curtain material, black paint or black tape, then trade was probably booming. For a short period local tradesmen did roaring business in food, clothing and bedding for the evacuees. Indeed trade also boomed as a result of panic buying and the inevitable hoarding that goes with the advent of any major crisis. But if you were a shopkeeper, open all hours, then blackening your window was not going to help your

trade. But the Bridgwater Mercury was able to seize this opportunity.

SPECIAL NOTICE TO TRADERS IN THIS AREA

Minimise loss of trade through darkened shop windows by displaying your goods in the columns of this newspaper

Publicity is essential for the Maintenance of trade

Whilst this may have presented a business opportunity for the Mercury, censorship didn't. It just created problems. If evacuees were heart broken, it was best if the Mercury failed to reflect the full extent. Many evacuated children actually went back home and faced their lot in the heavily bombed streets of London rather than suffer in an environment in which they were totally ill at ease. At least two boys started the long walk back within the first few days of arriving. This incident was reported more as a humorous story rather than a reflection of the size of the problem. In fairness, being the first week of the war, the full scale of the problem had yet to be realised.

Censorship also affected what you could do with your Mercury and where you could send it.

CENSORSHIP PERMITS

Private individuals are no longer allowed to post copies of news-papers to friends or relatives in Neutral Countries. Surmount this difficulty by placing your order with this office. We have the necessary permit to post this newspaper abroad.

Bridgwater' men on HMS Courageous, first maritime casualties of war

The war was just two weeks old when the news was received of the loss of the aircraft carrier HMS Courageous with 500 lives. It was Sunday, September 17th when the Courageous with many West Country men on board was sunk by a German submarine.

The Bridgwater Mercury reported *"The people of Bridgwater in common with those of other parts were shocked by the news of the sinking of HMS Courageous and the resulting terrible loss of lives and especially so because Bridgwater men were among those on board at the time. One of the lucky survivors is Mr. Charles Wood whose home is in Cecil Terrace, on the Westonzoyland Road. ... His parents reside in Polden Street and he has several brothers living in the town.*

... It was three minutes to eight on Sunday morning when the Courageous was struck 700 miles from Plymouth. A terrible explosion occurred and those who could jumped overboard when the order "Abandon Ship" was given and within a quarter of an hour the Courageous had sunk.

Mr. Wood clung to an oar for over an hour until picked up."

Less fortunate were Stoker Cecil William James who at the age of 50 had been recalled from his stoker's job at the Van Heusen factory, having earlier served 23 years in the Royal Navy. His life, along with two other local men were lost in the sinking of the aircraft carrier.

The other two Bridgwater casualties were both British Cellophane workers, until recalled into the navy in the June of that fateful year. Chief mechanic William Buttle of 13 Athlone road had already put in 25 years and 45 year old, Bridgwater born, Petty Officer Granville of 131 Rhode Lane had

retired just 5 years before. He left a widow and four children.

Another early Bridgwater loss was that of Marine Alfred John Croker whose widowed mother lived in Durleigh Road. He was killed in the gallant fight made by HMS Exeter with the German pocket battle ship, the Graf Spey.

Prisoners of war

Apart from the evacuees, other arrivals at Bridgwater station were the German and Italian prisoners of war. These arrived at night and were quietly trucked to their camps in Colley Lane and Goathurst until there were about five hundred in each camp. Here they were housed in new huts and were well looked after, receiving the same food as the soldiers that guarded them. They were put to good use in return, going out in working parties. They were frequently seen walking around Bridgwater with their yellow patches on their outfits to clearly distinguish them.

Women's Land Army

For the ladies the war brought new responsibilities and new freedoms. Many went to work filling the vacancies left by the men who had gone to war. For the first time women were seen to be encroaching on previously male dominated roles. My mother became a post woman, a role my father took on when he returned from Europe after the war. Others went to work on the land, using and repairing tractors and other farm instruments. There was really nothing beyond their capability.

The first air raid casualties

Generally speaking Somerset escaped very lightly from the bombing raids over England. Certainly Bridgwater and district was not a serious target, just a place over which German planes would fly on their raids to Bristol and Cardiff. If they encountered heavy resistance or lost their bearing, they would turn for home and drop their deadly loads on any convenient target.

The area's first bombing casualties were two killed at Burnham-on-Sea on 18 July 1940. For Bridgwater the first experience came with a huge bomb that landed some miles from the town at Northmoor blasting a forty yard wide crater in a field. The same crater can still be seen today serving a useful purpose as a pond.

Two weeks later there was a small air battle over the Polden Hills in which Bridgwater residents were able to witness the shooting down of a Heinkel over Puriton. The five German airmen were able to parachute to safety except for one being shot and wounded on the way down. They were all later taken to Bridgwater.

The first Bridgwater casualties came on the tragic night of 24 August 1940 when a German plane on its way back discharged its load of some 200 incendiaries. This it did as it crossed over Cranleigh Gardens and Colley Lane, creating several fires in the brickyards. Firemen fighting the blazes were machine gunned by German pilots. But the real damage came when a German plane off-loaded its heavier explosives over Old Taunton Road where nine houses were hit, some being destroyed, and killing seven including a lady by the name of Daisy Balham. Apparently when they found her, she was still sat up in her kitchen chair, paring knife in one hand and runner bean in the other.

The Mercury report for that week was only able to refer to 'a West Country' town being hit. It was not permitted to report any detail which might assist the enemy. It referred to a terrace of six houses being hit with three houses completely destroyed with bodies being recovered from the debris. Two houses in another row of six were rendered uninhabitable with two others severely damaged.

In one house, a bomb fell on a bed in which an eight year old boy was asleep. He awoke screaming that he was on fire. His mother and grandmother dragged him from the room and threw buckets of water onto the burning feather bed.

In another row of six houses, the only one to escape damage was number 13. One unfortunate resident killed in the raid had actually been advised by a nearby brickyard worker to go back in doors for fear of injury during the raid. Having retreated to the relative safety of his home, his house was one which took a direct hit. His body was the first to be recovered by the same brickyard worker.

Air raid shelters

Following the bombing, inevitably the need for shelters in public places was recognised. The local council agreed that twenty should be erected without further delay.

Much damage was done around the town on the night of 20 March 1941. Two landmines were dropped over the Meads near the Fairfield. Nearly fifteen hundred premises received some form of blast damage. Numerous town centre shops lost their windows and one person was killed.

Many bombs were dropped harmlessly around the area during the raids over England. Wembdon received its fair share along with Chilton Trinity. Some years ago I remember the bomb squad being brought in to Westonzoyland Road. An unexploded bomb was uncovered in the field next to the Clark's shoe factory, a good forty years after the war. My wife remembers there being one in a field in which she used to play at the top of Rhode Lane.

Unexploded bombs

At the time of writing this book, I became a grandfather for the first time. An unexploded bomb from the war could have prevented this happy event from coming to fruition. My granddaughter's other grandfather, Dennis Searle, could so easily have departed this world before he had even reached full manhood. On his way across the Meads, whilst walking home from Westover school, he saw an unexploded bomb, nose down in a ditch. Retrieving the object, he took it home where for safe keeping he put it under his sister's bed. As soon as his father found out, he put the bomb in a bag and cycled with it to the police station where he presented it to them on the counter. You can imagine how pleased they must have been to receive it!

The bombing raids remained the main topic of conversation for quite a while in Bridgwater. My mother arrived in the town for the first time in 1942 having moved up from Plymouth after her marriage to my father who was serving in the army at the time. One of her earliest impressions was how the townsfolk had been so effected by the bombing yet she found it hard to see where the damage had been. After her experiences in Plymouth, which was almost flattened by the Germans, Bridgwater seemed a positive haven of peace and tranquillity.

Cellophane windows

Needless to say, the raids created further opportunities for the imaginative. Fire buckets, window tape and sandbags sales increased dramatically. Even British Cellophane had its part to play with window protection. The Mercury for July 17, 1940 advised residents to protect their windows from the dangers of flying splinters of glass by 'gumming' a layer of Cellophane to the pane cut to the size of the window. The gum was to be produced using 1 lb. of Calcium Chloride, 1/2 lb. of Gelatine and 1 gallon of hot water. This paste was then to be used as when wallpapering, smoothing out the inevitable bubbles. A house on the corner of North Street and Penel Orlieu was used as a show house for this and similar safety ideas.

Shortages and food rationing

Throughout the war, food, clothing, petrol and other essentials were to be in short supply. Inevitably rationing was introduced, much of which lasted into the 1950's, well after the end of the war. "Dig for Victory" was the slogan aimed at encouraging garden owners to dig up their lawns and plant vegetables. By 1943, 600 new allotments had been created in a period of two years. Breeding meat rabbits and keeping chickens was soon common practice.

Hoarding became an issue as panic buying consumed early supplies. Whilst the government published notices encouraging people not to panic buy, the traders did the opposite, seizing every opportunity.

The G.I.'s arrive.

1943 saw the coming of the American forces to Bridgwater along with other Somerset towns. Major camps were set up. Taunton had a particularly large one and many homes were obliged to offer billet facilities. This meant taking in a serviceman for bed but not meals. For this the payment was 10d per day. British servicemen in billets were only worth 6d. Next to my first home in Branksome Avenue, just off the Bath Road, there was a garage on the corner called Tottle's. Petrol rationing was so severe that the garage served no useful role and so the building was turned over to billets. It may have been a mostly galvanised iron affair but it was better than a tent on a wet night.

In the main the G.I.'s were welcome. They were over here to help us finish a job. They contributed in no small way to the local economy and they offered male companionship to the local girls who were suffering the problems of having most of the menfolk away in the army. It was this latter point, more than any other, which caused the resentment.

"Overpaid, over sexed and over here" was the popular phrase when running them down. If they caused a nuisance, they were usually asked question about where they were during the first four years of the war.

Generally speaking, they were well received and recognised as some other mother's son, far from home and faced with the frightening prospect of war. Most families were able to relate to them and identified their problems with those of their own menfolk overseas. I know, for instance, that my own father was befriended by a Dutch family while he was serving in Holland. They suffered shortages and hardships far worse than over here. One way my father was able to repay their kindness was to smuggle, hidden in his gas mask, inner tubes for bicycles. The tubes were collected by my mother whilst he was away on service.

Dances were organised for G.I.'s at the Blake Hall and local factories such as British Cellophane. The YMCA, Blake Hall and Cranleigh Gardens acted as canteens. The local council as early as 1940 had already allocated the Town Hall to be used for dances to entertain the troops on Sundays.

British Cellophane on organising one of its dances sent out invitations to the American forces and the local girls. To their amazement when the G.I.'s turned up they were all young black American soldiers who served in separate units to their white counterparts. This came as an unexpected culture shock to the local girls with an embarrassing period of silence, until finally someone broke the ice and began to dance. They all enjoyed the rest of the evening.

There's a personal experience of my mother which I can relate here. My father was away with the forces in North Africa, during the time of the Rommell campaign. My mother had a parcel of soap to send out to him. If you kept the soap long enough, it dried, went harder, lasted longer and weighed less when you sent it. She was taking this sizeable parcel of soap to the Post Office in Eastover when she was the subject of amorous

134

advances from an American serviceman. Refusing to take 'no' for an answer, he put his arm around my mother and then learned yet another way of applying soap to the body. Mother brought the full weight of the soap parcel down on his head with as much commitment as she could muster. International diplomacy took a knock that day with mother departing the scene no doubt muttering "Overpaid, Over ....etc.".

More American servicemen arrived in April 1944 when the Westonzoyland airfield, previously used mainly for training our own pilots, was turned over to them. Its main use now was in providing a glider squadron for the D-Day landings. A truly awesome sight they made on their training runs with masses of towing planes and their attached gliders flying over the town.

Needless to say there were the inevitable romances between local girls and the young G.I.'s. Many of these affairs ended in tragedy when the G.I.'s went to the continent or back to the States, leaving behind young, expectant, unmarried mothers, a situation less tolerable than these more enlightened days. Others had happier endings with wedding bells preceding departure for America and a new life in the 'land of the free'. Carol Chapman and Rene Cornish, both from Athlone Road, were amongst those to make a new life overseas.

War effort at work

Local factories played their own role in the war effort. Cellophane was used to wrap ammunition going to humid climates in the Far East, and part of the factory was turned over to the production of 16,000 panels for Bailey Bridges, Asdic components for submarines, units for Mulberry ports used in the D-Day landings, gun mountings, turrets and other armour for cars. Landing craft were manufactured at Saltlands by Light Buoyant. The Trojan Works, based where Wellworthy now have their factory, made

shell cases. Then there were the locally made wicker baskets so resilient when dropped by parachute and, of course, high explosives produced at the Royal Ordnance Factory.

Fund raising was also a significant part of the war effort and a moral booster at the same time. During September 1940, the people of Bridgwater raised over £6400 in 31 days as part of the "Spitfire" fund. This meant the people of Bridgwater could boast a fighter aircraft with their name on it, albeit I have been unable to find any record of the plane's success or otherwise.

1941 saw the launch of "Warship Week" in which Bridgwater and district raised over £200,000 in loans. This earned the privilege of having a plaque placed on the bridgehead of the destroyer HMS Wolfhound, commemorating the townfolk's generosity .

Dad's Army

The Home Guard or Local Defence Volunteers was set up in May 1940. Their role was to protect the area against the invaders, should they arrive. Bridgwater had its own unit, the 10th Somerset Battalion, commanded from its inception to its stand down by Lieutenant Colonel R. Chamberlain. He kept up his public service after the stand down by assuming the role of mayor of the borough.

The Bridgwater battalion was based at the Drill Hall and was manned by almost two and a half thousand volunteers split into various platoons. British Cellophane was large enough to qualify for its own number 5 platoon. "6 Platoon" was reserved for the railwaymen. Their role was to defend the railway system and ensure 'Gerry' didn't suddenly appear coming up the line. 6 Platoon was made up of the railwaymen from both the GWR and S & D railways. Initially they were armed with just pick axe handles and an arm band with LDV on it. Hardly enough to stop 'Gerry'.

Later things looked up when Lord Wharton from Goathurst supplied them with a couple of double barrelled shotguns. However within a week one of these had been dropped and the barrel dented. Eventually uniforms, arms and other equipment arrived and the LDV started to look like a serious force. Three years on they were even supplied with grenades and, by then, knew how to use them.

The platoon drilled regularly in the grounds of Eastover school, convenient for both railways. There were also regular exercises. During one of these, against Cellophane's number 5 Platoon, someone misdirected a smoke bomb and managed to stop a passenger train which should have been passing through.

At the back of the railway station was a Spigot Mortar Gun emplacement. Another exercise involved a Scottish regiment which happened to be in the area. One of their number lobbed a thunderflash into the emplacement, setting fire to the seat of the pants of its LDV member. This was too much for the local lad who immediately resigned from the force. The neighbours weren't too pleased either. The Scots managed to blow out several windows in Devonshire Street and a freshly painted house had to be done all over again. The Scots moved on to the relief of the people of Eastover. With friends like that ....

Membership of the Home Guard was compulsory for certain qualifying towns people. Refusal to join was taken seriously as in the case of 42 year old Wilf Palmer, an employee of Hancock, the scrap metal merchant. His failure to enrol in August 1943 landed him a three month prison sentence with hard labour.

Bridgwater men held captive

The Bridgwater Mercurys from the first two months of the war reported on the loss of life of Bridgwater men. From then until 1943 there were virtually no lives reported as lost albeit the war memorial in King Square tells a different tale. It is not until 1943 when the war was felt to be swinging in our favour that the reports reappeared.

Among the early news was the return of three Bridgwater Royal Marines who had been captured at Tobruk and were reported as missing in September 1941. Henry Webber of Bath Road, Fred Hayman of Ashleigh Avenue and John Kerslake of North Street had all been taken ill in Italian prisoner of war camps and released as part of a prisoner exchange programme. All three were fit and well by the time they arrived home in April 1943.

Bridgwater men featured in strong numbers at Arnhem, when so many were shot or taken by the Germans. Trooper Fred Edney of Gloucester Road had been a glider pilot. After his capture at Arnhem, he was taken, with 50 others in a truck, to Stalag 12A where 550 prisoners were held in one marquee. Three weeks later he was moved to Stalag 11B where he met Private Hill, another Bridgwater man. The Germans used them to push trolleys in an underground chalk pit, up to their thighs in water. Underfed, neither man thought they'd survive. Eventually they were released by the Americans and billeted with German families who had express orders to feed them well.

Others captured at Arnhem and held at Stalag 11B included Private Donald Hill of Taunton Road. His leg had been smashed by a machine gun bullet. Despite his injuries, he had been made to work on railway repairs. Eventually released, he returned home pitifully thin and with sunken eyes, his body covered in sores and lice. He spoke of the cruel conditions and lack of amenities, one

136

tap for 500 men. Amongst those tending to the wounded at the camp was Private Bob Goodenough, a Bridgwater man in the medical corps.

Signalman Arthur Hale of Dampiet Street was another released from Stalag 11B but one who didn't get there was Private Norman Finch of the Cornhill. He escaped on the way from Arnhem to the camp and made his way back through the enemy lines.

Local mens' bravery recognised

Flying Officer Billy Hill was a Cellophane worker both before and after the war and lived in Wellington Road. He earned himself the Distinguished Flying Cross for his numerous missions over Essen, Hamburg and Berlin.

Brendan Baker of Camden Road also earned the DFC for his exploits over North Africa. Before the war he worked for Sellick and Dimmock, the accountants. He was involved in a dogfight during which he shot down two German planes before being shot down himself and forced to bale out. Wedged in his cockpit, he was unable to escape until 300 feet above the sea. Injuring his foot on landing, he was captured and held in an Italian prison near Naples. When the allies were advancing from the south of Italy, the Italian guards left to be replaced by Germans. The prisoners were transferred to a better defended site, except for those with injuries.

Baker was left behind but still well guarded. He and a British submarine commander and one other, used a table knife to dig an escape tunnel. After one month of digging, they heard the sound of British voices outside. The British had arrived.

Another DFC went to Pilot Officer Robert Hooper of Northfields. He was the pilot of an aircraft destined to attack Munich. Met by German fighters on the way, he lost his upper and rear gun turrets with his rear gunner

badly wounded. With his bomber heavily damaged and almost defenceless, he nevertheless escaped the enemy attack and continued to his target. Having discharged his payload, he was able to, once again, run the gauntlet and limp home.

Another act of high courage and gallantry earning the BEM, was that of Staff Quarter Master Sergeant John Coles of Kingscliffe Terrace, Taunton Road. He spent 19 days living side by side with death on an ammunition ship. The ship was at sea to dump unsafe explosives. Unfortunately one piece exploded killing one of the crew and wounding another. Many of the explosives were damaged. Any movement could set the whole lot off and blow the ship to kingdom come.

Fifty thousand rounds of ammunition had to be removed. Any one piece could have triggered the whole lot. John Coles was first to volunteer to dump the ammunition by hand, bringing it all up from the hold. Fortunately he lived to tell the tale and take up his job at Thompson's the ironmongers.

VE Day

Victory in Europe finally arrived. The town took on a colourful garb, bedecked in bunting and banners. Fireworks, dances around lampposts and kisses on the Cornhill were all in order from 10 o'clock in the morning to well gone midnight. Flags hung from every window, people danced to music of their own making with the Palais Glide proving most popular. The Cornhill dome was even painted red, white and blue.

The celebrations continued for two days and climaxed with a giant bonfire on the Fairfield. No more black outs now. Even the church bells rang once more with the factory hooters joining the chorus. The street parties went on for a week and the carnival committee announced "We're back!".

The sea drama of the century

Introducing Donald Crowhurst

Born in India in 1932, Donald Crowhurst lived there until its independence in 1947 when his family returned to England. The change of circumstances led him to join the RAF where he gained a commission but had to leave following a particular escapade. A similar situation followed in the army where having gained a commission he left under a cloud. Crowhurst's spirit of adventure, at all costs, was already revealing itself.

Then whilst working in the laboratories at Reading University, he met his wife Clare. Four children and several jobs later, he found himself employed as the Chief Design Engineer at Electro-Dynamic Construction in Bridgwater. By this time he had already developed a love of sailing and had purchased the 20 foot blue sloop, the 'Pot of Gold'.

He combined his love of sailing with his inventive skills and he was soon producing a number of safety and navigational aids. One in particular was the 'Navicator'. This development led him to set up his own company in order to produce and market this product. Despite the time required to set up 'Electron Utilisation', he still found time to successfully stand as a Liberal candidate for the town's Central Ward in the local elections.

The new business venture

The new venture appeared to flourish with the number of employees growing to eight before declining fairly rapidly to just one. The innovative skills were there but not those for marketing.

This was all happening around the time of Sir Francis Chichester's epic circumnavigation of the world. Chichester had returned a hero and was honoured with a knighthood. Whilst the nation basked in the glory of the venture, the Sunday Times announced its Around the World yacht race. With no yacht and no money, Crowhurst declared himself an entrant. All taking part had to sail between June 1 and October 31, 1968, otherwise the weather around the Cape would be too dangerous. Time was short and Crowhurst had to get sponsors and boat manufacturers into gear.

He made impassioned but unsuccessful attempts to get Chichester's boat, Gypsy Moth IV. Changing tack, he then opted for a trimaran. These vessels had a poor reputation at the time but despite this, having made the choice, Crowhurst waxed lyrical about their advantages as though he had been sailing them all his life.

Next he needed to find a sponsor. A major investor in Crowhurst's now failing business asked for a repayment on his share. Instead of this, Crowhurst convinced him to invest more deeply by sponsoring his entry in the race. The finance now being available, two manufacturers were identified to produce the required craft in what, with hindsight, was an unreasonable timescale. Too many corners were cut, too many compromises made. Sea trials proved disastrous and Crowhurst's plans based on the Trimaran's maximum speeds proved valueless with the trimaran unable to make ground tacking against head winds, lacking as it did the advantage of a conventional keel.

The three weeks before finally sailing turned out to be a catalogue of disasters. Crowhurst should not have entered the race. Unable to find an honourable way out, he bravely, and perhaps foolishly, proceeded.

He sailed on the latest permitted date, October 31st. His steering gear shook so much that screws rattled loose and were lost. One of the trimaran's floats was not watertight and soon became flooded. His electricity generator was flooded with sea water which breached a leaking cockpit. For weeks his progress was less than half of his expectation and he had no radio communication with which to report his situation.

The deception

Crowhurst, about this time, began to keep two logs of his voyage. One was a series of tape recordings for the BBC, the other his ships log book. The BBC version was full of heroic optimism. The ship's log however painted a different picture.

By December 5, the deception had well and truly started. On December 10, he telegraphed the Devon News in Exeter giving details of his daily mileage rates claiming 243 miles covered on one particular day. This would have been a record, had it been true,

and was the trigger to bring the "Teignmouth Electron", as he had named his vessel, into the headlines of the unsuspecting national press. They loved the story and kept it going for some while. Others however, including Chichester himself, expressed doubts about the honesty of the claims. In fact Crowhurst had covered 170 miles that day.

Later on December 17th, he telegraphed his position as being over the Equator when he was still 180 miles north and in a later telegraphed report he claimed a daily average of 170 miles on a day in which he had covered a mere thirteen.

Weeks and months of endless zig-zagging followed in order to stay out of shipping lanes, whilst all the time repairing the never ending string of faults. He spent a great deal of time listening into and decoding Morse messages in order to catalogue a global list of weather conditions - essential to his plan to fake the round world trip whilst biding his time in the Atlantic.

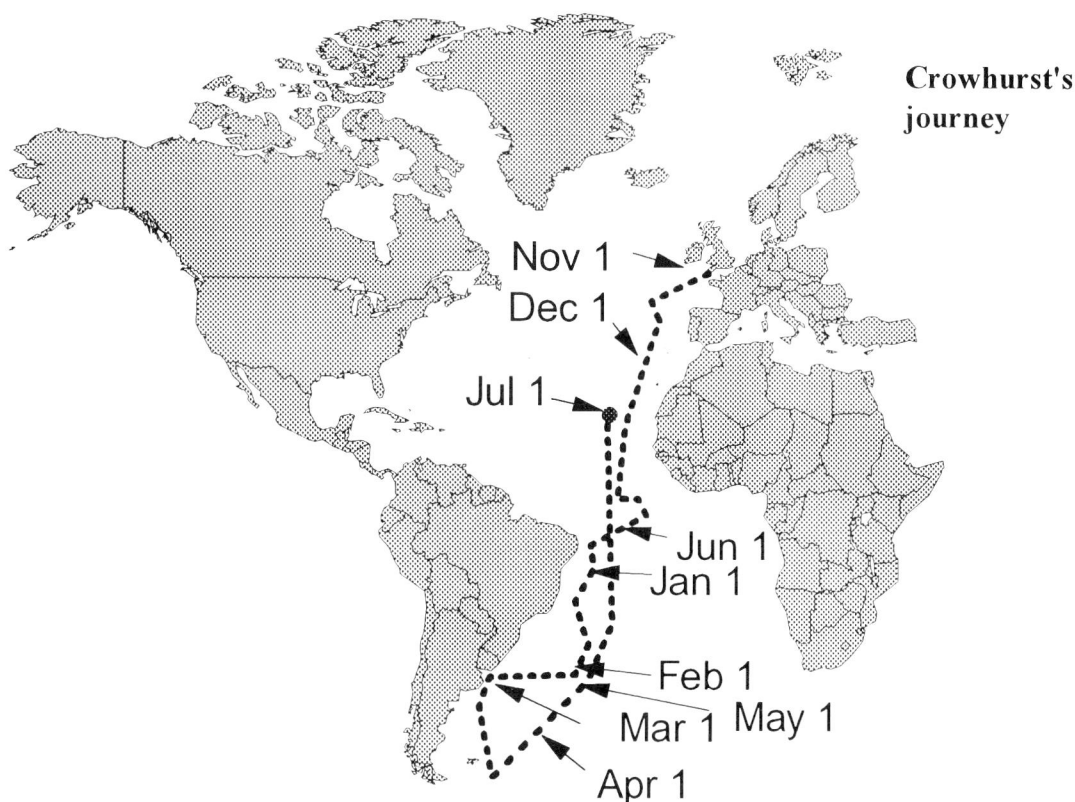

Crowhurst's journey

His own transmissions were curtailed, on the pretext of generator problems as it was always possible that the signal strength would give away his position.

A forced landing

As time went on, the difference between his actual and perceived position became further apart and by mid-January were a full 4,000 miles adrift. At the end of that month, the state of his vessel forced him to land on the Argentine coast. Most of February was spent approaching his destination. A small coastal village was chosen in the hope of not revealing his identity or position. Unfortunately, he misjudged his timing, grounded his craft as the tide rapidly cleared shallow waters and was spotted by the local, co-operative coast guard at Rio Solado.

Crowhurst was taken off the sand bank and towed to the safety of the harbour. Transport was arranged to a nearby community in order to pick up the plywood and screws he required. Although Crowhurst's deception thus far could be considered to be dishonest, this was actually the first time he had actually broken the rules of the competition thus disqualifying himself if the news got out.

Completing his repairs, he put to sea and spent much of March sailing around the South Atlantic. If that sounds like a bit of a holiday, it must be remembered that this part of the world can be very treacherous and demands the highest level of courage.

These ensuing weeks left Crowhurst unaware as to whether or not his landing in Argentina had been discovered. On April 9, he broke radio silence and telegraphed his position as "Digger Ramsey", requesting an update on the race. The brief reply reassured him that all was well and urged him on to the finish.

700 miles east of Buenos Aires, his next problem was to arrange a rendezvous with himself. His fictional route had to catch up with the actual one before he proceeded north into the more populated shipping areas. The zig-zagging continued until May 4 when he turned north to make a serious run for home.

His rivals

Robin Knox-Johnson had already arrived back in Britain taking the 'first home' trophy. Crowhurst's target now was for the fastest time. But to do this he had to overtake his rival, Nigel Tetley. This would give him tremendous publicity and at the same time put him under the spotlight. His voyage records would be thoroughly scrutinised. A much safer option, whilst still acquiring the publicity he needed for the voyage to be a business success, was to allow Tetley to win, but only just. He allowed his progress to drop dramatically. Unfortunately Tetley did as well. Believing Crowhurst was about to overtake him, he pushed his ailing craft to the limit. It was in fact in a worse state than Crowhurst's and gave up completely under the strain. He abandoned his sinking craft and took to the lifeboat to be rescued later.

Crowhurst heard the news on May 23. Victory was now unavoidable. The public spotlight would be focused on him and his log. The organisers would subject his records to the most detailed scrutiny. Meanwhile his domestic problems were increasing rapidly. Paraffin was low, food was running out and liquid was in short supply.

Over his rapidly failing radio, which he was continually rebuilding, he received a clear picture of a massive reception building up with national media coverage. The accumulating pressure and worries of how to react to this reception, combined with months at sea, apparently led to Crowhurst becoming mentally unstable, unable to cope with the position in which he now found himself. During the final week of June, Crowhurst wrote passionately, pouring out feelings, reflecting his gradual declining state of mind.

Homecoming preparations

Meanwhile back in Teignmouth, preparations for his return were reaching fever pitch. A naval minesweeper would escort him up the Channel, the Yacht Club would fire a salute, his trimaran would be towed along the seafront and back to the applause of the crowd before docking in the river. Helicopters from both television stations would be working overhead. A special postmark had been arranged, as had various dinners at which he would speak and postcards were produced to commemorate the occasion. The nation's press readied itself. Perhaps the most poignant article at the time was one by Clare Crowhurst, still waiting back in Bridgwater, prophetically entitled "My Life as an Ocean Widow".

Still becalmed, on June 25 he received a message from Portishead that his wife and family were doing well and looking forward to meeting him off the Scillies. His response to this was to insist they should stay at home. The radio operator, not understanding his reaction, requested confirmation. Clare assumed that perhaps it was for the sake of her and the children, avoiding the risk of sea sickness. With hindsight perhaps it was the first sign to the outside world of what Crowhurst had in mind.

His writings from that point on were just a confusion of expressions making little or no sense at all as he slipped into a psychiatric regressive and paranoid state.

His disappearance

Evidence later found aboard his vessel pointed clearly to Crowhurst's decision to end his own life. On July 1, 1969 he sat at his desk to make his final record. Everything he set down on paper was entered alongside the exact time of its recording. But none of it made any logical sense and it ended with the words "It is finished - It is finished IT IS THE MERCY". Then followed five phrases written in pencil telling God how he would do his duty, that his game had ended and the truth would be revealed. "I have no need to prolong the game".

As far as we know, at twenty past eleven, he stepped off the end of the trimaran into the Sargasso sea and watched the Teignmouth Electron slowly sail away from him at a pace just too fast for a swimming man to keep up.

She was eventually spotted and found abandoned. On July 10, the news was broken to his wife's sister Helen in Bridgwater, by two policemen who arrived at their Woodlands home. Helen fetched a nun from the nearby convent ready for Clare's return from walking the dog.

For the next month, Bridgwater saw a continuous stream of pressmen who in their relentless style, fail to leave those stricken with grief to mourn in private. A fund was started helping the Crowhurst family through their troubles, thousands of pounds poured in.

It will never be proven that Crowhurst died as we assumed. What can be assumed is that in his choice to end the voyage he certainly gained the international recognition he sought, but not in the way that he could have used or from which he could benefit.

Clare Crowhurst eventually accepted that her husband was almost certainly dead. Her courage and strength throughout the whole affair left her admired and respected by the people of Bridgwater who, had things turned out differently, would have been so proud to bathe in Donald Crowhurst's reflected glory.

Meanwhile, in Teignmouth, the cost of their support for this failed venture was being counted. However, when they realised they had gained approximately £1,500,000 worth of free publicity, they felt much better.

Bridgwater Carnival

The origin of Bridgwater Carnival

Bridgwater can proudly boast the world's largest and most spectacular night time carnival anywhere in the world. Every year on the Thursday nearest November the fifth, scores of giant floats parade through the streets of Bridgwater in an extravaganza of music and colour. There is nothing to compare with the spectacle that has developed over the centuries into the event it has become today. Crowds in excess of 120,000 come to the town and fill the streets to capacity. The carnivalites return the favour by putting on a procession over two miles in length with most entries using between 500 and 1,000 kilowatts of lighting each. Visitors and locals alike often wonder how it all began.

The Gunpowder Plot

Back in 1605, Guy Fawkes unsuccessfully attempted to blow up the Protestant parliament that was in power at the time. Guy Fawkes is the name that we all remember, another perhaps is that of Catesby. These were two of the five who attempted the demolition of that democratic house. There was however a lesser known name with a local connection.

The Gunpowder Plot is associated with November 5th, 1605 but the root cause for the unrest leading to this event goes back to the days of Henry Vlll.

Henry had a problem with his numerous wives failing to produce a male heir and it was important to him to be able to effect a divorce. However this was unacceptable to the Catholic faith and therein lay the cause for

Henry to declare the 1534 Act of Supremacy. This made Henry independent from the church of Rome and he declared himself the head of the church in England in opposition to the Pope. There followed a period of persecution and strong anti-Catholic feeling. These were dire times for those who preferred to adhere to the Roman Catholic faith, many of whom were burnt at the stake.

Henry was succeeded by his son, Edward Vl and his half sister Mary. She married King Philip ll of Spain, a staunch Roman Catholic. Persecution swung the other way and until Mary's death in 1558, it was the Protestants who perished at the stake.

Elizabeth l followed and her reign lasted 45 years until 1603. England experienced a long period of stability during which time Elizabeth resurrected the Act of Supremacy. The Pope declared Elizabeth a heretic along with all who followed her. England increasingly turned to Protestantism. Life was made virtually impossible for the Catholics. Fines increased from difficult to impossible and Catholics were declared traitors. It was a case of adapt or leave.

The Catholic faith in England was held together by Jesuit priests. These were trained in Douai, in France, the home several hundred years earlier of Walter de Douai after whom Bridgwater takes its name.

Elizabeth died in 1603 and was succeeded by James l. The son of the Catholic Mary Queen of Scots, he had married a Catholic and was recognised by the Pope as the legitimate heir to the throne. There was no way he would be anything other than a Catholic monarch. Life should have been easier for the Catholics but James was not of a strong enough personality to bring his influence to bear against a Protestant parliament whose power was growing all the time. The time had come for the Catholics to act.

Robert Parsons

Robert Parsons was a Jesuit priest born on June 24th, 1546 the son of a blacksmith in Nether Stowey and the sixth of eleven children. Raised as a Catholic, he was schooled at Stogursey, Taunton and finally Balliol College, Oxford.

Robert Parsons

He joined the Society of Jesuits on July 25th, 1575 and became a Jesuit missionary four years later. He followed a life of mystery and intrigue, plotting and scheming against the Protestants. On June 16th, 1579, he landed at Dover disguised as a soldier. There followed a period of intense activity with him effectively in an espionage role, continually and unsuccessfully hunted by government agents, a cross between a '007' and the Scarlet Pimpernel'.

During this period he used several aliases, the commonest of which was Robert Cowbuck. Some years were spent travelling around Europe drumming up support for the Spanish Armada. Certainly in 1605 he was instrumental in conceiving the Gunpowder Plot. Robert Parsons was one of the real brains behind the venture, one of many with which he was associated. Whilst Guy Fawkes, Catesby and three others carried the blame, Guy Fawkes was little more than a mercenary. Parsons was never held to account and after the plot kept his head fairly low. He died on April 15th, 1610. At that time he was serving the Pope in Rome where he was the rector of the English College.

One of his closest friends and co-conspirators was hung for his part in the plot. Parsons is reputed to have obtained the hangman's rope used to execute his friend and this he carried until his death as a reminder and perhaps a penance.

Apart from Parsons, there were other Somerset men involved in the plot, albeit they were on the winning side. A member of the local Popham family was chairman at the trial and it was Sir Edward Phelips of Montacute House near Yeovil who opened the case for the prosecution.

Bonfire celebrations

Right across the nation, the failure of the Gunpowder Plot is celebrated with bonfires. The bonfire tradition undoubtedly predates the Gunpowder Plot. They formed a part of the customs and traditions of the country perhaps right back to Roman times. There were always bonfires to celebrate the old 'new year' which was celebrated on All Saints Day, November 1st, the day after Halloween Night. The practice of throwing Guys on the fire was a simple variation of the old practice of burning effigies.

Remembering how Bridgwater favoured the Protestant Monmouth in later years, and remembering how the people of the town outside of the castle favoured the Protestant parliamentarians at the time of the Civil War, it is easy to believe that the bonfire and firework celebrations would have been as enthusiastic, if not more so, than anywhere else in the country. There was little room for Catholics in the West Country and certainly for many years there was no Catholic church in the town, the nearest being at Cannington.

The religious significance has long since disappeared leaving no explanation why the tradition is still so strong except that there is a quality in Bridgwater people that makes them more inclined to entertain than be entertained.

Boats and barrels

Certainly the bonfire and fireworks were the origin of our great spectacle. The foundation of the bonfire was traditionally a boat from the docks and as many as a hundred tar barrels. There was a time in the last century when the theft of old boats and barrels for the bonfire became a problem. As trade diminished at the docks, so did the number of boats and barrels which had reached the end of their days. The dockland community found that relatively new and certainly still useful ones were disappearing in early November. And so it became necessary to mount a guard during this vulnerable period.

One imagines that with such a foundation, any bonfire is going to burn bright and long. In the latter years of the bonfire, it may be safe to assume that it was a much better organised affair since we know that the lighting of it was organised by the Vicar of St. Mary's. The fire was never lit until the procession had gone past. Once that was out of the way, something like fifteen gallons of paraffin were thrown onto the bonfire and a group of young lads with tapers alight would approach and ignite the fire. This was not a very safe affair since the initial burst of flame would shoot about 200 feet up in the air and could certainly be seen from South Wales across the Bristol Channel.

The Cornhill bonfire was not the only one in the town. It was one of many but by far the biggest. At about 24 feet across the base and with all those tar barrels and a boat on top, it was going to take some beating. The revelries began at 7 p.m. when the fire was lit and continued until well beyond midnight. There were no bonfires during the war years.

Alas the bonfire - which was the centrepiece of the carnival - is no longer with us. 1925 saw the introduction of TarMacadam road surfaces to the town and consequently the demise of the traditional bonfire on the Cornhill. Attempts were made to move it to another site away from the centre of the town, in order to maintain the tradition. But the new site lacked the atmosphere and consequently the support of the local people. Perhaps the end of the bonfire worked in the favour of the procession in that all the focus of the gangs now went into the parade itself.

Whilst the bonfire lasted until 1924, there were attempts to kill it off much earlier. In 1880 there was an incident where the fire brigade were called to extinguish the fire at midnight. This did not go down at all well with the crowd who, having cut some of the hoses, turned those that were still functioning onto the firemen themselves. One of them was chased to the apparent safety of his home where the objectors took to breaking his windows.

The procession

The origin of the carnival procession goes back to the Guys Fawkes effigies which were burnt on the fire. These effigies, or Guys as they are now known, were put on the fire by gangs. Exactly what these gangs were or how they started is uncertain but they can undoubtedly take the credit for starting the procession tradition. The gangs were associated with the various drinking houses in the town and they would compete to produce the best Guy. In time, the Guys came to be paraded on the back of horsedrawn farm carts before being put on the fire.

In order to be more competitive, some gangs produced Guys which no longer followed the Guy Fawkes theme but instead wore a costume of a king or perhaps the national dress of some foreign land. Needless to say, if these were viewed as more interesting by the public, then in time all the Guys followed some new theme. Years went by and the Guys were replaced by wooden cut out models and the gangs took to wearing costumes of their own in which they would masquerade around the carts adding to the colour and vitality of their entry. When it came to the judging, each masquerader had to carry his own illumination, so a powder torch would be lit and held at arms length to show the competitor off to the best advantage.

From those early days have evolved our gangs and features. The gangs are those clubs which portray a tableau or still picture. The features (or groups of masqueraders as they are alternatively known) are the clubs which move and sing on the floats whilst portraying the theme of their entry. The floats, still locally called carts, are of course no longer horse drawn, the last appeared in 1948. Some explanation of carnival terminology is perhaps required. Gang is an expression now generically used to cover all clubs, both gangs and the features. Carts are of course floats and lamps are light bulbs (paraffin lamps were originally used to light the carts).

Size restrictions

Because of the limitations of the narrow streets in the towns of Somerset, and also to the laws and dictates of the Ministry of Transport, all floats are restricted in their dimensions to 100 feet in length, 11 feet in width and 17 feet 6 inches in height. The competitiveness of the event means that the full limit of these dimensions are achieved by the entries. Other techniques are also applied

to make the most of the space available with tractors and generators being incorporated into the entry and smaller yet more powerful generators are being used.

It is impossible to say when the procession became a serious affair. Journalistic records from 1865 referred to the number of 'disguises' being more numerous than ever. An 1857 reference gives details of a tableau which, having been in the procession, was subsequently thrown on the bonfire, so we can reasonably assume that the tableaux in those days were cut outs and not human as they are today!

Official organisation

After three centuries of spontaneous carnivals, the event became officially organised in 1881. It was however still a relatively small procession by today's standards. By 1900 it had grown and contained many trade entries, the like of which are not permitted today since neither space allows nor would they add anything to the spectacle.

Edward VII's coronation year of 1902 was particularly good as this theme encouraged a record number of entries. As in previous years, these were all horse drawn using - in the main - pairs of shire horses which were decorated to fit the occasion. Each horse had well polished collars with hanging bells which jingled as they moved. Shining harness, brilliantly polished hooves and coloured ribbons added to the charm and appearance. Special prizes were awarded for these magnificent animals. The local Bown family, who still have a strong association with carnival, were particularly known for the splendid turn out of their animals

One of the turning points in the standard of our procession came in 1913 when the first entry was illuminated by batteries. That same year an attempt was made by the local police chief to cancel the whole carnival affair, procession, bonfire and squibbing.

Police interference

Mr. W. J. Davey, the Chief Constable at that time, was a Welshman lacking any understanding of the town and its traditions. He had received a letter from the Home Office asking if it were true that there was to be a bonfire in the street with giant squibs being discharged. Davey felt it was his duty to cancel the event (rather reminiscent of our local police chief's involvement some eighty years later when the message in the local press was along the lines of 'shift it or lose it!').

Any goodwill between the local population and the Borough Police rapidly evaporated. Thousands congregated outside of the Mercury office to await any announcements. The council met in an emergency session. The best they could propose was to move the carnival to the 'rec' in Cranleigh Gardens. But the idea was not well received. The crowd made their feelings obvious. People power was to prevail over police interference.

Davey was adamant. If the committee continued with the organisation of the event, then some arrests would be necessary and charges would be made. The committee took legal advice and eventually found a solution. They knew that with or without officialdom, the carnival was going to happen anyway. The crowd outside the Mercury office raised a cheer when the committee published their announcement. They had written to the Chief Constable stating their disassociation with the event that was going to take place. In other words 'People Power' would rule the day with or without the committee and with or without Davey's interference.

The lead article in the following week's Mercury referred to the 'thousands of excursionists who visit Bridgwater every year to witness the carnival bear testimony to the admirable manner in which it is now organised and controlled, and the exceedingly good humour prevailing It is generally hoped, therefore that the seemingly uncalled for endeavour to prevent its continuance will prove unavailing'.

How true those words are even today!

The advent of generators

As the years have gone by, the batteries have been replaced by generators which have become increasingly powerful and are now anything up to a half megawatt. There was a time when the cold nights of November cut to the very bone of the performers on their floats. Some themes needed scantily clad maidens as part of the entry and these in particular were prone to the chilling effects of the wind, especially in the years when the winter took a grip a month or two earlier than the norm. Often these young girls would be removed from the float in an almost hypothermic state. The powerful generators of today have helped to reduce that problem. The half megawatt or so of power, whilst required principally for lighting, is actually mostly consumed in creating heat. Whilst the light bulb is very inefficient in that respect, it does help to create a friendlier environment for those performing.

In the same way horses have been replaced by tractors and the overall size of the entries increased up to the previously stated maximums.

The town prepares

Prior to the procession, the shop fronts lining the route were once boarded up along with Blake's statue, which still is. Scaffolding goes up for video filming and the numerous press photographers. Street traders from all across the country come to peddle their fast foods and novelties. To the stranger in the town, the boarded up shops must give the impression of an impending riot. Far from it.

The crowds are always well behaved how well they are entertained.

The present day carnival is about two miles long when fully stretched out and takes the best part of two hours to pass any point on the route. The total value of the entries must be in excess of a million pounds especially if the voluntary labour were costed in full. None of the entries are commercially sponsored and the clubs therefore are totally dependant on their ability to find new and innovative ways of raising funds.

War and conscription

The overwhelming majority of clubs are well established (very few are less than 25 years old) with most being formed in the post-war years. When the 'boys came home' from the last war, the carnival carried on almost where it left off. The partly made costumes were brought out and finished although naturally there were some who never returned and their costumes were used by others.

That first carnival after the war was celebrated with greater delight than many before it. The crowds turned out in record numbers. Ray Wadden in his history of Bridgwater Carnival remembers the old bus shelter on the Cornhill. Popularly known as the cowshed, it was used by scores of youngster as a grandstand to afford a better view of the proceedings. Unfortunately, and unexpectedly, it collapsed under the pressure causing those on top to descend more rapidly than expected onto those watching below. The ambulance service treated over one hundred casualties that night, many of them from burns since the practice of throwing squibs indiscriminately into the crowd was still prevalent.

It was a very difficult period for clubs. The years of conscription which followed the war meant that the young men of the town were going off to do their National Service at just the time they would otherwise have been at their most active on the carnival front. The 1960's saw the end of conscription and the resurgence of carnival and its growth to its present day position as the strongest and most spectacular in the world.

Whilst the competition is fierce between the clubs, there is a strong camaraderie which links them all. In times of trouble, they will always help each other out. The show comes first, the individual clubs second. One glowing example of this was the fire which a few nights before the big procession completely destroyed the entry of the Renegades Carnival Club. The fire, a deliberate arson attack, had left little more than the chassis and the wheels. Every single club in the town rallied to the cause. Money was donated, electrical items handed over, materials arrived from around the county and a multitude of members and helpers pitched in with three nights to go. When the show went on the road, the entry was not far short of the original expectation and the response from the crowd was tremendous.

There is great prestige in winning the major trophies. The cups themselves, many heavy in silver and of some considerable age, are valuable in themselves, but it is the honour for which the clubs compete. Carnival is such an important aspect of Bridgwater life. Hardly a family exists in the town which doesn't have a link somewhere.

The Bridgwater squib.

Squibbing is another element of Bridgwater Carnival which makes it unique. The squibs, giant fireworks, are attached to coshes. These are broom like items made of wood but where the bristles would be, the squib is attached so that when the cosh is held horizontally over the head, the squib points skywards.

On carnival night, after the procession, one hundred or so squibbers enter the High Street forming two columns down the road. The squibs are lit simultaneously and create an awesome sight and an unforgettable display when they shoot forth their sparkling fountains reaching well above the surrounding roof tops. The spectacle culminates in loud explosions following one after the other as the squibs finally extinguish. Once the squibbing has finished, the crowd linger a little longer while the committee determine and announce the winners of the night's performance.

The tradition of squibbing is a long one going back to at least 1716 and possibly right back to 1605. The earliest records show a man called John Taylor as a local manufacturer of the squibs but the event is recorded because of the tragic circumstances surrounding it. It appears that John Taylor failed to take adequate precautions in handling the explosives and managed to blow up himself - together with two of his children. The practice of making fireworks was carried out in many homes and gave the local authority great cause for concern.

The traditional squibs were very simple affairs. They varied in size up to two inches in diameter and twenty two inches long. The case made of rolled up paper was drawn in one inch from the top to form a choke of half an inch diameter. As the squib burned through, this choke widened increasing the size of the illuminated area as it went. Various forms of metal and glass filings were mixed with gunpowder in varying proportions but totalling three pounds in weight. The bottom end of the squib was then packed with two ounces of rock-powder to give the final loud report.

Prior to 1881, squibs were let off spontaneously throughout the day as and when the owners felt the urge. Many were hurled indiscriminately into the crowd. The formation of an official committee helped to control and organise this element of the festivities into an item of popular public interest.

The committee squibs were purchased from reputable suppliers and brought with them a higher cost than the home made affairs.

Traditional squibbing in costume

Consequently it was some while before proper control became the practice. Meanwhile the illegal, and perhaps bigger and better, squibs were still made. Fearing a repetition of the John Taylor disaster, in 1909 a raid took place on a house in Angel Crescent. There the Inspector of Explosives assisted by the Borough Police Force and a search warrant found 164 squibs weighing over a third of a ton. Each squib was two feet in length and weighed seven pounds.

This particular haul belonged to one gang and included all the equipment needed to produce these enormous squibs. The exact details were revealed at the Borough Magistrates Court on the Monday after the carnival. The guilty householder was fined £10 with £3, 1s and 6d costs and told how irresponsible he had been in putting the lives of several people at risk with enough explosives to blow up the whole of Angel Crescent.

In the true spirit of carnival, a collection was made and totalled exactly £18 1s 6d. The £5 surplus was donated to the Soup Kitchen Fund.

Last minute problems

The committee squibs of today are much safer as a result of stringent changes in relation to the use of explosives. The committee however leave nothing to chance and, before the public display takes place, a ten percent sample is tested to ensure the squibs perform within a safe standard. This practice dates back to 1987 when a serious problem with that years supply was found.

The Bridgwater Carnival Committee of 1894

The manufacturers had delivered on time and the squibs were stored in a secure place. A limited number had been released to local PTA's for use at the school bonfires with carnivalites present to ensure the safe firing of the squibs. Reports came back, however, detailing how four out of five of these squibs had exploded abnormally blowing the heads off the wooden coshes.

I was chairman of the carnival committee at the time and flew back from Canada where I was working, to help resolve the problem. Samples were taken from the main batch and fired. Sure enough, some of them exploded almost as soon as lit. They had been proven to be unsafe for use in a public place or anywhere else.

I contacted the manufacturer and described the symptoms. The following day the unsafe squibs were taken away and replaced with guaranteed safe items. The owners of the firework manufacturing company, a father and son partnership, had worked through the night to ensure the show went on. Naturally we tested a sample from the new delivery, a practice we have continued ever since.

There is unfortunately a sad ending to this tale. Whilst working on another customers fireworks, the son somehow must have caused a spark resulting in the building going up in a ball of flame as the explosive materials reacted to the catalyst. To the best of my knowledge, after this fatal accident, the father never put his hand to his trade again.

The concerts

For over a hundred years now the carnival concerts have been an integral part of Bridgwater Carnival and serve as yet another example of how Bridgwater's Carnival stays ahead of the rest. These concerts are performed by the Bridgwater clubs as part of their fund raising programme. Originally a fairly amateur affair, this annual fiesta has reached a very high standard of theatrical entertainment.

Such is the popularity of the show that a queue normally starts two days before the

Hope Inn Carnival Club, At the Races, 1954. The author, at 7 years old, is centre front.

box office opens and all tickets for the two week show are sold out in just a few hours.

The concerts help to emphasise the Bridgwater tradition of entertaining being just as important as being entertained. This becomes even more obvious when one considers that at each concert there are over 600 performers. On the other hand, the audience to which they perform numbers only 440. How many other events can boast more performers than audience? A phenomenon usually reserved for theatrical flops rather than consistent success. What a dramatic comparison with the first concert in 1883 which was staged for only two nights.

The clubs

The clubs themselves consist of ordinary people or there again perhaps they are not. To pass a carnivalite in the street or to meet one in the work place, they are the same as anyone else. Yet there is a something in those who take part in carnival that sets them apart. Get into conversation with one and you'll realise that you're talking to a different breed of person. They show tremendous innovation and energy, discipline and talent, dedication and loyalty. It's not surprising that in times of recession when unemployment runs high, carnivalites in general suffer less than most. The qualities that make them what they are just happen to be those that make them an asset to any employer.

Hundreds of hours are put into the building of the floats and the rehearsals for the stage show by virtually all the club members. Couple this with the hours of fund raising as well as meetings planning the show and you will realise that to be a carnivalite is an all year round, time consuming and energy channelling pastime. Bridgwater, with somewhere in excess of a thousand people directly involved in carnival, can proudly boast the most active and effective youth organisation anywhere in the west of England.

Gremlins Carnival Club – Features winners in 1993 with 'Morning of the Dragon'

Sydenham Manor House

Possibly Bridgwater's best kept secret, Sydenham Manor House is neatly tucked away in the centre of Courtauld's Cellophane factory. Built in 1500 as a yeoman's residence of blue lias in the Tudor style, the building is in stark contrast with the surrounding red brick factory buildings. The house was once the centrepiece of a 200 acre estate which had the River Parrett as one boundary and what is now the A39 as the other. Surrounded by orchards and pasture, the manor setting with its half acre pond must have been a most tranquil and pleasing spot until the troubled times of the mid seventeenth century.

The estate predates the house by some 500 years. Until the present century, it had over a thousand years of relative stability during which time only seven families were involved in its ownership and only twice was it sold.

Cheping's manor of Sibeda.

During the latter years of the Saxon era, Sydenham was known as Sibeda or Sideham which was Saxon for a 'wide meadow'. The area was virtually a coastal dwelling place, the sea coming in right up to and even past Dunball at that time. Its original value was set at five pence and its overlord, at the time of Edward the Confessor, was a Saxon called Cheping.

The Norman Conquest saw William the Conqueror sharing out parcels of land to his most loyal supporters. This resulted in the Cheping holding becoming the property of Roger of Arundel in 1086 and is documented in the Domesday Book. By that time its value had increased from five to fifteen old pence.

The property passed to his son and then a grandson called Robert, consequently Robert of Sydenham. He appears to have been the founder of the many Sydenham families throughout the county including those at Brympton, Bathealton, Dulverton and Combe Sydenham. To the best of my knowledge the last member of the Sydenham family to visit Sydenham Manor was Dr. George Francis Sydenham of Dulverton who spoke there in 1920, just three years before his death.

Caves and Percivals.

The property stayed in the Sydenham family for nine generations until 1450 when John Sydenham, the last of the line died with no natural heir. The property passed to his sister Joan who had married a local man, Richard Cave. It then survived in the Cave family for fifty years when once again no male heir was available.

This time, it was Alice Cave's marriage to Thomas Percival which resulted in another family line taking control in 1500 and it was Thomas Percival who had the present manor house built as a wedding gift for his bride. The coat of arms of the two families can still be seen over the door of the north porch, the oldest part of the building and a part of the

> **Domesday book entry for Sydenham Manor**
>
> *Under SVMERSATE Terra Rogerij Arundel Witts ten de Ro.una v trae in Sideha. Cheping tenuit T.R.E. Tra.e.l.car. Ibi.xv.ac.pafturae. Valet. xv denar.*
>
> William holds 1 virgate (a quarter of a hide) in Sydenham from Roger. Before 1066 it was held by Cheping (a Saxon lord). There is land for 1 plough with 15 acres. Its value was 15 pence.

Combined Cave and Percival Coats of Arms

original entrance to the manor house, the Percivals on the left, the Caves on the right. The Sydenham family coat of arms were described as 'argent - 3 rams passant sable', in other words three black rams on a silver background.

Candle auctions.

There is a local traditional candle auction held at Chedzoy every twenty one years which dates back to the local Sydenham family. It involves the renting of a piece of land owned by the parish council called 'Church Acre'. The proceeds raised therefrom go to the Church Fabrication Fund.

The practice started around 1500 when the will of Sir Richard Sydenham was proven. It appears he bequested the parcel of land for the use of the church based on the candle auction method, a method not uncommon at that time. Sir Richard was buried in Chedzoy church where there is a brass floor plate showing him in his armour with a lurcher dog at his feet. This indicates that he had served in the wars and returned alive, a lion would be used had he died in battle.

The practice at the auction in the Manor House Inn was to suspend a small board from the ceiling on which is placed a half inch of candle. The last bid before the candle expires gains the property for the next twenty one years. The last two auctions proved so popular that they had to be held outdoors and a miner's lamp was used to shelter the candle.

Richard Percival and the Spanish dictionary.

The last of the Percivals to hold the estate was Richard, born in 1550, the great grandson of Thomas. Richard was a bit of a lad who married beneath his station, much to the annoyance of his father.

The marriage was doomed to failure and Richard left his wife and family in the care of his relative, Roger Cave, before leaving for Spain. Within four years his knowledge of Spanish was at such a high level that he published the Bibliotecha Hispanica, perhaps the first English-Spanish dictionary.

By the time Richard Percival returned to England, his wife was already dead. His father would have nothing to do with him but he still managed to land on his feet. Cave's brother-in-law was the Lord Treasurer, Lord

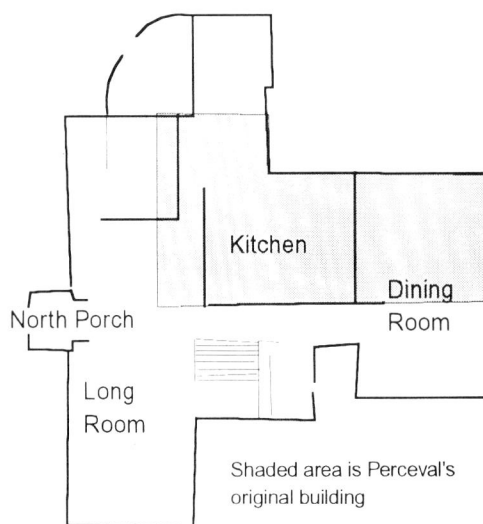

Sydenham Manor groundfloor plan

Burleigh, who in that role was deeply involved in foreign affairs and their funding. Richard Percival found a role for himself with the Lord Treasurer.

Meanwhile, out in the English Channel, the captain of one of the Queen's frigates was giving chase to a Spanish man-of-war. The year was 1586 and the gap between the two was closing. The Spanish captain was seen to throw a small wooden chest overboard. The English captain realising the contents of the chest were probably more significant than the Spanish ship itself, forsook the chase and retrieved the chest. He returned with it to Portsmouth and from there the chest was taken up to London and delivered to her majesty's court. The Queen took Burleigh's advice to give the documents contained therein to the Bridgwater lad, Richard Percival, for translation from Spanish into English and Latin.

This he did and those present were able to recognise the invasion plans for the Spanish Armada. The details of the ships taking part, from where they would sail and the nature of their duties were all contained within the documents. The release of this intelligence put paid to the attempt and the Armada had to wait another two years before the opportunity once again presented itself. Richard Percival's reward for translating the documents was the Duchy of Lancaster and a pension for life. Not bad for a day's work! Nothing is known as to whether or not the vigilant sea captain benefited from the exercise.

Another interesting link with the Armada is that of a beam which passes right the way across the kitchen ceiling and the main passageway in the manor house and is reputed to have been plundered from a captured Spanish galleon from the Armada.

Thus Richard became a hero and his father suddenly found it in his heart to forgive him and he was back in the will. On his father's death in 1613, Richard sold his inheritance including the estate at Sydenham and moved to south west Ireland where the name of

Sydenham Manor House, by courtesy of Courtaulds Films

Percival is now a common one in County Cork.

Manor sold to the Bull family

It was William Bull of Wells who bought Sydenham Manor from Richard Percival along with the manor house at Shapwick. The Bull family was a prominent one in Somerset and it was William's close relation, John Bull, who wrote the National Anthem. William's grandson, Henry Bull, became Member of Parliament for Bridgwater and, during the Civil War in 1654, he commanded a troop of royalist horse, for King Charles, which was garrisoned at the manor. Bearing in mind that Colonel Wyndham held Bridgwater Castle as a royalist stronghold, Sydenham Manor would have acted as an outpost. The Parliamentarian troops of Fairfax and Cromwell, however, had no trouble in capturing Sydenham Manor under the leadership of Captain Holborn. A hundred prisoners were taken and the damage of cannon shot can still be seen on the walls of the manor.

In those days there appeared to be two ways of punishing those who finished up on the wrong side of a Civil War or rebellion. Those with little or no money were prone to deportation or hung, drawn and quartered. Those with money, who by their very nature would be more influential, tended to be punished by having their lands and the income therefrom taken away for a period of time. So, the year after the Civil War, we are not surprised to hear that Henry's father William had his lands removed from his control for a year. It appears he managed to get time off for good behaviour. His lands were returned after nine months but only after he had paid a fairly substantial sum for the privilege.

The Bull family had a habit of backing the wrong horse. Forty years later, when the Duke of Monmouth came to town, Henry Bull rather fancied his chances. He decided to organise a party for the Duke and his

Monmouth's window, early Tudor with arched leaded lights

officers and sent one of his servants into Bridgwater to buy sufficient fare to do justice to the occasion.

The inevitable ghost

Monmouth is said to have stopped at the Manor House on his way to the battlefield. Whilst no documentary evidence exists to support this, it is known that he stopped on the way at about this point and since the house was known to be ready to welcome him, it seems likely that he would have taken advantage of the occasion. A room in the house is still named after him. The fact that the occasion is not documented is also understandable. If you were the householder, would you boast about it after the event knowing how Monmouth's supporters were treated?

Needless to say, Monmouth is said to haunt the house. However, of all the visitors that have stayed at the Manor, the only ones who have witnessed a ghost have all seen a lady. She is generally described as a young woman wearing a flowing robe and is seen on the first floor of the house. One variation to this comes from a Japanese visitor who was convinced he saw her as well. However his description had her wearing a kimono style costume and floating legless across the room. Apparently Japanese ghosts traditionally lack any legs!

Captain Blood

After the Battle of Sedgemoor, when the King's troops were rounding up the rebels, ready for trial by Kirke and Judge Jeffreys, a gentleman called Dr. Blood is said to have taken refuge at Sydenham Manor and was captured there. At the Bloody Assizes he was punished with deportation and transported to the West Indies where, pursuing a career as a pirate, he gained notoriety as the famous Captain Blood and became the subject of many a romantic novel.

The story has it that Blood was born of an Irish father and Somerset mother and had been trained as a doctor at Trinity College, Dublin. After his training he left for the continent where he apparently spent more time as a soldier of fortune than as a doctor.

At the time of his arrest, he was innocently treating a rebel's wounds and was not as such directly involved in the rebellion. He was arrested with a master mariner called Pitt and was eventually sold into slavery at the wharfside in Barbados for the sum of £10.

Pitt, Blood and others planned their escape and succeeded in capturing a Spanish ship and turned to piracy. It makes a nice story, well written by Rafael Sabatini, but can be no more than a story. Those interested should read Sabatini's "Saga of the Seas".

The Bull family ownership came to an end when the male line ran out in 1700 and Eleanor married George Bubb Dodington, Bridgwater's M.P. On his death in 1720, his nephew (of the same name) took control of the estate and followed in his uncle's footsteps pursuing a political career which proved to be a period of changing loyalties and deceit. This only became apparent when his diaries were released after his death.

It appears that from 1784, when the estate passed to the Marquis of Buckingham, there was a long period of disuse of the manor house albeit it stayed in the same family until sold by the Duke of Buckingham and Chandos in 1837 to Thomas Dymock. In the entire history of the manor this was only the second time it had been sold. It was sold five more times between 1837 and 1935 before the site was purchased by Courtaulds. During that period various parts had been sold off and the estate as purchased by Courtaulds had diminished to a mere 23 acres and the house had fallen into an desperately poor state of repair.

Courtaulds take control

Courtaulds used the site to develop their first cellulose film plant which became the largest in the world. How fortunate we are that Courtaulds avoided doing the obvious at the time - the demolition of the dilapidated Manor House. The option was actually considered due to the poor state of repair. Fortunately there was sufficient foresight to see its full potential and the building was spared. Today it serves as a guest house for VIP visitors and as a conference and training centre for the company.

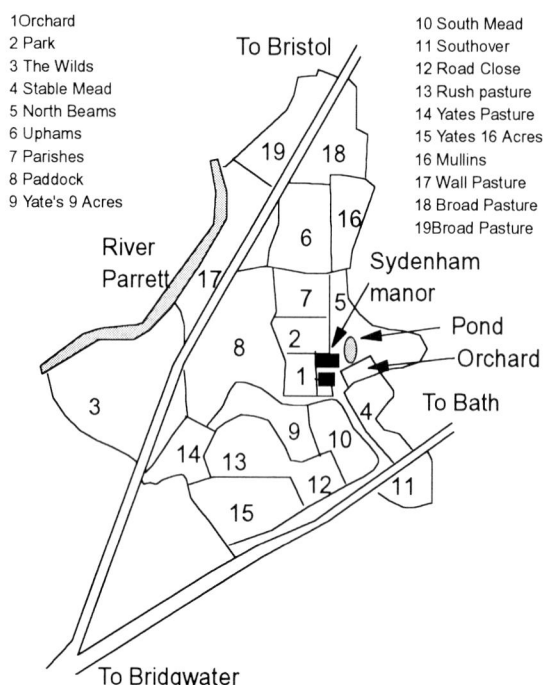

1 Orchard
2 Park
3 The Wilds
4 Stable Mead
5 North Beams
6 Uphams
7 Parishes
8 Paddock
9 Yate's 9 Acres
10 South Mead
11 Southover
12 Road Close
13 Rush pasture
14 Yates Pasture
15 Yates 16 Acres
16 Mullins
17 Wall Pasture
18 Broad Pasture
19 Broad Pasture

Sydenham Manor in 1837 before the railways came

Landmarks and place names

All Saints Terrace

The terrace takes its name from the church which still stands at one end and now serves as a Boys Club. All Saints church was opened in 1822 following the successful use by its congregation of a room in Edward Street. The church closed sometime before 1966 when the National Association of Boys Clubs found a new use for the building.

Angel Crescent

This was the site of the north gate entrance into the town, back when there were only four ways in. The crescent shaped row of houses were built in 1816 and were improved and brought up to standard in 1986 when the Angel Place shopping precinct was developed.

At the back of what used to be the Royal Clarence Hotel, now Royal Clarence House, there was a small public house called The Angel and this perhaps gave the area its name.

The Arts Centre

The Arts Centre at number 11 Castle Street was the first arts centre in Great Britain being set up in 1946.

The Baptist Chapel

The original Baptists were believed to have settled in Bridgwater during the sixteenth century. The middle of the seventeenth century was a difficult period for those of a Puritan persuasion. They used the Baptist Chapel for their pulpit and many who preached at Bridgwater were imprisoned under the Act of Uniformity. John Wesley, the grandfather of John and Charles Wesley who founded the Methodist church, was a regular preacher at the Bridgwater Baptist church.

In 1692 the Baptists erected a meeting house on the site of the present chapel. It lasted until 1835 when the present chapel was erected.

Binford Place

Running between the Town Bridge and the public library, Binford Place is one of the oldest streets in the town. Close by the bridge is the Langport Slipway dating back to 1488 when the Abbot of Glastonbury paid for its installation.

In the years after the Second World War, this spot was used by the local carnival clubs for a slippery pole contest. A long greasy pole was fixed to the bank and projected out over the river. A half crown piece was placed on the end which was several feet out over the murky waters of the Parrett. The carnivalites would 'sail' up the river from Dunball on the incoming tide following in the wake of the bore. Their boats were galvanised baths floated with oil drums lashed to the sides. Some of these flimsy affairs finished the route to the town bridge. Having arrived there, the carnival members would shinny out along the pole to collect the half crown. I cannot remember anyone ever achieving it.

Certainly my strongest recollection of that event was the appearance of the swimmers as they extracted themselves from the river along the West Quay. As they climbed up the steps out of the water, so the silt laden river water would run off their bodies giving the appearance of a khaki coloured layer of skin melting away from the body.

The Roman Catholic church of St. Joseph's, at the library end of Binford Place, was built in 1882 at the sole expense of a Mr. Philip of Langport.

Black Bridge

Designed by Brunel and built in 1871 to provide railway branch lines to the pottery, docks and brewery. A steam driven telescopic bridge, its history is dealt with in more detail in the section on road and rail.

Blake Gardens

Two and a half acres of gardens on the banks of the river, purchased by the corporation from Mr. R. C. Else in 1898. The picture above shows the old summer house, long since pulled down whilst below we have the also extinct arch, once the backdrop to so many wedding and carnival club photographs. The bandstand from the same period survives and is still used on the occasional Sunday afternoon.

Blake Place

Formerly St. John's Place, this short stretch of road runs along the front of St. John's Church.

Blake Statue

Bridgwater's best known landmark along with the Cornhill. Amazingly it was as late as 1900 before any monumental recognition was erected to Blake's memory. The statue was built in hollow bronze by F. W. Pomeroy. The £1200 cost was paid for by public contribution.

For decades its position was just in front of the Cornhill dome. Its much publicised move to its present position met very heavy resistance from the local population. They were not just resistant to change but fearful that in its new position it may have interfered with the smooth running of the carnival procession.

Blake Street

This street contains the home of Admiral Blake, purchased by the borough in 1924 to become the local museum and well worth a visit. Built around 1500, the museum's opening times are mornings and afternoons 6 days a week with Sunday afternoon affording another opportunity to view the artefacts. This building along with the Old Vicarage Restaurant and St. Mary's church are the only three buildings surviving in the town from the medieval period.

At the end of the street is the old 14th century mill which was an 'overshot' or 'breast' mill using Durleigh Brook for its supply of water. The brook in medieval times marked the southern boundary of the town. A system of half round gutters existed at one time to channel water from the brook to the town centre more or less where Blake's statue now resides.

The mill ground the corn for the castle which was the only place it could be purchased. Only one mill was permitted, so a monopoly was guaranteed for the castle governor.

A project is currently underway to extend the museum to incorporate the mill as a working feature.

Outside of the museum you may see a flag of somewhat unusual design. It is the Commonwealth Flag which was originally flown between 1649 and 1658 and this is one of only three places in the country where you will still see it flying. On the side nearest the pole is the cross of St. George. On the other side is the gold coloured Irish harp on a blue background. Although Scotland joined the Union in 1654, the cross of St. Andrew did not become part of the flag until 1658. It took the place of the Irish harp which was then featured on a shield in the centre.

The Cannon Junction of Bath Road and Bristol Road

Bond Street

This was the site of the bonded warehouses when imports and exports formed a significant part of the trade going through the Port of Bridgwater.

The Cannon

This was the popular name given to the junction where the Bath Road, Bristol Road and Monmouth Street all join, shown in the old postcard above. The name came from the Russian cannon which was placed there until its metal was required for the war effort. It was at this point that the old Great Western Railway line crossed the Bath Road on its way to the docks.

This junction is still referred to as the Cannon by members of my generation albeit the name appears to be dying out.

Castle House, Queen Street

Unfortunately Castle House in Queen Street, formerly known as Portland Castle, is in a very poor state of repair having been left empty for many years and it eventually became the victim of a fire which has virtually gutted it. This was a sad end to a building which, whilst being hideous in design, was once one of the most significant buildings in Bridgwater.

Built by William Akerman in 1851 for Board and Co., its purpose was to demonstrate the benefits and potential for pre-cast concrete - using Portland Cement which had been patented in 1824 - and so attracted many visitors from all over the West of England. Thus Castle House was little more than a folly acting as a real life trade catalogue for the Portman Cement Company and demonstrating the different ways concrete could be used in building houses.

It was the first example of the use of reinforced pre-cast concrete and was almost a century ahead of its time as pre-cast concrete did not really take off until after the Second World War. It was also a brave move to venture such a design in a town which for so long heavily depended on the traditional brick and tile industry.

160

Castle Street

Possibly the finest Georgian Street in the West of England, it was built in 1723 by the first Duke of Chandos, James Brydges. The architect, Benjamin Holloway, built his own house around the corner in West Quay at the Lions.

The street remained cobbled until well into this century and its early Georgian features were sufficient to attract the attention of a film company who produced parts of the film Tom Jones in this area.

Apart from the Arts Centre at number 11, another well known Bridgwater landmark in Castle Street is the former Mary Stanley hospital, only recently closed down as part of the cut backs in the National Health Service. From 1920 to 1988, the Mary Stanley was the birthplace of most of Bridgwater's present generation.

The Cattle Market (Newmarket)

The old cattle market, originally in Penel Orlieu where the Classic Cinema stands today, moved to its present position off the Bath Road in 1935. The demand for cattle sales had outgrown the space available and the mixture of A39 traffic and so many animals was not a good one. However, no sooner had the move been affected, than the decline in the use of the market began.

Chandos Glass kiln

Built in 1726 by the Duke of Chandos, it proved unsuccessful as a glassworks venture and was converted to a pottery kiln. Listed as an ancient monument, it was originally 125 feet high, 75 feet across the base and 6 foot across the top. In 1942 it was demolished to provide brick rubble for use at Westonzoyland airfield. The remains are now the subject of a preservation order. A reproduction of the interior can be found in the section on the brick and tile industry.

Chandos Street

Named after the Duke of Chandos, the man responsible for the building of Castle Street and the construction of the now conserved glass kiln. The street was originally known as

The old cattle market at Penel Orlieu

North Back Street when Castle Street was known as Chandos Street.

Chapel Street

The Wesleyan Chapel in Chapel Street was built in 1816 with columned porticoes. Its use today has been relegated to that of a furniture warehouse. John Wesley had a significant impact on the town.

In 1746 he made his first visit to the town on September 18th and preached late in the afternoon. He repeated his visits during the following two years preaching not only in Bridgwater but also in many of the surrounding villages. According to his diary, his schedule was a busy one and it was his normal practice to preach at three different venues in any one day. His diaries show a gap of ten years or so from 1749 to 1759 with his reappearance in 1760 when he described Bridgwater on a wet and windy day as a dead and uncomfortable place at best. With comments like that he was lucky indeed to have two Wesleyan chapels operating simultaneously in Bridgwater right up to the

middle of the present century. His final visit came in 1769. Wesley's followers set up a small chapel in Eastover before building the Chapel Street premises.

Clare Street

Originally known as Orlove Street and then Back Street before taking its present name.

Cornhill

The Cornhill is the historic centre of the medieval town. Originally there was an octagonal market cross on the site being one of two crosses in the town. The other was the Pig Cross at Penel Orlieu. The Cornhill market cross, erected in the late 14th century when the Cornhill was known as Cornchepyng, was perpendicular in style with a roof supported by eight pointed arches and a central pillar.

The market cross or High Cross as it was known was repaired in 1567-68 and the roof had a water tank added in 1694 from which the town centre was supplied with water.

Bridgwater. Cornhill

High Street, Bridgwater. No. 12104

Richard Lowbridge of Stourbridge used an 'engine' to take water from Durleigh Brook to the High Cross through a system of hollow elm pipes.

The market cross carried the motto "Mind your own business" on one of its pillars. Perhaps it had a friendlier meaning in those days. The old cross was pulled down in 1827.

There was another cross in this area. This was St. Mary's Cross at the corner of the churchyard. This was moved in 1769 to the Penel Orlieu and was demolished in 1830. Its circular base can still be seen in the churchyard and a replica now takes pride of place where Fore Street meets the river.

The Cornhill was the meeting place for all local businessmen, the Rialto of Bridgwater, the Piccadilly Circus of the town. Here the Duke of Monmouth was crowned King of England and the infamous Judge Jeffreys vented his wrath. Here the bonfire burned on those carnival nights up to 1924 and Admiral Blake still takes pride of place.

The present Cornhill building was built in 1826 by a local builder by the name of Hutchings. The National Provincial Bank premises on the Cornhill was another of his successes. The pineapple on top of the dome is a symbol of welcome. On market days, sheep were traded in West Street, pigs at Penel Orlieu, cattle in the High Street and fish, foul, vegetables and other fair at the Cornhill. The building still serves much the same purpose even today. At one time railings were necessary around the market to keep the produce and the beasts apart. These were finally removed in 1895. This snippet of knowledge proves quite useful when dating pictures of old Bridgwater which almost invariably depict the Cornhill. Blake's statue is another one, that item being installed in 1900.

Wednesdays and Saturdays were the traditional days for auctioning goods at the market which for many years was one of the last bastions of pounds, shillings and pence.

There was a lady called Mrs. Ash who was the auctioneer at the market for more years than I can remember. When the rest of the nation converted to decimal coinage, Mrs. Ash stuck to the old ways. For years after, by which time most youngsters only understood the new decimal way, Mrs Ash continued with her "Right, who'll give me two bob? Yes sir, thank you, do I hear half a crown? Yes madam, half a crown it is, three shillings anywhere?". She never changed, eventually retiring and no doubt proud of having kept to the old ways.

The 4-storeyed buildings on the south side of the Cornhill are from the first half of the 19th century and are in the renaissance style with elaborate window mouldings and quoins.

The National Westminster Bank was built originally for Stuckey's Bank in the Baroque style. The Stuckey family made their money out of trade. In 1707 the firm of Stuckey and Bagehot was started in Langport. They concentrated on trading up and down the river. The successful growth during the 18th century is reflected in Mr. Stuckey being able to open his own bank.

Next to it was Bridgwater's premiere hotel, the Royal Clarence built in 1825 in Regency style. The plaque attached to the front of the portico was a souvenir from the old town

Shell porch on the Unitarian Chapel

bridge and depicts the borough coat of arms in their original colours. When the present bridge was erected in 1883, parts of the old bridge were sold off to help pay the bill and thus the coat of arms found its home over the portico of the Royal Clarence. The Royal Clarence was built on the site of two former inns, the Crown at the front facing the Cornhill and the Angel at the rear.

Court House, Queen Street

An early 19th century building of limited architectural interest.

Court Street

Leading from Fore Street to the Court House, this was originally known as Coffee House Lane until 1890 when its name was changed to Queen Street before its change to its present title.

Dampiet Street and the Unitarian Chapel

A medieval street originally called Damyate meaning by the way of the dam. This probably refers to a dam built on Durleigh Brook for the purpose of the corn mill at the bottom of Blake Street.

The Unitarian Chapel dates back to 1688. That was when the original chapel was built and a stone taken from the original bearing that date can been seen as a feature of the new chapel which was built on the same site in 1788. There was an earlier church on the same site which was circular and seated 400 people. In 1683 Colonel Stawell, from Cothelstone Manor, raided the chapel, apparently looking for weapons. On his insrtuctions all the seats were burnt. The Bill of Rights introduced by William and Mary in 1688 finally allowed freedom of worship.

The chapel was twice used by the poet Samuel Taylor Coleridge in 1797 and 1798 to preach from its pulpit having come on from his home at Nether Stowey. The entrance has a fine shell porch dating from 1688 mounted on carved console brackets. The pews inside are the originals with small doors through which to enter them.

Danger's Ope

This is the narrow lane running between the High Street and the back of St. Mary's church. The origin of the name is unknown although ope is an archaic word for open.

Eastover

Eastover - from the Saxon ufer meaning bank, i.e. the east bank of the river. The name probably dates back to about A.D. 682 when Centwine left a Saxon outpost here. The named is used to refer to the general area on the east side of the river, roughly between the river and the railway lines, and also to the main street on that side of the bridge. This is perhaps the oldest street in the town and used to lead to the East Gate.

The street was known by many names before it took the name of the general area. 'Beyond the bridge', 'between the bridge and the river', 'within the east gate' were all titles used before 'Eastover' was adopted in the mid 14th century.

There used to be a midsummer horse fair held here each June 24th and this is described more fully in the section on fairs and markets.

The White Hart Hotel in Eastover is perhaps the longest serving building in the street and has remained unchanged in its use for a considerable period. It certainly served as a coaching house and there is an amusing tale relating to that period.

The White Hart at one time was kept by a Mrs. Francis. She carried out the practice of cooking her meat on a spit of the type which was turned by a dog inside a caged wheel. Whilst this may seem cruel these days, the dog was kept well away from the heat and it is no different to the exercise hamsters take quite voluntarily.

Mrs. Francis by way of novelty used a fox which she had raised as a pet. One day the inevitable happened and the fox escaped. It headed towards Westonzoyland and the moors where its wild instincts took over. It didn't realise the harm it was doing in killing the domesticated ducks and geese on the farms and found it difficult to understand why the landowners became so hostile.

To the fox's horror, the foxhounds were brought out and chased it across to Athelney, from there up on to the hills at Enmore, down into North Petherton and back into Bridgwater. Once back in the town, it soon recognised Eastover and the White Hart Hotel. Here it made the wisest decision of its life. A quick dash through the legs of the customers, out into the kitchen and straight back into its cage at the turnspit.

Another tale of the White Hart takes us back to 1850. Political feelings in the town were running high and the White Hart was a haunt of the local Tories. A band of Whigs outside the White Hart and a band of Tories inside was good enough cause for an argument. As the situation developed, skittle pins and balls were hurled through the windows in both directions. The outcome of this affair was the reading of the Riot Act by the Mayor and the temporary introduction of Martial Law.

Eastover Park

Popularly called 'the rec', short for the recreation ground. There is a positive Victorian air to this park with its proud Horse Chestnut trees surrounding its boundary. The park used to have its own bandstand and an informal zoo for the local squirrels.

East Quay

The older buildings along East Quay include a former warehouse, a temperance hotel and next to that the old post office which served the community until 1909. From here the London stage left at between 5 and 6 o'clock each evening for its journey to London.

The medical centre marks the site of Carver's Yard, formerly a dry dock for ship building. Here was built the last ketch to be launched from Bridgwater, the Irene. The dry dock fell into disuse and became water filled. That was the way it stayed until 1959 when tragically a young lad fell in and drowned. Thus in 1960 it was filled in and the area subsequently developed.

Fore Street

Predominantly 19th century in style of buildings, the street survives from medieval times and earlier. Indeed it is one of the oldest and best used roads in the town. Numbers 2 to 6 feature an Edwardian facade using attractive two tone terra cotta blocks.

Particularly interesting is the unusual chimney with its serpents heads bursting forth.

Number 14 is an earlier site of the Bridgwater Mercury office which suffered a fire with tragic consequences. The story of this is told elsewhere in this publication. Fore Street was once the site of the old police station and town gaol. The newly erected cross at the bottom of Fore Street is a reproduction of the Pig Cross, or Pea Cross as some called it, which resided outside of the Blue Boar in Penel Orlieu. Its original position was in St. Mary's Churchyard when it was known as St. Mary's Cross. It was moved to Penel Orlieu in 1769, demolished in 1830 and replicated in Fore Street in 1989.

In medieval times Fore Street was known as 'Between Church and Bridge'.

Friarn Street

Friarn Street - the site of the Grey Friars priory. One of the oldest streets in the town containing many buildings of interest.

Bridgwater, Fore Street.

166

Bridgwater High Street

The Plymouth Brethren, who moved to the town in the 1840's, moved to Friarn Street in 1868 from their Gloucester Place premises.

George Street

Formerly known as Ball's Lane. It was the original home of the Bridgwater Mercury.

Gordon Terrace

This terrace was the first site of a Roman Catholic church in the town after the nation accepted the Church of England. Catholics had been persecuted in the 17th and 18th centuries. In 1845 Catholics practised in the privacy of their own homes. In 1846, the Reverend Capes, first vicar of St. Johns, took to the Roman Catholic faith and was instrumental in the opening of the church of St. Joseph in Gordon Terrace. It now serves as a workshop, the Roman Catholic congregation having moved to Binford Place in 1882.

Green Dragon Lane

A narrow lane running between Friarn Street and Little St. Mary's Street. The alley takes its name from the Green Dragon Inn which marked one end and at the time of writing carries the name of 'The Snuffbox'.

High Street

Dating from medieval times, the High Street could once boast a row of houses right down the middle. Today evidence of this is still present where the depth of pavement goes back in the area around the front of the shopping precinct. There are quite obviously two lines of shop frontage denoting the original line the furthest from the road and the new line where the pavement narrows down. Whilst this may give the impression of an exceptionally wide road in the early days, that perception is far from the truth, in fact the additional space was taken up by a row of houses right down the centre line of the road. Thus there were in fact two narrow streets where now we have one.

In the 13th century the High Street was known as Great Street. The island down its centre was called Cokenrewe and survived until the early 19th century.

The High Street was very much an area for cattle. At one end, in the Blue Boar area, pigs were sold and down through the street, cows and occasionally horses. One of the old public houses which survived until the development of the Angel Place shopping precinct was the Bull and Butcher. This was particularly appropriate for the type of trade carried out in the street, the row of houses down the centre being known as the Shambles, the traditional name for the butchering area of market towns. There exists an alternative opinion of the Bull and Butcher name and that is as a corruption of the Boleyn Butcher being a reference to Henry Vlll and his treatment of Anne Boleyn.

One of the oldest buildings in the street is the Valiant Soldier which dates back to 1583. Little of the original building remains, perhaps only the doorway arch.

The Mansion House also has a significant history. On the site there was originally a house belonging to the church which was given to two townsmen. In 1722 the upper storey was used as a grammar school and was still there in 1788. At the end of the 18th century it was used as a soup kitchen and since at least then, if not earlier, has served the role of a public house.

The High Street is the place to come on the night of Bridgwater carnival when after the procession over a hundred squibs, giant fireworks, are simultaneously let off whilst held above head height on coshes, an amazing spectacle which nicely rounds off a spectacular evening.

Horsepond Lane

Just off Friarn Street it is quite simply the lane leading to the horse pond which certainly existed in the fourteenth century when this lane was called 'wayhur' which translates into horse pond.

King Square

King Square forms a significant part of the site of the old castle. Two sides of the square, the development of which started in 1820, feature some fine early 19th century architecture and these have been complimented on a third side by a 1976 addition in the form of Bridgwater House which has been carefully designed to maintain the character of the square. This has been well achieved and the premises now form the home of Sedgemoor District Council.

On the same side of the square is the Masonic Lodge built in 1912 (quite close to the police station!). This features narrow vertical slots in the side facing the square through which visitors or intruders can be viewed. How appropriate that their home should be 'on the square'. The early nineteenth century buildings were erected as homes for local well to do businessmen.

The centre piece of the square is the war memorial, conveniently situated only a matter of yards from the Royal British Legion in Castle Street. Erected in 1924 and unveiled by Lord Cavan to commemorate the dead of the First World War, the memorial features the statue of a mother and child representing civilisation. Beneath the mother's feet, if you look carefully, can be seen the tiny and almost neglected figures of strife, bloodshed, corruption and despair. In one hand she holds a globe of the world and in her lap is the Book of Law.

Amongst the names featured in the list of those lost serving their country is that of Andrew Barr, Bridgwater's most recently lost son whose life was taken in the Falklands Conflict in 1982.

King Square

King Street

Formally called Coffee House Lane, this street runs between Fore Street and Dampiet Street.

Lamb Lane

This is the short lane running down the side of the Duke of Monmouth Inn which was originally known as the Lamb Inn. In the first half of the nineteenth century, the Lamb Inn also served as the offices for the local agent dealing with assisted passage to Australia.

Lime Kiln Inn

The Lime Kiln Inn more or less marks the site of the old lime kilns which served the town. The process of lime burning was an unpopular one if for no other reason than its appalling smell. The kilns were therefore sited outside of the old town boundary. Records show that lime was dug and burnt in this area around 1497.

Market Street

Originally known as Orlove Street and then Prickett's Lane, it was the junction of this street and Pynel Street which gave Penel Orlieu its name.

Newmarket

The new cattle and corn market was built in 1935 just off the Bath Road. Market day has always been Wednesday. I have many memories of this place as a youngster. Living in Branksome Avenue, only a matter of yards away, this was effectively my playground. Wednesday morning always brought with it a procession of cattle trucks coming into the market.

Cattle sales were predominantly of young Friesian calves or fat stock for the slaughterhouse. Pigs used to be high in numbers. Wessex Saddlebacks were the most common, unfortunately being noticeable by their absence these days as with so many of the older breeds.

The Malt Shovel Inn

You could buy most things here, certainly on the farming front, and many food items could be purchased and killed on the spot. Wild rabbits were sold as indeed were the much larger domestic meat rabbits such as the New Zealand Whites. These could be purchased alive or, for the more squeamish, the sales lady would dispatch them at no extra cost.

Newtown

The name given to the suburb established in the 1880's to provide housing for the dock workers.

Northgate

The original Northgate was an arched entrance way into the old town. Its position was at the present junction of Angel Crescent and the present day Northgate. This was one of only four entrances into the partly walled, partly moated old town.

Starkey, Knight and Ford had a brewery here which closed in the 1950's. I remember as a youngster going to the brewery to dig for the small brandling worms in their heaps of spent hops. These were perfect for a young angler.

Another childhood recollection is of the salt fish which was brought in through the docks. Barrels of this could be seen each morning outside Whitehead's shop in Northgate awaiting the proprietors return. Meanwhile every dog in Christendom appeared to pass the shop leaving its mark on the boxes. We never ate salt fish in our house!

North Street

One of the oldest streets in the town. Until the 1840's the housing at this end of the town reached as far as the Malt Shovel, shown in the postcard above, and no further. One amusing aspect of this road, unnoticed by most locals, is the terraced house next to the North Pole Inn which appropriately carries the name of The Igloo.

Penel Orlieu

Penel Orlieu - the junction of what used to be Pynel Street and Orlieu Street.

Orlieu Street (more recently Clare Street) is from the family name of Orlove. It used to run from Pynel Street straight down to the town ditch on the west side of the castle, parallel with the High Street. Pynel Street dates back to the fourteenth century when John Pynel or Pagnel had property in the area. The meeting of these two streets combined the names of the two.

The corruption of Pynel into Penel is easily recognised. The change from Orlove to Orlieu is also easy to comprehend if we consider the Norman's inability to pronounce Saxon names. Inevitably many of them took on a French variation.

In the 15th to 17th centuries there was a St. Anthony's Cross somewhere on the west side of the town. By 1689 it was known as the Pig or Pea Cross and had been moved to Penel Orlieu. Many older residents of the town still refer to this area as Pea Cross or Pig Cross, a reference to the old market cross sited in the area. The cross, a simple shaft in style, probably served as a boundary marker and a replica can now be seen at the river end of Fore Street.

In 1769, the old Pig Cross was demolished and replaced with St. Mary's Cross from the churchyard. This in turn was demolished in 1830.

Provident Place

A street of small terraced houses built around 1851.

Public library

Bridgwater public library was built in 1905 financed with an endowment from Andrew Carnegie, a Scot who emigrated from Scotland to America and made his fortune in the steel mills of Pittsburgh. Towards the end of his days, having acquired considerable wealth, Carnegie's conscience began to play on him and he did much to benefit the working classes of the nation of his birth.

Millions of pounds were endowed to assist with the education of the people of Britain.

171

One of the towns to benefit was Bridgwater which was able to boast one of the best free libraries of the time in the country. Taunton also benefited similarly. Carnegie's name is best immortalised by Carnegie Hall in the United States, famous world wide as a cultural and entertainment centre.

The local library was built in an octagonal form as an Edwardian variation of the Cornhill.

Rope Walk

This was the site where J. H. Waddon had his rope works which were certainly here in 1865 and survived on the site until 1951 when fire destroyed the premises. The rope walk was a long covered gallery where rope was manufactured by twisting it over a considerable length. The business was very prosperous during the successful decades of river traffic with ships coming to and fro and always needing to replace their heavy ropes.

Another rope walk also existed half way along Chilton Street.

St. Francis of Assisi church, Saxon Green 1960

The parish of St. Francis was formed in 1965. The church was designed by a Taunton man, Peter Bradley. The spire was added in 1984.

St. John's Church (1845)

St. John's church in Eastover was opened on 9 April, 1845 by its first minister, the Reverend J. M. Capes and the Reverend E. W. Estcourt. Its presence is due to the generosity of the Reverend Capes of Balliol College, Oxford. He responded to the news that there were 3000 people in Bridgwater who were not catered for by the church of St. Mary's and put up the money for the building. The ground itself was gifted by a Mr. Sealy, the owner of one of the many brick and tile pits in the town.

The church is built from Bath stone in 13th century Early English style with lancet windows and an open timber roof with hammer beams. The stained glass windows were made partly in France and partly in England. The architect was John Brown of

St. John's Church

Norwich whose original plans to cap the tower with a spire were thwarted due to poor foundations The organ was built by a Mr. Bates of Ludgate Hill in London.

St. John's Street

St. John's Street - leading from the site of the Hospital of St. John set up by William Briwer the younger in 1216. The street owes its development to the presence of the railway which came in 1841.

The Mariners' Chapel was built in St. John's Street in 1837, the society having been formed in 1817. The Mariners' Christian Society was formed by a former Methodist minister. The society ceased in 1857 although the chapel continued until 1960 when it was sold and became a motor cycle shop.

St. Mary's Church

Bridgwater's most famous landmark for several hundred years originates from the thirteenth century albeit its most obvious features, the tower and spire, are of the fourteenth century. The earliest known reference to the present church building is 1220. There are earlier references to St. Mary's going back at least to the days of Merleswain, i.e. before 1066.

The church, in Early English and Perpendicular style, is almost a local geological exhibit with three very distinctive stones used in its building. It owes much to William Briwere for its present day appearance.

The tower, the oldest surviving part, is 13th century and built of red Wembdon sandstone. The spire, 176 feet high was made in 1367, just twenty years after the Black Death, at a cost of just under £144. It contains eight bells, three medieval and the rest mainly Elizabethan. The tenor bell weighs just short of two tons.

Work on the spire began on June 28th, 1367 and when the task was complete, Bridgwater

could boast a most unusual spire in that it is exceptionally high relative to the tower, almost twice its height in fact. The original bells were cast in Bridgwater and at least one other Bridgwater bell can be found in the United States. The clock, installed in 1869 was made by S. & W. Cope of Nottingham.

The fawn colour stone was floated down the river from Langport, having been quarried at Ham Hill. The Bristolian Nicholas Waleys commenced the erection of the necessary scaffolding on top of the tower using timber from the royal forest at North Petherton.

Records of repairs to the church appear for 1414 and 1415 with stone being quarried at Pidsbury in Langport. There it was loaded onto barges at a quayside by the quarry, on the River Yeo, and floated downstream to the town bridge.

The weight of the stone used in the tower proved excessive and thus the tower had to be significantly strengthened with heavy buttresses. The lead for the roof came from Wells. The walls of the main church are made from the blue lias stone of central Somerset. The squint windows were to allow lepers to view the altar without entering the church.

In 1813 there was a major hail storm which did much damage to the spire. The following year the spire was struck by lightning with the weathercock ending up in Blacklands field some distance away. The next year it was decided to correct the damage.

A local sea captain by the name of Gover was sought for advice on how best to scale the spire. His advice was to place poles around the base of the spire and lash them together around the spire. In this way a solid base closely resembling ships rigging was put in place. Further poles were lashed to the tops of these until sufficient height was gained. Rope ladders were then fastened from pole to pole and the task was completed.

Unfortunately when all the scaffolding work had been brought down it was realised that the weather cock was not turning. Wedges placed to stop it spinning whilst the work was carried out had inadvertently been left behind. To overcome this problem, a kite was flown over the church until it draped over the weather cock. The kite string was let out allowing the kite to descend, a larger rope was attached to the string and this pulled up over the weathercock. Gover was honoured with the task of ascending the top of the spire using this rope and removing the wedges. The steeple itself was repaired by Thomas Hutchings, a stonemason.

Repairs were again necessary in 1887 when the weather cock required regilding.

Inside the church, one of the most striking features is the painting of the Descent from the Cross. The origin of this magnificent painting is uncertain but it is probably Italian, Guido or Carraci maybe. It is believed to have been taken as part of the plunder from a captured Spanish vessel and was then auctioned at the quayside in Plymouth. Fortunately for Bridgwater it was purchased by the local Poulett family and it was the Honourable Lord Anne Poulett who donated it to the church in 1783. (The Honourable Anne Poulett was actually a man who suffered the misfortune of being named after Queen Anne, his godmother).

The painting itself is unusual in that it depicts Christ without a beard. It shows John the Baptist leaning over the body of his cousin, the Virgin Mary having fainted into the arms of Mary of Magdelene and Mary, wife of Cleophas with a tear touchingly falling down her cheek. The hair style of Mary Magdelene, and the blue band which crosses it, are suggestive of the Spanish School of painting rather than Italian. Such is the magnificence of this piece that Sir Joshua Reynolds came to Bridgwater many times when in the West Country just to study the artistry.

The furnishings include the Corporation Pew which dates back to James 1 and the font in which Blake was baptised. The back of the mayor's seat has the seal of Bridgwater which was that of William Briwer.

Outside the church, a large circular stone remains amongst the tombstones looking something like a large millstone. It is in fact all that remains of the original Pig Cross which was situated during its working life just outside what is now The Blue Boar Inn and is now replicated at the bottom of Fore Street.

The oldest grave in the church grounds is that of James Hartnell who died in 1866 at 102 years old, an incredible age today let alone back in the nineteenth century.

St. Mary's Street and the Old Vicarage

St. Mary's Street contains a line of 14th century cottages including the Old Vicarage Restaurant which was given in the 16th century by Edward de Chedzoy to be used as a vicarage. That was how it remained until the last century. It is a particularly interesting building, the original wattle and daub walls being open to the public view both on the front of the restaurant building and on a side wall under the arch which gives access to the rear of the building. Also preserved on the front wall is a hole with wooden surround through which beverages were passed to the drivers on awaiting coaches.

Back in the days of coach travel, the stage coach would have pulled up outside of the restaurant and frequently whilst the passengers were allowed inside, the driver would have to stay with the coach and horses. This bottle shaped slot through which the beverage was passed is therefore set high enough to make it convenient for the driver who was set well up on the front of the stage.

Opinions differ as to why the bottle shape was necessary. The obvious answer is to facilitate the transfer of a bottle without having an overly large opening. The one I prefer is that the narrower slot at the top (the neck of the bottle if you like) is to take a

Judge Jeffrey's House, Marycourt

mulling iron. Stage coach drivers in cold weather would surely have been given a hot drink. The custom was to mull port and ales. This was achieved by putting a mulling iron or rod into a fire and when hot enough it would be put into a pewter tankard of the required beverage. This kept the refreshment warm for a much longer period. The bottle shaped hole is perfect size and shape to facilitate the transfer of a pewter tankard with protruding mulling iron.

Another feature of the Old Vicarage is the fire insurance plate clearly visible from the road. This basically entitled the owner to fire insurance including the use of the fire brigade. Without it, the fire brigade would not attend.

The house known as St. Mary Court, shown above, is reputed to be the place where Judge Jeffreys stayed on his visit to Bridgwater. Historians argue that this was never the case. Local legend has it that it was so and certain stories are associated with his stay there. However those same stories exist in respect of Colonel Percy Kirke who definitely did stay in the town. Almost for certain, any lingering tales should be credited to Kirke and not Judge Jeffreys.

The Rose and Crown Inn dates back to the 14th century. The Tudor restaurant, which is not Tudor at all, dates from around 1600 and the Waterloo Inn is early 18th century.

The Baptist Chapel built in 1837 is in the fine classical style with neo-Greek pediments, a low pitched gable over a portico on ionic columns.

Saint Saviour's Avenue

This late 19th century avenue more or less marks the site of St. Saviour's church which stood outside the south gate from about 1530 or earlier until at least 1703.

Salmon Parade

Possibly named after the fish, certainly there was a time when salmon ran up the river. In 1803 the Reverend William Holland in his diaries published under the title 'Paupers and Pig Killers', refers to the price of Bridgwater salmon having risen from four old pence per pound to two shillings, a six fold increase. This would suggest that salmon were rapidly becoming scarcer even in those days.

The row of cottages are 19th century.

Bridgwater hospital, or the infirmary as it was originally known, dates back to 1813 when the need for a local hospital was recognised and acted upon. The first hospital as such was that of St. John's at the junction of Eastover and Broadway which lasted from 1216 to the dissolution of the monasteries in 1546. In 1813 a hospital was started in Back Street, roughly behind the present Town Hall. By 1820 the demand had outgrown the premises and the hospital as we know it was founded at Salmon Parade, the site being purchased for £700.

In order to fund the hospital, subscribers were required. For each one guinea paid per annum, the subscriber could recommend four outpatients or their equivalent, one inpatient being worth two outpatients. Each inpatient then had to pay 5 shillings and 6 pence per week. By 1830 the rules had changed to cater for longer term patients. After three months as an inpatient, a fresh recommendation was required and each patient was required to pay one months board in advance. They were also required to supply their own linen and 'bedside' requirements.

The hospital grew regularly from then to the end of the nineteenth century. In 1837 two new wards were added, a female ward was introduced in 1847 and in 1876 the frontage was altered to add the now present portico. A new operating theatre was added in 1902 along with X-ray equipment for the first time.

Salmon Parade was the home of Wills Engineering, a long established Bridgwater engineering company. Much of the success of this business was based around the shipping that went on in the town. So successful was the enterprise and so skilful

the engineers that Mr. Wills built a motor car in the same year that Henry Ford first built his Model T. We all know what happened to the Ford Motor Co. and must wander what might have happened to Bridgwater had Mr. Wills had the inclination to push his venture further. Perhaps we're better off without it.

Salvation Army Church

Situated in Moorland Road on the Sydenham Estate, the Church building was originally built for the Mariners Chapel in 1961. The building was transferred to the Baptists in 1965 and later to the Salvation Army who are still very active there.

The Salvation Army came to the town in 1880 and took over the Zion Hall, now demolished, in Friarn Street. They stayed here until their move to Moorland Road in 1970.

Town Hall

Opened on 6 July, 1865 it was built by C. Knowles using Bridgwater Brick, Wembdon red sandstone and Bath Stone where more demanding architectural features were required. In Georgian style, it stands three stories high with a stucco frontage.

Valetta Place

Named after the capital of Malta in the Mediterranean, this row of houses was built in the mid-late 19th century for the use of our local sea captains. Numbers 4 and 5 feature curved brickwork. For many years the house nearest the river was the home of a basket weaver who could be seen all year round in his workshop producing various wicker items many of them for export.

Victoria Park

Originally called Malt Shovel Park, it was in those days twice its present size. This was the home ground of the Albion rugby club, popularly called the Sappers, prior to its merger with the Bridgwater club. It was also the site of the original town football club and a rather unusual site was that of the twenty two players all sharing an open air galvanised bath of hot water after the game.

Victoria Road

Originally known as Malt Shovel Lane.

Wembdon

Wembdon is a Saxon name, referred to in the Domesday Book as Wadmendun. The Wad was the Saxon name for the bundle into which woad was made up before it was crushed to extract the dye. Woad is a plant yielding a blue dye and presumably was readily available in the area. Thus it would appear to be the dwelling place where woad was made; it doesn't sound much like the 'much sought after' residential area as now described by our local estate agents.

The village grew quite dramatically in the nineteenth century, multiplying four fold in numbers in the first seventy years. As a result of the increased demand, Wembdon School was built in 1871 being officially opened on April 24th, 1872. Numbers of just over forty in the first week increased to almost a hundred by September but then plummeted when the fair came to town. Absenteeism was one of the schools greatest problems, the pupils being predominantly from rural families with agricultural ties. Harvest time, sowing time, the blackberry season, all had their impact on the numbers attending.

The situation improved as the importance of education became recognised and by 1900 over a hundred and seventy regularly attended.

West Quay

Probably the most important feature on West Quay and yet the least noticed is the old watergate from the river to the castle. Situated between numbers 11 and 12 West Quay, down a short narrow passage, the old walls of the castle are still clearly visible and give a indication to the thickness of the defences.

The Lions, further along, was built in 1720 by the architect of Castle Street, Benjamin Holloway. This is a grade 1 listed building and is currently the home of a firm of architects and the Citizens Advice Bureau. There is a local legend which claims that the lions which stand either side of the entrance come down from their pedestals each night to drink from the river. Knowing how many public houses there were at one time along this stretch of the river bank, it is not difficult to imagine where the story started.

The wharves along this side of the river, and likewise the East Quay, at one time extended for a mile downstream from the town bridge.

The Fountain Inn is a late 18th century house built with high gables emulating the Dutch influence. This style is repeated in many buildings in the area and is perhaps an indication of Dutch and Flemish immigration related to the wool trade and the drainage of low lying areas.

There used to be a regular timber trade with the Black Sea area and the sailors from those parts often used the Fountain Inn. It was during those times that a young Joseph Stalin

The Lions, East Quay

The Bridge, Bridgwater

is said to have frequented the Fountain Inn. Although it cannot be proven, the confidence with which the story is told leads one to accept the possibility.

The raised walls along the river bank are a recent addition. At on time the top of the bank was level with the road and thus flooding was a regular occurrence.

Witches Walk

Witches Walk - the original Witches Walk was in the area of the fields below St. Matthew's field. There was a common belief in witches right up to the nineteenth century. They were considered to fall into two categories. The white witches practised good by way of cures and the black witches were of a wicked nature and took the blame for many events that would now be considered to have natural explanations. Cattle dying or a cow's milk drying up, the presence of a facial blemish, a miscarriage, an unexpected death, a house fire; all these events were likely to be blamed on the unpopular black witches.

York Buildings

Leading from the Cornhill to Kings Square, York Building date back to 1823 on the site of the old castle bailey, the only land based entrance from the town to the castle, the other entrance being the watergate from the river.

The dentists premises on the right hand side of this short piece of road has two unusual features. To the side of the steps leading to the front door the railings feature a built in foot scrape which was a well used addition in the days before tarmac roads. Also worth a look are the lions heads featured on the guttering.

Bridgewaters in the U.S.A.

The emigration years of the nineteenth century saw Somerset folk leaving to start new lives in America, Canada and Australia. We know of at least seventeen other Bridgewaters around the world. It is however only our own which is spelt with just the one 'e'. This is not an argument that the other Bridgewaters therefore cannot be connected. Indeed we know for certain that most of them are. Consider the number of times our own town name is spelt incorrectly. Consider the American way of spelling even simple words in a different way to ourselves. There was never really any chance that the town name would survive elsewhere without being 'corrected'.

The greatest number of Bridgewaters is in the States which can boast thirteen, then Australia with three and one in Canada

United States of America

The depressed conditions of nineteenth century England contributed to many West Country folk leaving for the New World. In the England of 1849, the farming community were suffering from the import of low price grain. This de-stabilised local agriculture, brought prices tumbling, saw hundreds unemployed and brought about the Corn Laws. The problems coincided with the goldstrikes in America. What better reason to chance your luck and cross the Atlantic in search of a better life. This led to a peak of emigration in the mid-nineteenth century albeit emigration was not uncommon from the mid-seventeenth century onward. Understandably most of the thirteen Bridgewaters in the United States are therefore towards the east coast of America.

Such was the trade in emigration that new ships had to be built to deal with the traffic. In 1852 an 800 ton clipper built barque, the Pathfinder, was launched from Bridgwater

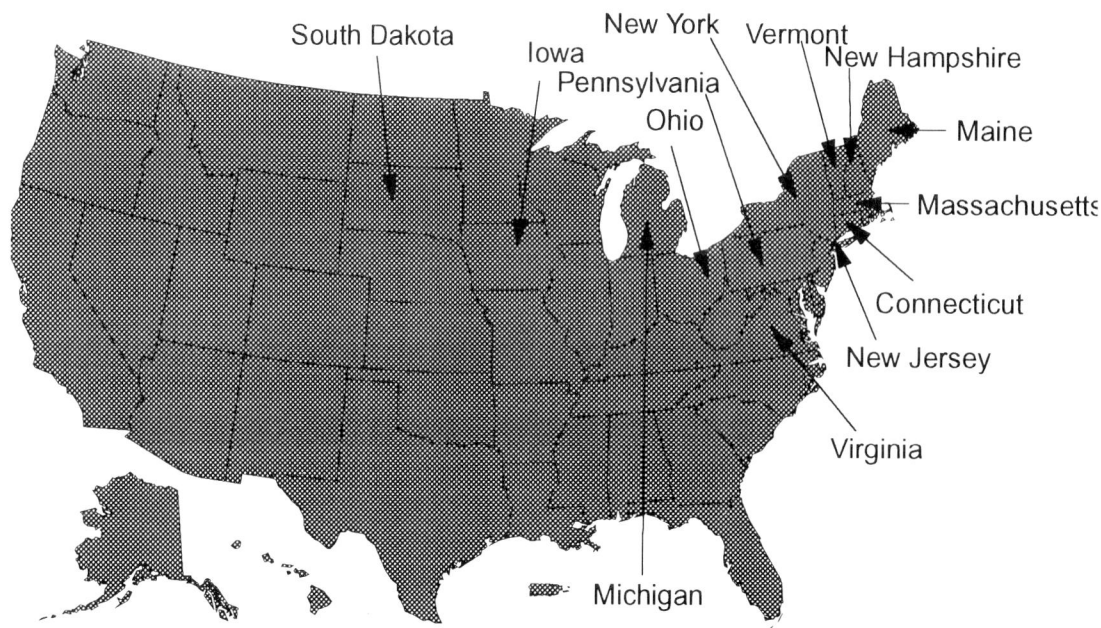

South Dakota · Iowa · New York · Vermont · New Hampshire · Pennsylvania · Ohio · Maine · Massachusetts · Connecticut · New Jersey · Virginia · Michigan

with over 5,000 spectators lining the river banks to witness the occasion. She was purpose built to carry one hundred and thirty emigrants from the West Country to New York and left with her first load on Sunday, March 8th. The journey, under the command of William Loveless, took 30 days.

Bridgewater, Connecticut

In 1722, Samuel Clark (a good Somerset name) had his land surveyed in the southern part of an area known as Shepaug Neck. This was to become Bridgewater, Connecticut which really began to grow in 1803 and grew steadily until it was incorporated as a town in 1856. It was then that it separated from the township of New Milford. It is bounded on two sides by the Housatonic River and Town Hill brook and its hills include Second Hill, Hut Hill and Wolfpit Mountain.

Horace Sanford was one of the local heroes of Bridgewater. He took a very active part in the Civil War fighting under both Generals Grant and Sheridan at the battles of Cold Harbour, Winchester, Fisher's Hill, Cedar Creek, Fort Fisher and Petersburg before Lee's surrender.

The town consisted predominantly of farmsteads, many of them needing the native Indians to be cleared from their camping grounds before the farms could be established. Nowadays the town is a 1,654 strong agricultural community looking out over wooded hills and cultivated valleys. The name of the town describes the fact that it was necessary to bridge a river in order to enter the area.

If we look for similarities with our own town, then it does have a fair albeit a country fair, similar to our now defunct agricultural show. And it has the Burnham library which proved so useful in providing information for this book.

Bridgwater Town Hall, Connecticut

Bridgewater, Iowa

One of the smaller Bridgewaters, with just 225 population, can be found in Adair County. It was built by the railroad company in 1885 starting with a hotel followed by a church, school, cafe and lumber yard. Board sidewalks (pavements) came later along with two more churches.

Today the railroad has gone and the town is dependant on agriculture, particularly cattle. It has its own feed and grain operation serving the whole area. Facilities include agricultural and automobile servicing, a petrol station, cafe, grocery store, bank, welder beautician, post office and primary school.

The community centre also houses the volunteer fire brigade which dates back to 1910 when the original town buildings were destroyed by fire. The town well was dug at the same time.

A two hundred and fifty foot bridge was built by the railroad company to span the Nodaway River. For four days following its completion, torrential rains swept away the roads leaving the bridge surrounded by water. This gives us one theory on the origin of the town's name. An alternative theory is based on the fact that the town can only be reached by crossing a bridge.

The town is surrounded on three sides by farm fields and on the east is the county lake called the Mormon Trail Lake, the trail passing right through the town. Apparently many of the old wagon wheel ruts are still there showing the route that Brigham Young took with his followers, the trail being clearly marked by the local historical society

Bridgewater, Massachusetts.

This city, population 22,000, dates back to at least 1656 when it became 'incorporated' albeit the land was granted in 1646. It can proudly boast that it was one of the first 'interior' settlements in the colonies.

The West Country connections here are obvious with the city being in Plymouth county and coincidentally ten miles from Taunton, Massachusetts. The story of Bridgewater, Massachusetts goes back to shortly after the landing of the Pilgrim Fathers. They set sail from Plymouth, Devon and landed in America in 1620 in what was to become Plymouth, Massachusetts, for twelve years the only town in the colony. Then a few small settlements sprang up along the coast including Taunton in 1637. Between Plymouth and Taunton was hill country, the home of a friendly Red Indian tribe whose chief was Massasoit, later called Ousamequin.

In 1645, Miles Standish, a man from Duxbury, another coastal town, received permission to purchase sixty four square miles of land called Satucket from the Indians. The price paid to Ousamequin was seven coats, nine hatchets, eight hoes, twenty knives, four moose-skins and ten and a half yards of cotton. The deeds were signed in 1649 and thus started the settlement which was to become Bridgewater.

Settlers moved inland from the coast from 1650 onwards. Many of them were from the West Country and undoubtedly included some from Bridgwater, Somerset. Amongst the names of those early settlers were the Mitchells, Hoopers, Bryants and Allens, all prominent names in our own home town during that period and even today.

Being the first inland township in the colonies is not Bridgewater's only claim to fame. In 1791 Calvin Phillips was born there. Apparently he is still the smallest mature man for whom there is an accurate record. At only two feet, two and a half inches he weighed a mere eleven pounds.

By the early nineteenth century industries were springing up producing anchors and nails using iron from two foundries. Cotton gins, boots and shoes were also manufactured here.

The Old Meeting House, Massachusetts, 1760

Along the same lines as our own town, Bridgewater Massachusetts reaped the benefits of the railroad from Boston in 1846 (just five years after its Somerset namesake had welcomed the railroad to its town). From 1810 to 1830, the population grew from 1,234 to 1,855. By 1895 it had reached 4,686 and has grown steadily ever since. At the end of the nineteenth century, a local newspaper was launched, The Bridgewater Independent which was to last from 1876 to 1958. Coincidentally Bridgwater, Somerset had its own weekly Bridgwater Independent from 1885 to 1933.

Bridgewater, Maine

Bridgewater, Maine, population 1200, is situated very close to the Canadian border, twenty miles north of Houlton in Aroostook County. It is spread over a six mile square and its economy is based on agriculture and timber. It was incorporated in 1858.

Its origin is quite interesting and gives it an indirect link with Bridgwater, Somerset. The State of Massachusetts, around 1647, passed a law that towns of a hundred families or more should have a grammar school. Eventually the need for higher education was felt and academies were established. In order to financially support these academies, grants of land were made. One land grant in Maine was made in 1803 to the Bridgewater Academy in Massachusetts. Thus the land in Maine became known as Bridgewater, after the town in Massachusetts which in turn had been named after Bridgwater, Somerset. In actual fact, half a township was granted to the Bridgewater Academy and the other half to the Portland Academy in Massachusetts. However, Maine already had a Portland, so the whole area was called Bridgewater.

In 1827, the town was a forest covered wilderness. Then Nathaniel Bradstreet arrived and built himself a house and timber mill at the confluence of two streams, the Presque Isle (pronounced Prestile) and the Whitney. In the winter of 1829 he moved his family to the site. Whilst winter may seem an odd time to move to a wilderness area, in this area travelling by ox drawn sled on the snow and ice was easier than summer travel.

Once the mill was up and running, he next cleared land for farming. And thus the town began to develop to its present size with good churches, schools, clubs and modern homes.

Bridgewater, Michigan

This Bridgewater in Washtenaw County, founded in 1898, is reasonably close to Detroit, the nearest significant place being Ann Arbor just to the north. With a population of about 500 it is one of the smallest of our namesakes and forms part of the Scio township.

The Bridgewater Bank Tavern is perhaps the hub of the old town which is mainly agricultural with a lumber yard, mill and factory manufacturing cosmetic containers. Although it has a church it has no school and perhaps uniquely amongst all the Bridgewaters, it has no bridge! This makes the origin of the name most interesting but none the less untraceable thus far.

Bridgewater, New Hampshire

In Grafton County, this small community, population 610, can date itself back to 21 June 1766 when the nineteen year old Thomas Crawford built a log cabin here having purchased 400 acres of land. It was apparently he who gave the place its name based on the fact that one cannot reach it without crossing a bridge although it is referred to locally as being named after a town in England. His father settled in the neighbouring territory two years later, followed by Robert Crawford in 1769 and Jonathan Crawford in 1771. The second settler, John Mitchell, arrived in 1767.

The town, which became incorporated in 1788, is situated on the banks of the beautiful glacial Newfound Lake, one of the cleanest lakes in the world. The lake, seven miles by four, is in the foothills of the White Mountains, 30 miles north of the state capital of Concord. It is fed by both streams and springs, accounting for its cleanliness. Well blessed with trout, typically between eight and fifteen pounds but occasionally up to twenty five, it also boasts landlocked salmon.

The trout spawn in the autumn along the shore of the lake, at which time they are very approachable and hence easy prey for the spears of the indigenous Indians who once were the only inhabitants here. They would then salt them down for the winter. The lake is frozen from January to April and the fish are taken through holes in the ice.

Although the first settler arrived in 1766, military expeditions passed through what was yet to become Bridgewater on their expeditions from Massachusetts in search of Indians to destroy, as early as 1703 and from then right through to the 1750's.

These were hard times in a hostile environment. An ancestor of a family still living in Bridgewater, George Browne, sent for his wife to join him in 1764. On the way she fell, with her baby, into the river when her horse stumbled. Needing time to dry, she lost the light at the end of the day without reaching her destination. She was obliged to shelter in a cave for the night. During the hours of darkness a group of Indians held a pow-wow above the cave. Much of the night was spent smothering the sounds of the crying child, almost suffocating her in the bargain. Her Bridgewater home was safely reached the following day.

It was a tough breed of individual who pioneered this territory. Virgin woodland had to be cleared with a just hand axe. Crops had to be planted around the stumps of the fallen trees. And all the time the settlers had to contend with the Indians. It certainly developed the hardened resilience required when the Revolutionary War against the British came a few years later.

The town is situated between Bristol and Plymouth, with Plymouth just 7 miles away. Other West Country place names nearby include Dorchester, Lyme, Exeter and Portsmouth. The town is split and the postal address on the west side is Bristol whilst that on the east is Plymouth. It is therefore easy to surmise that that there is probably a link with Bridgwater, Somerset albeit not proven.

The town owns its own 50 acre forest with nature trails where bear diggings, squirrel nut shell piles, beaver dams and woodpecker cavities are amongst the numerous clues to the abundant wildlife.

The original settlers were agricultural people, mainly of English origin, who cut back the forests in this rocky, hilly area to produce a vibrant farming community. As an agricultural area, it was well adapted to grazing and growing corn, oats and potatoes.

The numbers peaked around 1830 with a population of 783, but then during the 1840's and 1850's, the numbers declined as the west opened up. In 1861, with the start of the Civil War, Bridgewater's finest young men went off to join the fight. Fourteen enlisted in 1861 with thirty more in 1862. This left just eleven able bodied men to do the farming.

The young men from Bridgewater joined the thousand strong Twelfth New Hampshire regiment. By the time the Gettysburg campaign was over, the Twelfth New Hampshire regiment was reduced to just sixty nine effective soldiers and thus began a more rapid decline of Bridgewater's population. Ever since then the land has gradually reverted back to forest.

The head man of the town is called the Select Man, the small town's equivalent to our mayor.

Bridgewater, New Jersey

"Founded" on April 4, 1749 by royal charter of King George ll, it has a population at 32,509 very similar to our own and is in Somerset County which was created in 1688.

Founded in this case really means established. Bridgewater was actually founded in the English sense in 1687. A Bridgwater man by the name of Daniel Coxe went to America and became a partner of the famous William Penn. Daniel Coxe laid out the 'County of Somerset' in the state of New Jersey after his home county in England and gave Bridgewater, New Jersey its name.

The thirty three square miles was originally bought from the local Delaware Indians by the early settlers. They were a peaceful tribe and called themselves the Lenni-Lenape. They had no grasp of land ownership. They worshipped the air, soil and all aspects of nature. When they 'sold' their lands, their understanding was that they were doing little more than granting hunting and fishing rights. The land was purchased in 1664 and transferred to early settlers in 1682.

Early settlers here were a mixture of Dutch, English, Scottish and Irish. The roads formed by the wagon trails of those early settlers form the basis of Bridgewater's current road network.

The first recorded meeting of Bridgewater inhabitants was in 1750 at the home of George Middaugh. At the approach of the American War of Independence, Hendrick Fisher, a Bridgewater resident, was one of the signatories on a declaration of support to the Boston Patriots stating "Our committee is well disposed in the cause of American freedom". He also gave the first reading in Bridgewater of the American Declaration of Independence and for this the British put a price on his head and declared him an "Outlaw and enemy of the Crown".

By 1777, the revolutionary war was under way and Bridgewater had two encampments. The first, lasting just 35 days in 1777, the second was in 1777 - 1778. During this latter period there was a winter encampment at what is still called the Middlebrook Encampment. George Washington and every

officer under his command stayed here during this period. When the Stars and Stripes was adopted as the nation's flag (this was the Betsy Ross 13 star version), it was first raised over George Washington's headquarters at Bridgewater's Middlebrook encampment. This was on June 14, 1777.

During the nineteenth century the town was mainly agricultural. The population was 3,550 in 1830. The latter part of the nineteenth century saw the arrival of the railroad and the growth of both industry and population in its wake, almost mirroring the development of our own town's growth. Bridgewater was incorporated in 1899.

The township has two sites of historic importance. The first is the Middlebrook Encampment referred to earlier, the second is Van Veghten House. The latter, built in the Eighteenth Century, is now in the hands of the Somerset County Historical Society and was used to entertain Washington during his stay.

One prominent resident of Bridgewater's Finderne district was Antoinette Louisa Brown, the first ordained woman minister in the United States. In 1856 she married

Van Veghten House, Bridgewater, New Jersey

Samuel Blackwell and it was as Mrs. Blackwell that in 1911, aged 86, she marched down Fifth Avenue in a Suffragette parade. In 1920 at the age of 95, she cast her vote at the first election in which women were recognised as equals. She was the oldest surviving suffragette and died the following year.

The town is in the flat Raritan River Valley with several mountain ridges nearby and has developed to the north of the river. Several man made lakes have been developed in the area. The township can be found at the intersection of State Highway 287 and 78 giving easy access to the mountains, valleys and rivers.

Bridgewater, New York

Bridgewater, Oneida County has a population of 1,600. A mainly agricultural community of some 24 square miles, it is positioned in the centre of New York State about 15 miles south of Utica, its nearest major town. Sheep, cattle, hops, potatoes and grains make up the greater part of the economy.

In March 1789 the settlers arrived on their ox sleds, first from Connecticut, then Rhode Island and Massachusetts. By 1797 the township was officially formed and continued to grow at the crossing of the Cherry Valley Turnpike and the Utica to New Berlin Turnpike, not unlike our own Bridgwater acting as a convenient location on the stagecoach routes.

With the founding of the township, social organisations sprang up with the Masonic Lodge, Congregational Church and Art's Club. In 1922 the Bridgewater Historical Society was founded and remains active.

One claim to fame for the town is the success of Dr. Stephan Moulton Babcock (1843 - 1931) who as a professor of agricultural chemistry discovered a device and method to accurately determine the butter fat content of milk. Another claim to fame for Bridgewater is that it returned the first black mayor in New York State.

Bridgewater Center, Ohio

Bridgewater Township in Ohio is a small, totally agricultural community situated in Williams County, a few miles south of the Michigan border and about ten miles east of Indiana. It began in 1835 when Tucker's Clearing was established in the dense forest, albeit short lived. In 1837 the Smith brothers, Daniel, Anson and Asa, were the first to put down permanent roots, others following the next year.

It was a difficult place to settle taking two weeks to voyage up the St. Joseph River which was only navigable to within nine miles of the developing township. The forests were bountiful providing game in the form of deer, turkey, rabbits, possums, coon and porcupine. They also contained rattlesnakes and Pottawattamie Red Indians, the former being the most feared.

As the town grew, it took on a postmaster and a doctor, William Stout, in 1846. Unfortunately for his patients he just loved to go deer hunting and their ailments had to await his return. The school teacher, Miss McCrillus, also had problems. She would stay up late with her boyfriend most evenings and consequently fell asleep during her own lessons. The pupils took advantage each time and just up and left. Miss McCrillus received her marching orders in July, 1841.

At this time the community didn't even possess a horse. Everything was done with oxen, including taking crops to market. The first horses came in 1842. Corn and wheat were the main crops; cattle, sheep and chickens coming later.

Bridgewater Ohio remains a small agricultural community even today. Its one time store has disappeared although the gas station carries basic provisions. It has no post office, fire station, school or railroad. The town swimming pool is an enormous gravel pit

Bridgewater, Pennsylvania

Situated near Beaver in Beaver County about 35 miles to the north west of Pittsburgh, this Bridgewater, on the banks of the Ohio River, has 1,292 inhabitants.. Its economy is based on the steel mills albeit many of these have closed down in recent years. The origin of the town and its name are unknown. It is known, however, that in the last century it was very much a ship building base and as such was occasionally visited by George Washington. Boat races are still one of the features of this riverside community.

Bridgewater, South Dakota

During my research I spoke to Evelyn Shrogg at the City Hall in Bridgewater, South Dakota. Evelyn is the mayor's wife. We discussed our respective towns and my perception of hers rapidly changed. The Americans use the term city more liberally than the English. The city of Bridgewater, South Dakota has a population of 533. It is a predominantly agricultural town in a very flat farming area. It has its own small meat processing plant, a nursing home and five churches. That sounds a lot of churches but they do of course satisfy the needs of a very widely spread rural community.

This Bridgewater is based in the eastern part of South Dakota about forty miles west of Sioux Falls, the state's largest city. Its name has no connection with our own town. Apparently its original name was Mation but in 1880 the railroad came to town on its way to more important destinations. Just outside of the town, there is a small ravine and river over which the railroad workers built a bridge to carry their daily water needs. That, quite simply, is how the name took place.

Bridgewater, Vermont

A dormitory town of 895 where most of the townsfolk work out of town, commuting to the nearby Killington Ski Area or the famous tourist attraction of Woodstock. The most

Relative sizes of world's Bridg(e)water's

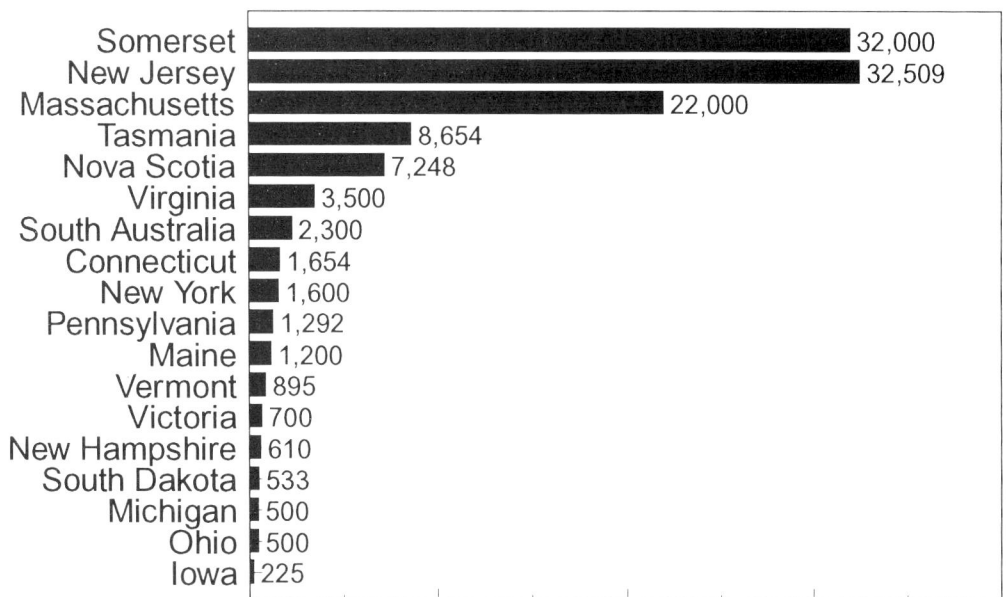

Location	Size
Somerset	32,000
New Jersey	32,509
Massachusetts	22,000
Tasmania	8,654
Nova Scotia	7,248
Virginia	3,500
South Australia	2,300
Connecticut	1,654
New York	1,600
Pennsylvania	1,292
Maine	1,200
Vermont	895
Victoria	700
New Hampshire	610
South Dakota	533
Michigan	500
Ohio	500
Iowa	225

attractive part of this area is the untamed wilderness called Chateauguay.

The town was chartered on July 10, 1761 under the reign of King George lll. A condition was that all white or other pine timber within the town which was fit to be used for ships masts should be left untouched until licenses were issued for their felling.

The first settler was Asa Jones who surveyed his land in September, 1779. He moved his family in the March of the following year having built a house entirely of wood. No glass for the windows, no stone for the walls and even the nails were made of wood. It must have provided good shelter none the less. The snow was four feet deep when they moved in, hauling their belongings by hand on sleds by men wearing snow shoes.

The reason Asa was keen to move in during such bad weather was to harvest the sap from the maple trees which had to be done during March and April. This was then used to produce sugar. Life was difficult in this wilderness country and made more so by the Canadian Indians to the North. During the Jones family first summer, four men from Barnard, the next town to the north, were captured by the Indians and taken into Canada. Another nearby settlement, Royalton, suffered a similar raid.

By 1786 two saw mills and a grist mill had been set up. The town grew steadily to a peak of 1363 in 1840, but from there on it declined, particularly after the Civil War.

In common with other New England Bridgewaters, there is a Plymouth not far away.

Bridgewater, Virginia

This must be one of the most scenic of all the Bridgewaters. The Shenandoah Valley lies between the Blue Ridge mountains and the Allegheny Mountains with Bridgewater close

to its centre.

The town was already a settlement in 1749 when John Magill had settled on his three hundred acres. His brother William lived on the other side of the river. The river crossing at this point is still known as Magill's Ford. Jacob Dinkel built the first bridge and bought the land which was to complete the town.

As in Somerset, Bridgewater served as a base for river transportation and from this upper limit pig iron, hides, skins and grain were transported down the Shenandoah River to Harper's Ferry and thence down the Potomac to Alexandria.

Although the town has a population of only 3,500, it boasts all the services of a larger town with a police force of five officers.

The proudest boast of the town is Bridgewater College, established in 1880. The college serves the need of 900 co-ed students from over 20 States and overseas. Offering Bachelor of Arts degrees in 28 subjects on its 40 acre site, it seems amazing to English eyes for such a small town to support such a significant establishment.

The other Bridgewaters

Australia

The first emigrants to Australia were the convicts deported to Botany Bay in 1788. As the colony developed and the potential for land development was recognised, so the British government encouraged the strong and healthy to travel to the far side of the globe and develop Australia. Many families went from all around the country. Those with young children had the expectation that half the children of four years or under would fail to survive the journey. Fortunately for Somerset children they seemed to fair better than most with only one in eight dying en route.

The busy years were from 1839 to 1854 with most emigrants sailing to Port Philip Bay in Victoria. The opening of the railway line to Bridgwater in 1841 made it possible for the locals to travel to London at an acceptable cost. This increased the Bridgwater emigrants to Australia with the cost of the train travel being included in the package.

At the same time the Colonial Land and Emigration Office in Victoria had set aside large parcels of land for development. These were sold at a very attractive price in 320 acre lots. The owner of such a piece could buy the passage for immigrants to work on his land at £20 each. Thus landowners of English origin would naturally look for immigrants from their own home area. No wonder that we find other Bridgewaters in the developing areas.

One example of this is the Sheppard sisters from Bridgwater, Mary Anne and Emma who, aged 20 and 23 respectively, sailed on September 17th, 1852 from Plymouth on the barque 'Time and Truth' along with 279 other emigrants. The ship was brand spanking new, built no doubt to help cope with the demand for emigrant ships. However, it was small and the passengers suffered from overcrowding. Dysentery and whooping cough took their toll with six children dying on the voyage before the remaining passengers finally arrived in Australia on January 5th, 1853.

There, after a period of quarantine on board ship, they joined John Cullen of Bridgwater, a butcher - grazier, and his wife Martha. They lived and worked in Newtown, Victoria where they were paid £25 a year with rations. They would have had no difficulty finding a husband at such a young age. Ladies were in great demand and, in the same year that Mary Anne and Emma arrived, the Bridgwater Times published an article stating that even women of gone forty could find a husband in the new territory!

Two others who went from Bridgwater were Jeffrey and Ann Gillingham. Jeffrey, 25, was a coachmaker and took up employment with a Mr. Gilbert in Geelong. Jeffrey and his wife must have been an asset to any employer since they were both able to read and write, not too common in those days.

In all, there are three Bridgewaters in Australia.

Bridgewater, Victoria

On the far west coast of Victoria we have Cape Bridgewater (named after the Duke of Bridgewater) and Bridgewater Bay. It was in this area of Australia that the majority of assisted passage emigrants arrived in the

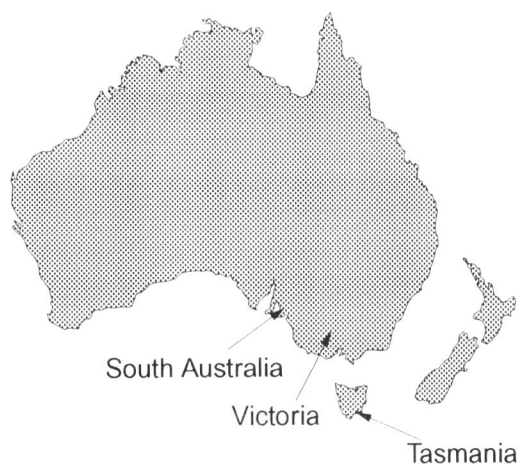

South Australia

Victoria

Tasmania

nineteenth century. Most of them landed in Port Philip Bay where Melbourne is situated.

Some 120 miles inland from Melbourne and 20 miles from the major city of Bendigo, Bridgewater can be found on the Loddon River in north central Victoria. Straddling the river, the town is split between two administrative areas. Part is in the shire of Marong and part in Korong. It lies on the Calder highway between Inglewood and Bendigo.

The population of 700 are employed mainly in farming with the Waterwheel Flour Mill being the other industry. In their spare time, the locals enjoy fishing and water skiing on the river. This facility is shared with the visitors to the town's one hotel and two caravan parks.

The town was founded by a Bridgwater emigrant called "Big" Clarke and its presence arose out of sheer need. Gold was discovered in an area known as Catto's Run at nearby Inglewood. A sizeable nugget of ten stone in weight was found and called the Welcome Stranger. This was in 1860. Unfortunately for the miners, they managed to pollute their own water supply by their mining activity. It was therefore necessary to camp on the Loddon River at some distance from the goldfields. In 1862 a bridge was erected replacing the punt used to transport

stage coaches across the river. Next came the brewery apparently with disastrous effects on the local aboriginal population.

1873 saw the opening of the mill which survives even today despite a chequered history. In 1892 it burned down and was rebuilt. In 1905 it doubled its capacity only to burn down again in 1934. It was again rebuilt and today employs sixty people.

The nearby Yarraberb estate was witness to a most peculiar sight in 1860 when twenty camels, with Indian drivers, and wagons piled high were seen approaching. This most unusual convoy was the famous Burke and Wills expedition. The following day the party left on their ill fated journey. Some years later a solitary camel passed through retracing its earlier steps.

Bridgewater, South Australia

This Bridgewater is a dormitory suburb in the area of Stirling District Council in South Australia, a part of the Mount Lofty Ranges. Its population of 2,300 depends on the major city of Adelaide only fifteen miles away, although it does have its own primary school, Anglican, Roman Catholic and Lutheran churches. Situated in the gently rolling mountains of the Adelaide Hills, it boasts an historic water wheel, part of a restored mill housing the wine making and maturation plant for "Petaluma's" premium sparkling wines.

It was founded in 1840 only four years after the first wave of colonists. They arrived in December, 1836 and for the most part lived in tents. One of the early pioneers was a Scot called Robert Cock and the area around Bridgewater took its name from him becoming corrupted to Cox's Creek. The exact position was determined by the need for bullock drays to cross the creek at the fording place that was found here in order to move supplies of timber required by the settlers.

A hotel called The Deanery was built at the crossing point which caused those moving the timbers to stop awhile and thus the small community began to grow. For several years the area suffered from the criminal activities of bushrangers, in particular three characters called Curran, Fox and Hughes. They were eventually captured at the Crafer's Inn (named after another early pioneer) after they had provided free drinks to everyone and ended up too intoxicated to resist arrest. The area was able to boast more than its fair share of villains, much of the town being built by their endeavours.

We know that in 1855, the local hotel was already called the Bridgewater Hotel. Its owner was James Addison. He may well have been a Bridgwater man himself for we know that the settlement's first Post Master, William Radford was from our own Bridgwater and had named his Post Office after his home town for sentimental reasons. Cox's Creek's Bridgewater Hotel and Bridgewater Post Office were both named after Bridgwater, Somerset.

Thus Addison introduced the name in 1855, Radford reproduced it somewhere between 1858 and 1862 and John Dunn, a Bideford man who formally laid out the township, renamed it officially in 1873 as Bridgewater.

During the 1880's a camp was set up for navvies. These created a number of problems and there were many court cases in the town, mainly for drunkenness. The town had no prison and, in one case in 1881, the convicted offender was chained to a log overnight for safe keeping. In the morning, the prisoner with chains, log and all had disappeared. He carried the log for three mile to Summit Station before he rid himself of his burden. After this event, a local cottage was converted to a lock up.

In 1883 the railroad arrived and land prices went up ten fold. The population grew steadily to its present day level.

Bridgewater, Tasmania

With a population of about 8,654 this is an important market town twelve miles north of the principal city of Hobart on the bank of the River Derwent. Its origin was the building of a causeway and later a bridge across the River Derwent. This was in the early 1830's and involved the use of one hundred and sixty convicts. These unfortunates were used to wheelbarrow two thousand tons of stone and clay. Those who were deemed to be putting in less than the required effort were locked up in Bridgewater's prison. This can still be seen today in the Old Watch House which now serves the local community as a petrol station. It boasts the smallest cell in Australia at twenty inches square and six feet high. Most were slightly bigger at seven feet high and two feet square but they had the inconvenience of a floor sloping at forty degrees.

We know that in 1831 there were at least 160 men working in chains. Those who behaved well were permitted longer chains allowing greater freedom of movement. Shorter chains led to chaffing and infection, and to become ill was considered a crime.

The original bridge from which the town probably took its name was built in 1849 and replaced in 1946. It is the site of the first permanent crossing over the Derwent, Tasmania's largest river. The Derwent valley was one of the first lines of settlement in Tasmania. Therefore Bridgewater's situation at the crossing point was quite strategic.

Apart from its importance as a stock selling centre, Bridgewater remained a fairly small settlement until the 1970's, indeed its population was a mere two hundred people when the State housing commission purchased land for subdivision and housing development. The population rocketed to 7,000 in 1976 and then gradually rose to today's 8,000 plus.

The local paper, by coincidence one imagines, is called The Mercury. Copies from 1977 refer to unsuccessful attempts to have the name of the town abolished.

Canada

There is perhaps less known about emigrants to Canada than those to Australia and the United States. Canadians seem to have a lesser need to understand their roots than the other former colonials. This perhaps explains why less is known, or perhaps it's just that fewer people went to Canada.

We know that in 1831 there were at least two sailings of emigrants direct to Canada from Bridgwater and that three hundred and sixty people went on board the vessels "Friends" and "Euphrosyne". The following year, the Euphrosyne was advertising again for direct sailings to Quebec. Her master was Joseph Sampson who lived in Northgate and she had a 500 ton capacity, a large vessel to enter Bridgwater.

Bridgewater, Nova Scotia

Described as Canada's Ocean Playground, Nova Scotia is known for its hospitality and humour. Rich in scenery and marine life, it's an ideal place to go to fish and hunt or just watch whales. Like ourselves it knows the effect of high tidal ranges with tidal variations

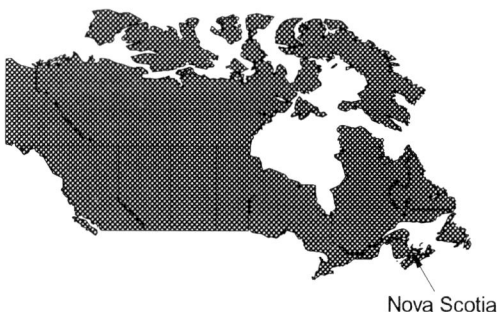

Nova Scotia

reaching 54 feet. Also in common are wicker and basketry.

Centrally located in western mainland Nova Scotia, Bridgewater is one of the larger Bridgewaters in the 'colonies' with a population of 7,248 in 1991. Two miles by three, it sits astride the tidal La Have River fifteen miles inland reminiscent of our own town in Somerset.

Its economy is based on manufacturing, forestry and tourism. The main manufacturing plant is the Michelin Tire Company, the town's largest employer. In the forestry industry, their Balsam Fir Christmas Trees are exported all over North and South America as well as, surprisingly enough, Europe.

Bridgewater is situated in Lunenburg County which takes its name from the home of the German settlers who moved in around 1780. They settled around the mouth of the river and over the years spread inland along the banks of the La Have, eventually reaching the navigable head of the river where Bridgewater began to settle in 1800.

Its first church and school were both built around 1830, following the timber bridge which was erected across the river in 1825. This was replaced in 1867 and again with the present bridge in 1891, a similar story to our own town.

In 1858 the road from Halifax, Nova Scotia's capital, was opened up and the effect of this was like the railroad coming to Bridgwater in 1841. The population has grown steadily since the days of its purchase from the Micmac Indians (once the only inhabitants) and was incorporated in 1899.

In that same year the town was struck by a disastrous fire. On the night of 12 January, the entire High Street was razed to the ground, the flames fanned by the bitterly cold winds. Amazingly no one was killed and the town survived. It learned though from its mistake and when the town was rebuilt, one bank of the river was left as clear open land. Potentially even more disastrous was the forest fire of 1955. The mostly timber houses were threatened for a full two days while the townsfolk fought a tinder dry forest fire which completely surrounded the township.

The growth of the town came with the demand for its timber and in the late nineteenth century Bridgewater boasted the largest sawmill in Nova Scotia. Lumber and woodpulp are still important but the main industry now is the Michelin tyre plant whilst tourism plays an increasingly important role.

Today the town's biggest attraction is the annual South Shore Exhibition in late July and early August where events such as ox and horse pulls can be seen. Salmon fishing on the La Have is another popular seasonal offering.

H.M.S. Bridgwater

In 1928, the Royal Navy introduced a class of sloops. Bridgwater was honoured by having not just a naval vessel taking its name but the whole class. HMS Bridgwater was the first in the class to be launched in 1928 followed by the Sandwich; 1930 saw the Fowey, Hastings, Folkestone, Penzance, Scarborough and Shoreham; 1931 had the Bideford and Rochester followed the next year by the Dundee, Falmouth, Milford and Weston.

This wasn't the first naval ship to carry the town's name. We know that in 1747, Admiral Alexander Hood was sailing on the Bridgwater.

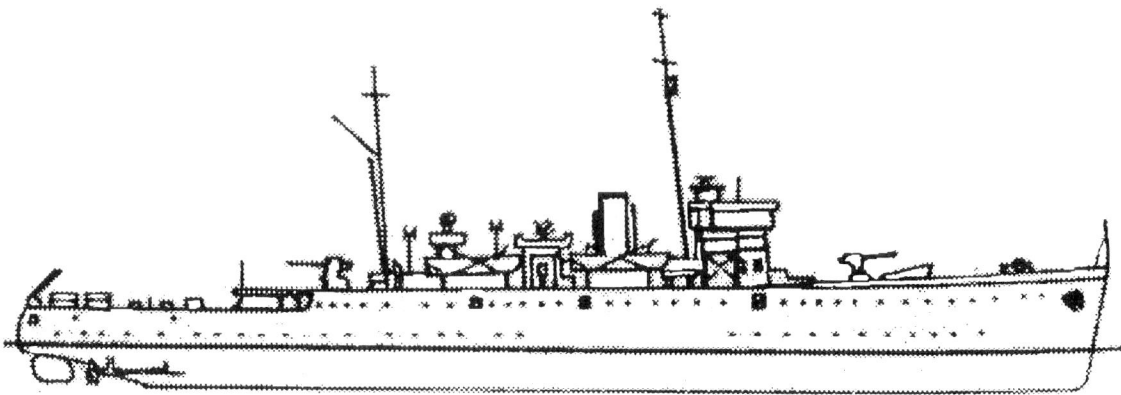

Bridgwater class sloop   1928 - 1932
1,105 tons   266 feet by 34 feet   Guns 2 at 4" A.A., 4 at 0.5" A.A.
2,000 h.p turbines, top speed 16 knots

Bridgwater dialect

Perhaps "Bridgwater dialect" is a pretentious heading being little more than "central Somerset". Professor Higgins in Shaw's 'Pygmalion' claimed he could pin a London accent down to its street of origin. He would find it very difficult these days where the mobility of the population and the influence of television has had such a diluting effect on dialects. The best place to hear good dialect in its strongest form is the school playground, before the youngsters are "improved".

However, where dialect is concerned, it is still relatively easy to pin a person down to a county by the way they sound. Think of Gracie Fields for Lancashire, Freddie Truman for Yorkshire, and so on. Having identified the county, to pin the dialect down more accurately, one has to recognise the local popular use of certain words and expressions.

Using prepositions to end a sentence is certainly more commonly practised in and around Bridgwater than elsewhere. For example, "Where are you going to?" instead of "Where are you going?".

But starting with the sound of words, the Bridgwater accent is that of central Somerset and can be heard as much in the town as on the moors around the area. A comedian portraying the "Somerset Yokel" deliberately emphasises the hard 'a' sound and the hard consonants. Almost every impersonation will start with "Oo-ar" and contain the words "Zummerzet zyder" somewhere.

But within the area, it's more subtle than that. In the Bridgwater area, the consonants which are sounded hard elsewhere in the county are frequently dropped all together. Thus "I can and you can't" becomes "I kin and you can'."

with the 't' dropped from "can't" and the vowel sound and its inflection being used to differentiate between the positive and the negative. As you move north across the peat moors towards the Mendips, so "cassun" becomes used for "cannot".

Learning a foreign language conventionally starts with the verb "to be". Perhaps the same applies to the local dialect since the Bridgwater version of "to be" is nothing like the "English" version and as such is almost unrecognisable to the outsider. For example, "are you" becomes "Izzee", "aren't you" becomes "Innee" and so on. Even more confusing "you" becomes "he" and "he" becomes "'ur". Very difficult to follow!

If the English-Somerset dictionary is ever published, this would be the verb "to be".

Somerset	English	Somerset	English
I iz	I am	Iz I	Am I
You iz	You are	Izee	Are you
'E iz	He is	Iz 'ur'	Is he
We iz	We are	Iz uz	Are we
Day iz	They are	Iz'um	Are they
I ain't	I am not	In'I	Am I not
In'ee	Are you not	In'ur	Is he not
Innuz	Are we not	Innum	Are they not

These examples take us into dialect rather than accent. The words are actually different rather than just sounding different. The next step in dialect is into colloquialisms.

Somerset	English
Anyroad	Anyway
Cack handed	Left handed
Cart	Carnival float
Colley	Blackbird
Crane	Heron

Croopied down	Squat down
Diddikies	Gypsies
Dimpsey	Half light, dusk
Dishy washer	Wagtail
Fair t'middlin	So so
Fuddled	Confused
Gang	Carnival club
Leastways	Anyhow
Look so	So it appears
Minded	Inclined
Nottled	Cold
Reckon	Believe
Ruttles	Peat stacks
Scrumpin'	Stealing apples
Snobbin'	Stealing apples

How appropriate that there should be room in the local dialect for two words meaning stealing apples. No wonder most of the orchards have disappeared!

Vowel sounds, apart from becoming hard, also become prolonged and can become two syllables where one would normally do.

> Last becomes laast
> File becomes Vy-yul
> Dear becomes Dee-yur

The 'a' on the end of a word also attracts an 'r'. Thus 'idea' becomes 'idee-ur'.

Another local trick is to swap the vowel and the consonant in the middle of a word.

> Great becomes gurt
> Wasp becomes wapse

This leads to one theory on the origin of the name of Bridgwater. The 'water' is definitely after Walter of Douai. The bridge however is debatable. Some say it means simply bridge but another theory is that as a borough it was once called Burg, pronounced 'burj', meaning borough, thus the borough of Walter. And that has a natural ring to it as an explanation.

In fact if you listen hard to Bridgwater people pronouncing the name of their own town, you can just hear some of them saying 'Burjwalter'.

The hardening of the consonants turns 's' into 'z' and 'f' into 'v'.

> After becomes adder
> Three becomes dree
> Father becomes vadder
> Forget becomes vorgit
> Forward becomes vord

Other local corruptions change the form of the word.

That	thik
That one	thiky one
That one there	thiky one thur
Yours	yorn
Instead of	sted'a
Himself	'Eezelf
What's on then	Wasson den

It could be argued that any of the above could be heard anywhere in Somerset and I guess that's true. They are just my own observations and experiences. I would argue however that "proper fair weather" is uniquely Bridgwater. Anywhere else it means long sunny days, but not here. At the end of September, the annual St. Matthew's Fair is held and local perception is that it always rains for the fair. True to say that in recent years it hasn't been too bad, but many a year in my life time it's been Wellington boot weather as one treads a weary path through the mud on the Fairfield. Somewhat in keeping with the St. Swithin's tradition, the local belief is that if it rains on the first day of the fair, it will rain for all four. And that's "proper fair weather"!

Well, if you've kept up with the lesson so far, then you should be able to follow the tale below which I found in the Somerset Year Book for 1925 and relates to a stormy night in Bridgwater town not long after the first world war.

Thic Betzy-Jane Affair

A midnight adventure at Bridgwater   Related by Tom Nutty

From little words that I've yeared dropped, I
vancy you mid care
To hear me just tell up the rights o' thic
Betzy-Jane avair -
Then do'ee listen, there's good zouls, vor
mabby if you try
You mid explain a little thing gets auver Zal
an' I.

Well, look-'ee-zee, 'twar like this here, - I 'ant
a got no call
To vix the date exactly, - but twar latter end
o' vall,-
We both went into Burgewater and vixed it
up alright -
That as we shooden a-done 'til late, to sleep
in town thic night-

Zome dear old vrends o' ours that lived down
near the river-zide
Pervailed on we to stop wi' they, - now hear
what did betide.
You know what's like when old vrens meet,
ov news there's zitch a ztock -
How arter zupper, chattin' on, the han's crope
'roun' the clock -

Well that's jist 'bout how 'twar wi' we, time
zlipped by unawares,
The clock did warny loud for twelve avore
we went upstairs.
Mind narry one o' us till then had zlept zo vur
vrom whoam, -
You knaw, in zich perdicaments what vunny
vancies roam.

Zal, thinking o' th' chillern, did a quiet little
weep,
But as we both war tired right out, we soon
valled vast asleep.
But vearvul 'ruptions woked us 'bout th' zmall
hours o' th' night,
That caused our hair to stan' on end an' ztiver
up wi' vright!

It made us trem'le zo by gars, the bed
beginned to zhake.
Whatever 'twar a-gwine on 'twar rough
works, no mistake.
Twar bad as any 'lection row you ever yeared
about, -
Var wuss than Matthus-Vair time when the
zhows be coming out;

Vust I pinched Zal - then Zal pinched I, to
prove that twarna dream,
Then both clinged hold each other tight, too
tarrivied to zcream.
That night war wet, an' dark as pitch, the
wind zo loud did blow,
We on'y yeared by vits an' ztarts what passed
down there below.

But ztartin 'twar we yeared enough to make
our blood urn cold, -
You'd creamy right vrom top to toe if on'y
half war told.
"Whatever can it be?" zays I - "'tis vearvul
work no doubt,"
Vor every now an' then we yeared a 'ooman's
name called out.

Zal took an' jumped to it at once and made a
straightish guess,
Zays she "They'm drunk an' vighting Tom -
zome 'ooman's in a mess."
Twar "Betzy-Jane, hoy! Betzy Jane!" we
yeared 'em zhout an' bawl,
But zim to I that Betzy-Jane didden zome
how yeed their call.

Then all at once it lashed on I - I had it in a
twink, -
Twar zome poor ooman bin zar'd out - an'
zhe the wuss vor drink!
I vancy I catch'd half a word - vrom which -
poor zoul - did zim
Zhe'd more than zhe cood carry well, which
put her out o' trim.

Zhe gied 'em no back-answers, though they
hollered theirzelves hoarse.
Lar, what they did be-call her, too - their
language was so coarse.
But they tell I twar always zo, that vrom her
kirsening day
Zhe never answered as zhe zhould whatever
vokes mid zay.

No doubt zhe warden up to much, but I want
this point clear -
What right had they to zar her zo, an' no one
interveare?
"Hold on her head - now slew her roun' zhe's
gwine too vur" they cried.
"Look out, her nose is in the mud! Zhe's
auver on her zide!"

Then if you'd yeared the vearvul works they
men droved up wi' her
I'm bound you'd zay 'twarn Betzy-Jane, but
they that went too vur.
Ees, when you've yeared their gwines-on
you'll own they zar'd her bad.
Vor twarn to zay, the zpitevul twoads, 'twar
just a lark they had.

D'zim they went an' got a rope about her
waist made vast,
Then zet to haulin' her about - Zal looked at I
aghast.
Thay zim'd to zar her how they liked - I
veared they'd never ztop,
"Let's car' her in agen the wall" - zays one -
"an' then we'll let her drop."

An then another wretch yell'd out - the
viercest o' th' gang -
"Let's make her vast, and lash her Jim, then
let the beggar hang!"
Then in the blustrin' o' th' ztarm we yeard
another zhout -
"Come on here wi' a ztouter rope an' take an'
pay her out."

I gied a groan but cooden budge - the zweat
rolled off in beads -
To think that zo-called Englishmen could do
zich vearvul deeds.

The one who zim'd to take comannd gied
arders plain an' vlat,
To "take an' let the bull-dog come an' vetch
her out o' that."

"Zhe's tough," zays he, "altho zhe's old - but
ztill 'twill never do
"To let her lay like that all night - she'll break
her back in two."
"That's it, ztan back - she's commin' round -
zhe veels the breeze a bit.
"Now zlacken ztays, Bob" - "Lar," zays Zal -
"they've droved her in a vit!"

Then come one more blood-curdlin yell that
blanch'd our cheeks wi' horror -
"Jist zhove her head in th' basin Jim' - there's
lots o' water vor her."
The thic ring-leader chap, agen - he boldly
ups and speaks,
"I guess zhe've had enough to-night to lay her
up vor weeks."

You'd scarcely think zitch things coud be, in
zitch a Christian land'
An' nar a blessed 'ooman near to len' a helpin'
hand.
A vearvul clatter vollered then - but vur as I
made out -
Thic veller at the head o' em zeed vear wi' out
a doubt.

"Oh never mind her zlack," bawls he - 'bove
all the noise an' din,
"As zoon as zhe's come to a bit, we'll take an'
turn her in.
"We've had enough ov her to night -
tomorrow in the dock
"We'll keervully examine her" - that war the
vinal zhock:-

Thic veather broke the camel's back - to
vinish up their zport
They must take the poor old creetur up, an'
lug her into court!
Thinks I, there's more than one can play at
thic geame any rate,
I'll up an' veace the lot o' em 'vore any
magistrate.

Wi' that I stopped up both my ears an' croped aneath the clothes,
An' tried my best - although 'twar in vain - once more to zeek repose.
Vor dozin' off I dreamt I zeed the cruel Rooshun knout
A-weltin' zome poor 'ooman's back - I yeared her cryin' out -

An zo I woked - but mussy me twar wusser than I veared,
Twar Zally war a shriekin' out - an' that war what I yeared.
"Oh Tom" - says zhe, "they've done vor her" an' then zhe yelled aloud -
"I've yeared 'em zay they'd get a board and zee about the zhroud!"

"I'm sure they bin an' murdered her by haulin' her about.
"Tis wuss than laying o' her up, they'm gwine to lay her out!
Wi' that I jumped out in a crack, an' oped the winder wide -
There, in the dimpsy light, I zeed 'em moving 'bout outzide.

"You viends o' darkness," I blared out - I let 'em have it straight.
"You midnight murderers, by you - this poor zoul's met her vate.
"A purty piece o' work indeed - you'd 'let her zwing' you zaid -
"You'll vind the tables tarned, my lads, you'll zome o' ee zwing instead.

"If I'd got 'ee down in Poun' Vield, wi' a 'oss whip in my han',
"I'd pay 'ee out, you mitchin' rogues - I'd make 'ee understand'
"Though bark's a good med'cin - there's no doubt - that every vool admits -
"Still don't quite volly bull-dogs be the proper cure vor vits.

"That I aint a-got my hand on 'ee mid thank your lucky ztars, -
"we'd zee how zome o' you'd bear up - I'd put 'ee 'bout by gars,

"I'd lay thee up - but never vear - jist mark me what I zay.
"I'd pull the rope mysel' but what the law zhall have its way,

"Don't think bist gwine to hush it up - I know jist what I'm 'bout.
"Too much is wrapt up nowadays that ought to be rapped out!"
I zpose I war in a tar'ble tan - I can't tell half I zaid -
Vor zudden zummit went off snap! - an' I war off my head.

- - - - -   - - - - - -   - - - - -

When I vetched 'roun agen I vound my head had bin close shaved,
An' on my vor'head ice war put, an' quite dree days I'd raved.
"O Betzy-Jane" an' "Bull-Dog," too - zo vearvul war my yells -
'Twar works th' world Zal ztopped the voakes from zen'in' me to Wells.

'Twar long time 'vore I got about - but one day by the post,
A newspaper war zent to me, - an' down the bottom most
A little paragraph war marked wi' a gurt black cross in ink,
An' there I read as plain's could be - whatever do 'ee think?

THE SCHOONER BETSY JANE, - We hear that the schooner Betsy Jane, that in the recent gale got stranded in the river, is ready now to sail, having repaired the damages, which after all proved slight, that she incurred in entering port that wild tempestuous night. The owners feel most grateful and their thanks are here conveyed, for the steam tug "Bull-dog's" services and efficient timely aid. We learn that Mr. Nutty, who, our readers are aware, formed an awkward misconception of the Betsy-Jane affair, and whose health has been in consequence precarious of late, is approaching convalescence at a satisfactory rate. We venture to express the hope that this episode may tend, to check the rash impulsiveness of our bucolic friend.

I read it auver more'n once to see I'd got it right,
By no means 'twarn a easy job to understan' it quite,
Zal ztuck there ztarin' all the time as 'ooden as a owl.
I didden quite zee the joke o' it - I'm veared it made me scowl -

Though mabby they newspaper chaps be very knowing birds -
I didden half like bin bully-rag'd in dictionary words.
But zlowly as the truth o' it dawned - it cut me ten times more,
When Zal tarned roun' an' zaid "Oh Tom - what a vool thee bist vor zure."

The Bridgwater Limerick

Although nothing to do with dialect, I found this limerick and had to put it somewhere.

There once was a girl from Bridgwater
Who remembered most things that were taught her
And she didn't forget,
When her young man she met
To remind him how long he had sought her.

The Town Bridge with the former YMCA building

Chronological history

682	Centwine, king of West Saxons, pushes Britons beyond the Parrett.
800	Saxon chronicles indicate definite presence of Bridgwater as Bruggie.
878	Danes invade at Combwich
1080	Domesday book shows Bridgwater as 5 hides being 5 extended families.
1200	Bridgwater Borough incorporated.
1200-1210	Castle built
1204	King John visits
1205	Grant of free market
1212	William Briwer serves with the King.
1216	St. John's hospital founded.
1220	Earliest reference to St. Mary's church.
1227	William Brewer died. Castle passed to Broase family.
1230	Grey Friars priory founded
1231	Death of William Brewer, senior.
1236	Death of William Brewer, junior.
1246	Michael of Bridgwater appointed Sacrist of Newenham Abbey.
1250	Henry lll visited the town.
1276	Great earthquake at Bridgwater
1278	Timber granted from North Petherton forest for Franciscan Friary.
1280	Complaint from people of Langport that the Lord of Aller was stopping free passage of river traffic.
1298	Geoffrey de Monk first recorded master of hospital of St. John's. Earliest record of Bridgwater school.
1330	Influx of Flemings
1346	Town supplied vessel and 15 marines to Edward lll's fleet to Calais
1348	Black Death Earliest record of Bridgwater as a port but linked to Bristol.
1367	Spire added to St. Mary's church
1381	Religious unrest; disturbances in town during Watt Tyler's rebellion. St. John's hospital attacked. Two rioters heads 'spiked' on town bridge.
1402	Bridgwater declared a port in its own right, no ties to Bristol.
1424	Castle passes to Earl of Pembroke by marriage of Anne Mortimer
1450	Death of John Sydenham, last of local line. Sydenham Manor passed into Cave family
1460	Bridgwater manor possessed by crown.
1463	St. John's hospital brethren found guilty of 'misbehaviour' and punished in stocks.

1464	Humphrey Stafford, Earl of Devon, appointed constable of castle.	**1531**	Sir John Popham, Chief Justice of England, born at Huntworth.
1468	Edward IV substituted a mayor and two bailiffs for a reeve.	**1535**	Riots, four ringleaders executed.
1469	Humphrey Stafford beheaded in Castle. John Kendall elected as first mayor of Bridgwater.	**1536**	St. John's and Grey Friars closed under Suppression of Monasteries Act. Four men executed in town after uprising in Taunton.
1486	Lord Daubenny married Lady Arundel	**1538**	John Leland, chronicler of English towns, visits Bridgwater. Henry Daubenny made Earl of Bridgwater.
1487	Henry VII granted charter making town a county.		
1488	Langport slipway built.	**1539**	St. Giles hospital closed. Quarter of body of Richard Whiting, Abbot of Glastonbury, displayed in Bridgwater.
1500	Sydenham Manor built. Approximate date of Blake's house being built.		
1503	Lord Daubenny made constable of castle.	**1546**	Robert Parsons, reputed instigator of Gunpowder Plot born at Nether Stowey. St. John's hospital dissolved. Residents request a free grammar school.
1507	Death of Lord Daubney.		
1520	Jane Seymour, third wife of Henry VIII, reputedly born at Durleigh.	**1561**	Bridgwater Free Grammar School, Castle Street, founded by Queen Elizabeth.

Binford Place and the Langport Slipway

1578   The 'Emanuel' of Bridgwater joined Frobisher's voyage to discover the North West passage.

1583   "Valiant Soldier" public house believed to have been built..

1586   Charter granted for Bridgwater Fair. Richard Percival of Sydenham Manor translates early Armada plans for Queen Elizabeth.

1588   First news of Armada reaches England by Humphrey Blake's ships arriving at Bridgwater on July 21st. Bridgwater's ship the 'William' sailed to join the fleet against the Spanish.

1598   Admiral Blake born.

1600   Baptist Chapel founded.

1605   Gunpowder plot, origin of Bridgwater Carnival.

1607   Heavy flooding from broken sea wall at Burnham causes extensive flooding right in to Bridgwater and beyond. Numerous deaths.

1613   James l grants royal charter for regular fair and confirms all previous charters.

1617   John Egeston, Viscount Brackley, created Earl of Bridgwater.

1620   Sir Francis Kingsmill buried at Bridgwater. His granddaughter married Samuel Pepys.

1625   The plague hits Bridgwater and river traffic brought to a standstill.

1626   Charles l granted manor and castle to Sir William and George Whitmore.

1638   Blake returns on death of his mother.

1640   Blake enters Parliament.

1643   Royalists capture Bridgwater. 17 soldiers buried in the town. Blake at siege of Bristol.

1644	Blake at siege of Lyme. Blake holds Taunton.	1685	Monmouth Rebellion. June 21st, Monmouth arrives in Bridgwater, crowned by mayor. July 2nd, Monmouth returns. July 6th, Battle of Sedgemoor. July 15th, Monmouth executed. Bloody Assizes.
1645	July 20-22, Cromwell and Fairfax take town and castle. Blake captures Dunster castle. Blake becomes MP again for town.		
1646	Castle demolished..	1686	King James visits Bridgwater. Bridgewater, New Jersey, started.
1648	Blake takes up appointment as General-at-Sea. Sir Thomas Wroth, Bridgwater M.P., moved the impeachment of Charles 1 but refuses to act as judge.	1688	New Unitarian Chapel built (later replaced in 1788).
		1692	Baptists open meeting house, replaced in 1835.
1649	Duke of Monmouth born. Bridgewater, Massachusetts, started.	1694	William Penn holds a Quaker meeting in the town.
1649-72	Trade tokens issued locally.	1716	Earliest record of squibbing although it could go back much further than this. Record refers to John Taylor blowing up his family making squibs.
1652	Blake defeats Tromp.		
1653	Blake defeats Tromp again. Blake seriously wounded.		
1654	Blake becomes involved in war with Spain.	1717	St. Mary Street riot.
		1720	"The Lions" built on West Quay
1656	Bridgewater, Massachusetts, incorporated.	1720-23	Castle Street built.
1657	Blake's final battle at Santa Cruz. August 7th, Blake's death.	1722	Friends Meeting House built in Friarn Street. Enlarged in 1801.
		1723	Dr. Morgan's school founded.
1671	Admiralty approve Bridgwater for ship building.	1725	Closure of Duke of Chandos soap works. George Bubb Doddington donates fire engine to the town. Earliest known record.
1673	John Oldmixon, historian, born in Bridgwater.		
1680	Monmouth's first visit to West Country.	1726	Glass kiln built by Duke of Chandos.
1683	Pulpit and seats from Unitarian Chapel burnt on the Cornhill by Lord Stawell and his militia, putting 'fanatics' under house arrest.	1730	Jack White sentenced to death at Bridgwater Assizes for the murder of Robert Sutton. Bridgwater Turnpike Trust founded.

1733 Failure of Duke of Chandos glass kiln.	**1787-1817** Trade tokens return.
1739 Reverend George Whitefield hosed by fire brigade whilst preaching provocative sermon.	**1788** Current Unitarian chapel constructed. Bridgewater, New Hampshire, incorporated.
1741 Parliamentary election scandal.	**1789** John Walford sentenced in Bridgwater to death by hanging (Walford's Gibbet).
1744 Town's pillory and stocks moved from High Street to the Cornhill.	
1746 John Wesley's first visit to town. Various visits until 1769.	**1794** Bridgwater Volunteer Infantry formed.
1749 Bridgewater, New Jersey, established. Bridgewater, Virginia, settled.	**1797** First iron bridge over river. Samuel Taylor Coleridge preaches in Bridgwater (also in 1798).
1761 Bridgewater, Vermont incorporated.	**1800** Approximate date of origin of Bridgewater, Nova Scotia.
1766 First known record of Bridgwater built ship, "Nancy", a brigantine. Start of Bridgewater, New Hampshire.	**1801** Quaker's meeting house built.
	1803 Bridgewater, Connecticut, started. Last Duke of Bridgwater died - Earldom becomes extinct.
1769 Old Pig Cross (St. Anthony's) at Penel Orlieu demolished and replaced with the new Pig Cross (St. Mary's).	**1807** Work starts on King Square.
1773 John Symons & Co. established.	**1809** Sarah Crocker sentenced to death at Bridgwater Assizes for stealing Sacramental Plate from Butcombe church.
1776 Bridgewater, New York State, founded.	
1777 Stars and stripes flown for first time over Bridgewater, New Jersey	**1810** Unsuccessful attempt to launch a scheme to build a canal from Combwich to Bridgwater.
1782 Town's pillory and stocks return to original High Street position.	**1811** Bridgwater's first paper, The Taunton and Bridgwater Journal, first published. (Closed in 1816.) Henry Prince, founder of the Abode of Love, born at Bath.
1783 "Descent from the Cross" donated to St. Mary's church.	
1785 Bridgwater first to petition Parliament for abolition of slavery. (Success came in 1807). John Clark born, inventor of "MacKintosh" technique.	**1813** St. Mary's church spire severely damaged in thunderstorm. Bridgwater Infirmary opened in Back Street (now Clare Street).

1815 St. Mary's spire repaired.	**1826** Cornhill dome erected.

1815   St. Mary's spire repaired.

1816   Angel Crescent built.
Wesleyan Chapel in King Street built.
It was later to close in 1980.

1820   Scheme put to Parliament for
Bridgwater to Taunton Canal.
Bridgwater Infirmary moved to
Salmon Parade.
Bath Brick manufacture started.

1821   Birth of George Williams.

1822   All Saints Church opened.

1822-23   Bristol Road constructed
avoiding Puriton Hill.

1823   Bath Brick patented
York Buildings built.

1825   Bridgwater and Somerset Herald first
published. (Closed 1831.)
Royal Clarence Hotel built.
British School opened in Mount
Street. (Probably closed in 1853.)

1826   Cornhill dome erected.
Bridgwater Herald first published.

1827   Canal opened from Taunton Firepool
to Huntworth
Old High Cross, Cornhill demolished.

1829   Russell Place built.

1830   National Infants School opened near
Angel Crescent.

1831   The Alfred, London Weekly Journal
and Bridgwater and Somerset General
Advertiser first published. (Closed in
1833)
Approximate date Bridgewater,
Tasmania founded.
Mr. Bennett's shop premises in St.
Mary's Street wrecked by a
gunpowder explosion.
Sailing ships 'Friends' and
'Euphrosyne' departed Bridgwater
with 360 emigrants bound for Canada.
Launching of the 'Britannia'.

1832   Riot Act read after disturbances at
general election.
Cholera outbreak.

1834 Bridgwater Borough Police force formed.
Small pox outbreak, 40 deaths.
Gas works established in Old Taunton Road.

1835 Bridgewater Centre, Ohio, started.

1836 George Williams, founder of YMCA, moves to Bridgwater.

1837 Royal assent granted for canal to be extended to Bridgwater.
Mariners Chapel erected and Baptist Chapel rebuilt.
Corrupt general election voting proven.

1838 Northgate Workhouse established.
Ox roast takes place on frozen river.

1839 Holy Trinity church built.

1840 Bridgewater, South Australia founded.

1841 Canal completed to Bridgwater.
Docks opened.
Bristol and Exeter railway arrives.
Serious outbreak of Cholera.

1842 Bristol and Exeter Railway extended to Taunton.
Albert Street built.

1844 'Bertha' built, a steam dredger used in the docks now housed in Exeter Maritime Museum.

1845 Borough given responsibility for navigation along river.
Horse tramway installed from railway station to riverside wharf.
St. John's Church opened.
St. John's School erected.

1846 Bridgwater Times first published (closed 1861).
St. John's parish created.
Riot Act read at White Hart, Eastover when Tories and Whigs attacked one another with skittle balls and pins.
St. Mary's School, Mount Street, erected.
Roman Catholic church opened in Gordon Terrace.

1849 Railway carriage works opened at Colley Lane.

1850 YMCA established in Bridgwater.

1851 Castle House built.
Terraced houses erected at Bristol Road, Bath Road and Monmouth Street.

1852 The 800 ton clipper built barque 'Pathfinder' launched in Bridgwater.
Immediately sails to New York with cargo of emigrants.

1853 Local wages inflation in wake of high rate of emigration.
John Clark, inventor, died.

1854 Bridgwater Horse races revived.

1856 Bridgewater Conn. incorporated.

1857 St. Matthew's fair extended to three days.
Russian captured cannon presented to the town (resided at Town Bridge until 1886).
Bridgwater Mercury first published.
190 ton sailing ship 'Admiral Blake' launched.

1858 Bridgewater, Maine incorporated
Dates of chartered fairs moved by Act of Parliament.

1859 160 lb sturgeon caught in river.

1860 Approximate date Bridgewater, Victoria founded.
Wesleyan Chapel, King Street, rebuilt.
Town's first telephone tried in Eastover.
Bridgwater School of Art opened in George Street.

1861 Peak year for river and dock traffic.
Bridgwater Standard first published. (Closed in 1870.)
Turkish baths opened in York Buildings.

1864 400 ton barque, 'The Cesarea', launched from John Gough's yard.
Telegraph office opens on West Quay.

1865 First mention of Bridgwater troop of West Somerset Yeomanry.
Corrupt election practices proven in general election.
Town Hall opens.

1866 Cholera outbreak caused by contaminated wells.

1868 More corrupt election practices.
Plymouth Brethren move to Friarn Street.

1869 Bridgwater disenfranchised.
Clock added to St. Mary's church.
Possibly the last year of horse fair in Eastover.
Devonshire Street built.

1870 Black Bridge opened (officially March 1871).
Eastover school erected, enlarged in 1894 and 1897.
Bridgwater Turnpike Trust abolished.

1871 Bridgwater Gazette, Somerset and Devon Chronicle and West of England Advertiser first published (became Bridgwater Independent in 1885).

1872 Wembdon School officially opens.

1873 Eastover School opens.

1875 Disastrous flooding effects the whole of Sedgemoor when ten foot bore sweeps up the river.
Unsuccessful attempt to introduce Somerset and Dorset railway.
Police station moves from Fore Street to High Street.
Bridgwater Rugby Club founded.
Corn Exchange opens.

1876 Great Western take over Bristol and Exeter Railway.

1877 George Parker publishes 'Ancient History of Bridgwater'.

1879 Ashford Reservoir opens.

1880 Salvation Army comes to Bridgwater.
Fire hoses cut in unsuccessful attempt to put out Cornhill bonfire.
Approximate date of Bridgewater, South Dakota.
Albert Street school erected.
Edward Street built.

1881 First officially organised carnival (previously spontaneous event).
Bridgwater Bicycle Club formed.
Bonfire lit on frozen river.

1882 Somerset Union of Rugby Football founded in Bridgwater.
All Saint's Church built in Westonzoyland Road.
St. Joseph's church built, Binford Place.

1883 Present town bridge opened.
Mercury office fire.
First carnival concerts.

1884 General Booth, founder of Salvation Army, visits the town.

1885   Bridgwater Independent first published. (Closed in 1933.)
Bridgwater Guardian published.
Bridgewater, Iowa, founded
Bridgwater vote in general election (first time since disenfranchisement).
Bridgwater Dramatic Society formed.

1886   Severn Tunnel opened, start of decline in river and dock traffic.
Unsuccessful 8 week brickyard strike.
Russian cannon re-sited at Bristol Road and Bath Road junction.

1887   George Williams Memorial Hall built.

1888   Work started on Somerset and Dorset Railway link by Bridgwater Railway Company.
School of Art opened in Blake Street.

1890   Somerset and Dorset railway arrives.
600 brickyard workers on strike.

1891   The Albion Rugby Club founded.
Art and Technical College established in Blake Street.

1893   61 tramps admitted to Workhouse in one week.

1895   River Parrett frozen, ox roast on river.

1896   Total brickyard strike, troops brought in and riot act read to strikers.

1897   Roseberry Avenue built.

1898   Blake Gardens purchased for town.

1899   Bridgewater, Nova Scotia, founded.

1900   Blake statue unveiled.

1902   Bridgwater Echo first published. (Closed 1904.)

1903   Board of Trade grants licence for supply of electricity to the town.
St. Mary's parish hall opens in King's Square.
Bridgwater Motor Company and Bridgwater Steam Laundry opens.

1904   Somerset Bridge completed.
General Booth visits the town.
Electricity introduced.

Tidal bore at Barham's Brickyard

1905	Public library opens.
1906	New Clare Street fire station opens. Three second earthquake shakes the town. Starkey, Knight and Ford open brewery in town after closing one at North Petherton. Cranleigh Gardens built.
1907	"Irene", last ship to be built in Bridgwater. Last commercial barge runs on canal.
1908	Bandstand opens in Blake Gardens.
1909	Police raid illegal fireworks factory. First taxi service launched by Bridgwater Motor Company.
1911	Police station moves from High Street to Northgate. Monmouth Street Methodist church built.
1912	Masonic Lodge opens near police station. Bijou Theatre opens in St. Mary's Street.
1913	Electric lights introduced to carnival procession. Unsuccessful attempts by police to ban carnival activities.
1916	Palace Theatre opens.
1918	Quantock Jam factory opens. First World War ends, Bridgwater had lost 308 men.
1919	St. Matthew's Fair extended to four days.
1920	Old Morganians RFC formed.
1921	Tarred road surface trials

between Bridgwater and North Petherton

1922	Bridgwater Carnival recorded on film.
1924	Quantock Road constructed. Last bonfire on Cornhill. Blake's house bought for museum. War memorial unveiled.
1925	TarMacadam introduced. Bijou Theatre reopens.
1926	Blake Museum opens to the public. Bridgwater Races revived at Durleigh (survives only three years).
1927	First council houses built on Newtown Estate.
1928	'S.S Mauren' capsizes entering dock.

1910 General Election - declaration of poll

1929   Arcade cinema opens in Eastover.

1930   Dr. Morgan's Grammar School moves to Durleigh Road from Mount Street.

1934   Last sailing craft uses Bridgwater quaysides.

1935   Petrol driven fire engine introduced. Cattle market re-sited in Bath Road

1936   Odeon cinema opens.

1937   Westover School opens. (Closed in 1973 when premises were taken over by Friarn School.)

1938   Typhoid outbreak. British Cellophane plant opens. Durleigh Reservoir opens.

1939   Vernon Bartlett, Independent M.P., elected. Severely criticised by German press for anti-Hitler stance. War breaks out. Evacuees arrive at Great Western Station. Bridgwater men lost with sinking of HMS Courageous and on HMS Exeter. Leffman's brassiere factory opens.

1940   Wembdon bombed. Bridgwater bombed, seven killed in Old Taunton Road. Fireman fighting blazes machine gunned. Home Guard set up. Palace Theatre reopens to entertain troops.

1941   High explosive mines land on Meads.

1943   American G.I.'s arrive. Chandos glass kiln demolished.

1945   Crowds celebrate end of war on the Cornhill

1946   Nation's first Art Centre founded in Castle Street, Bridgwater.

1947   Last recorded commercial use by shipping of Bridgwater quaysides. C. & J. Clark open shoe factory.

Salmon Parade and the Hospital

210

1948 Last horse drawn float in carnival procession.
Crypton Equipment factory opens.

1951 Bonded Fibre Fabrics opens.

1952 Bridgwater branch of the Somerset and Dorset railway closes to passenger traffic.
Hamp and Sydenham infant and junior schools opens.

1953 Coronation street parties.

1954 Somerset and Dorset railway closes to goods traffic.

1956 Hamp Secondary Modern School opens (Changes to 'Blake' in 1957.)
Elmwood School opens.

1957 Blake Bridge opened for the last time.

1960 Broadway swimming lido opens.
St. Francis church opens.

1961 Severe water shortages, supplies switched off during daytime.

Work starts on Mariners Chapel in Moorland Road (now the Salvation Army church premises).

1962 Sydenham Secondary School opens.

1964 Fire Brigade moves to Colley Lane.
Traffic wardens arrive.
Starkey, Knight and Ford's Northgate brewery closes.
Broadway link road between Taunton Road and North Street opens.

1965 Barham Brother's last brick kiln firing.

1966 Somerset Inland Waterways Society formed with purpose of returning canal to navigable waterway.
Chilton Trinity Secondary Modern School opens.

1969 Last coal delivery to docks.
Disappearance and presumed death of Donald Crowhurst.
Bower infant school opens.

1970 Tom King elected M.P. for first time.
18 year olds able to vote in the U. K.

A view along West Quay towards the Town Bridge

High Street

1971   Docks officially closes.
        Penrose School opens.

1972   Bower Junior school opens.

1973   Local section of M5 opens.
        Dr. Morgan's Grammar School for
        Boys changes to Haygrove
        Comprehensive.

1974   Formal end of Borough of Bridgwater
        with local government reorganisation.

Blake Gardens with ornamental arch

IN BLAKE GARDENS. BRIDGEWATER.

Bridgwater Worthies

Dr. Alleyne John Allen 1660 - 1741

A physician at Bridgwater who wrote numerous medical and scientific works. These were translated into French and German and published in 4 different countries.

Lieutenant Colonel Jeffreys Allen

Commandant of Bridgwater's Volunteer Infantry around 1807.

Henry Arundel, 1st Earl of Bridgwater (died 1548)

Made the first Earl of Bridgwater in 1538. Flamboyant courtier who spent so heavily he had to sell most of his properties to pay for his debts. He died without offspring, the title thus became extinct. His wife, the Countess of Bridgwater died 1553.

In South Petherton church there is a tomb ascribed to the Earl of Bridgwater. It lies in a transept and is made of Sienna marble with effigies in brass of a gentleman and lady. At there feet is the inscription "Sis tertis ete qd nan jacet lopis iste, Corpus ut onetar ... ".

Roger of Arundel

First Norman holder of Sydenham Manor around 1086.

George Aubrey

Publisher of Bridgwater's first newspaper, The Bridgwater and Somerset Herald in 1825.

Robert of Bampton

Successor to Walter de Douai in lordship of Bridgwater during the late 11th and early 12th centuries.

Jim Barrington

Founder of local solicitors firm. Bridgwater and Albion rugby player who gained international honours between the wars.

Vernon Bartlett

Independent M.P. for Bridgwater, 1938-50, who gained national recognition for his outspoken attitude towards the peace deal between Hitler and Chamberlain.

Robert Blake 1599 - 1657

General-at-Sea, perhaps England's finest. Son of Humphrey and Sarah.

Captain Blood

Fictitious character of Rafael Sabatini supposed to have lived at Sydenham Manor during the Monmouth Rebellion of 1685.

John Board 1802 - 1861

Mayor and brickyard owner.

John Bowen

Philanthropist and critic of Bridgwater's workhouse around 1834.

John, Marquis of Brackley, Duke of Bridgwater

Second Duke of Bridgwater. Title passed to his brother Francis on his death in 1747.

Captain George Lewis Brown, RN.

The man responsible for bringing home Nelson's body. He was a close friend of Nelson and served with him at the Battle of Trafalgar. It was his duty to hoist the signal which should have read "Nelson Expects". However an apparent lack of flags led George Brown to hoist the now well known message "England Expects". Captain Brown's portrait and that of his mother can be found in the Presbyterian Chapel in Dampiet Street along with a commemorative plaque.

James Brydges, Duke of Chandos (died 1744)

Creator of Georgian Castle Street and Chandos Glass Cone.

William Briwer or Brewer (died 1226)

Lord of Bridgwater at time of King John, responsible for Bridgwater Castle and free borough status.

William Briwer (died 1233)

Son of William Briwer above, responsible for foundation of Grey Friars in Friarn Street.

Graecia Broase

13th century daughter of the younger William Briwer and inheritor of Castle.

John Browne

19th century brickyard owner and patentee of the Bath Brick.

John Bull 1563 - 1628

Resident of Sydenham Manor, composer of the National Anthem.

Reverend J. M. Capes

Oxford gentleman responsible for the funding and building of St. John's Church in 1845.

Bampfylde Moore Carew 1693 - 1770

Notorious 'King of the Gypsies.'

Andrew Carnegie

Not strictly a Bridgwater worthy but the man whose endowment in 1905 financed the building of the Bridgwater Free Library in Dampiet Street.

Roger Cave

Inheritor in 1450 of Sydenham Manor by marriage to Joan Sydenham.

Duke of Chandos 1673 - 1744

Builder of Castle Street and the Chandos Glass Kiln.

Cheping

Saxon Lord of Sydenham Manor before Norman Conquest.

John Clark 1785 - 1853

Inventor of Eureka machine to make Latin sentences in perfect iambic pentameter and patentee of waterproofing later exploited by MacKintosh.

Samuel Clark

Founder of Bridgewater, Connecticut in 1722.

'Big' Clarke

Founder of Bridgewater, Victoria in 1860.

Samuel Taylor Coleridge 1722 - 1834

Poet. Preached in many local churches, in particular the Unitarian Chapel in Dampiet Street. An occasional guest of John Chubb.

Roger of Courcelle

11th century Lord of various manors around Bridgwater after Norman Conquest.

Daniel Coxe

Founder, in 1687, of Bridgewater, New Jersey.

B. Crompton-Wood

Conservative M.P. 1924-29

R. P. Croom-Johnson

Conservative M.P. 1929-38

Donald Crowhurst 1932 - 1969

Inventor and yachtsman at centre of 'Round the World Yacht Race' scandal.

Lord Giles Daubney (died 1508)

Constable of Bridgwater Castle

Bob Dibble

Perhaps the finest rugby player Somerset has ever produced gaining 19 international caps and the captaincy of the national side around 1901.

George Bubb Doddington 1691 - 1762

MP for Bridgwater, famous for his corrupt ways. Described himself as 'sore grieved by having to comply with the low habits of those venal wretches of Bridgwater'.

Walter of Douai, also known as Walscin (died 1107)

The Norman lord from who Bridgwater takes part of its name.

J. T. Dunsford

Editor of Bridgwater Mercury who lost family in tragic newspaper office fire of 1883.

Corporation Pew, St. Mary's Church

**John Egerton, Baron of Ellesmere,
Viscount Brackley, 1st Earl of Bridgwater
(died 1649)**

The title of Earl of Bridgwater had become extinct. James 1 resurrected the title on May 27, 1617.

John Egerton (died 1686)

2nd Earl of Bridgwater, his son John became the 3rd Earl. His son Scroop was elevated to Duke of Bridgwater.

Scroop Egerton, Duke of Bridgwater (died 1727)

1st Duke of Bridgwater succeeded by John Marquis of Brackley.

R. C. Else

Owner of Blake Gardens prior to purchase in 1898 by corporation.

Thomas Fairfax

General in Cromwell's Parliamentarian Army, leader of forces at siege of Bridgwater Castle in 1645.

T. E. Francis

Bridgwater and Albion rugby player who gained international honours between the wars.

Richard Godfrey

Local man who led Monmouth across moors to battlefield in 1685.

Francis Joseph Grimshaw 1901 - 1965

Roman Catholic Archbishop of Birmingham.

Roger Hoar

One time Monmouth rebel who escaped the gallows in 1685 to later become Mayor of Bridgwater.

Benjamin Holloway

Architect of Castle Street around 1720.

Captain Hucker

Man who fired shot giving away rebel position at Battle of Sedgemoor.

Judge Jeffreys

Judge at trial of Monmouth's rebels, notorious for his ruthlessness and high rate of executions.

King John

Frequent visitor to Bridgwater Castle in early 13th century.

John Kendall

First Mayor of Bridgwater in 1469. Served in that position on at least five occasions.

Tom King

Conservative M.P. 1970 and still holding that position at the time of writing having held numerous government posts including Secretary of State for Northern Ireland.

Alexander William Kinglake 1809 - 1891

Historian of Crimean War and MP for Bridgwater.

Colonel Percy Kirke 1646 - 1691

Fought under the Duke of Monmouth in 1683 and then came to Bridgwater after the Monmouth Rebellion to 'mop up' the rebels. Notorious for his ruthlessness.

C. Knowles

Builder of Bridgwater Town Hall in 1865.

George Laughton 1736 - 1800

Published the History of Ancient Egypt before most of it had been discovered.

John Leland

Chronicler of English towns who left a most useful description of Bridgwater on his 1538 visit.

Thomas Maddicks

Engineer responsible for construction of Bridgwater to Taunton canal, 1837.

Major General Massey

One of the leaders of Parliamentarian forces at siege of Bridgwater Castle, 1645.

Merleswain

11th century Saxon overlord, owner of Bridgwater before Norman conquest.

John Morgan (died 1723)

Founder of Bridgwater Grammar School for Boys.

Thomas Morgan (died 1743)

A doctor who wrote several volumes on moral philosophy and physico-theology.

W. E. Morse

Liberal M.P. 1923-24

John Oldmixon 1673 - 1742

Poet, historian and Collector of Customs. Once described Bridgwater as 'life not worth living'.

George Parker

Author of 'Ancient History of Bridgwater' published in 1877.

Robert Parsons 1575 - 1610

Jesuit priest of Nether Stowey believed to be the instigator of the Gunpowder Plot.

Richard Percival 1550 - 1620

Resident of Sydenham Manor. Author of the first Spanish-English dictionary. Translated the Armada plans for Queen Elizabeth, granted the Duchy of Lancaster.

Henry Phillpotts 1778 - 1869

Became the Bishop of Exeter.

Andrew Plimer 1763 - 1837

Painter of miniatures.

Henry W. Pollard

Holder of record number of mayoralties, six in total. Responsible for reading the Riot Act to striking brickyard workers in 1896.

F. W. Pomeroy

Creator of Admiral Blake's statue, erected in 1900.

Colonel Edward Popham 1610 - 1651

General-at-Sea and a Bridgwater man who served alongside Blake.

Sir John Popham

Benefactor of St. John's Hospital in 1330, resident of Huntworth.

Reverend Arthur H Powell

Historian of Bridgwater around 1908.

Lord Anne Poulett 1711 - 1783 or later

MP for Bridgwater, Knight of the Garter, donor of the Descent from the Cross in St. Mary's church.

Vere Poulett

One of three parliamentary candidates involved in at least one corrupt election, 1741.

R. E. Prescott

Bridgwater and Albion player between the wars who gained international honours.

Reverend Henry Prince (died 1899)

Founder in 1846 of religious sect at the Agapemone, or Abode of Love.

John Pynel or Pagnel

14th century Bridgwater property owner from whose name Penel Orlieu partly derives.

William Radford

Whilst not the founder, responsible for giving Bridgewater, South Australia its name in 1855.

Sir Robert A. Sanders

Conservative M.P. 1910-23

Jane Seymour

Wife of Henry Vlll, reputed to have been born at West Bower Manor.

Reverend John Hugh Smyth-Pigott (died 1927)

Successor to Henry Prince as leader of Agapemonites.

John Somer or Sumner

Franciscan monk at Bridgwater in 1380 who wrote a calendar with astronomical tables for Joan, Princess of Wales, wife of the Black Prince.

Lord Humphrey Stafford 1439 - 1469

The Earl of Devon, appointed Constable of Bridgwater Castle in 1464 where he was beheaded on August 17, 1469.

Mary Stanley

The lady whose name was immortalised with the Mary Stanley nursing home in Castle Street which functioned as Bridgwater's nursing home from 1920 to 1988. Subsequent to its closure, the maternity wing in Bridgwater hospital took her name. Mary Stanley was a contemporary of Florence Nightingale and served with her in the Crimea. The diaries of Florence Nightingale indicate a strong dislike of Mary Stanley. Florence Nightingale trained nurses in England and took them to the Crimea. Mary Stanley took trained nuns.

There appears to have been a clash of personalities or professional conflict. Florence had a very low opinion of Mary who perhaps was a threat in terms of stealing Florence Nightingale's thunder. On Mary Stanley's return to England, she set about opening the nursing home in Bridgwater.

John Sydenham (died 1450)

Last member of Sydenham family to hold Sydenham Manor.

Robert of Sydenham

12th century son of Roger of Arundel, Lord of Sydenham Manor. First member of Sydenham family to carry the name.

John Taylor (died 1716)

First recorded death caused by explosion whilst manufacturing carnival squibs.

Jonathan Toogood 1783 - 1870

Founder of Bridgwater Infirmary.

George Trevor 1809 - 1888

Friend of Benjamin D'Isreali. Well known author and writer of the "Catholic Doctrine of the Holy Eucharist". Son of a Bridgwater Customs Officer.

Sir Thomas Trivett

Responsible for completion of three arched stone bridge crossing River Parrett in the 13th century.

Lt. Colonel C. K. K. Tynte

Commander of Bridgwater troop of West Somerset Yeomanry in 1868.

John Walford (died 1789)

Charcoal burner from Nether Stowey, condemned to death in Bridgwater for murdering his wife.

John Wesley

Methodist leader and frequent preacher at Bridgwater Baptist Church.

Henry Westropp

Central figure in corrupt voting practices in 1868 which lead to Bridgwater's electorate losing their entitlement to vote through disenfranchisement.

Reverend George Whitefield

Extrovert Non-Conformist preacher who, in 1739, was hosed down by local fire brigade for provocative content of sermon.

George Williams 1821 - 1905

Founder of the YMCA movement who started his career in Bridgwater.

Sir Gerald Wills

Conservative M.P. 1950-70

W. A. Woodley

Instigator in 1857 of Bridgwater's oldest surviving newspaper, the Bridgwater Mercury.

Sir Charles Wyndham

One of the parliamentary candidates guilty of corrupt voting practices in 1741.

Mrs. Christabella Wyndham

Wife of Colonel Wyndham who came close to killing Cromwell prior to siege of Bridgwater Castle in 1645.

Colonel Edward Wyndham

Governor of Bridgwater Castle at time of siege and its fall.

Works of reference

The ancient borough of Bridgwater	Rev. Arthur H. Powell	1898
The ancient history of Bridgwater	George Parker	1877
A Bicentennial History of Bridgewater, New Hampshire	Thomas S. Curren	1988
Bridgwater Alfred		1831-33
Bridgwater and Albion RFC centenary year book		1975
Bridgwater and Somerset Herald		1831
Bridgwater Borough Archives 1200-1400	Thomas Bruce Dilks	1933
Bridgwater Borough Archives 1468-85	Dunning and Tremlett	1971
Bridgwater brick and tile industry	Catherine Wells	1984
The Bridgwater brickyard strike of 1896	Brian Smedley	1986
Bridgwater docks and the River Parrett	Brian J. Murless	1983
The Bridgwater election inquiry - Report of the Commissioners		1794
Bridgwater General Hospital		1970
Bridgwater in the latter days	Rev. Arthur H. Powell	1908
Bridgwater Independent		1907-28
Bridgwater industries past and present	Edmund Porter	1970
Bridgwater Mercury		1857-1992
The Bridgwater Railway	J. D. Harrison	1990
Bridgwater Railways	Sydenham Junior School	
Bridgwater Standard		1861-70
Bridgwater Times		1846-61
The Bristol Channel	Brian Waters	1955
The Charles Tite collection of Somerset books	Somerset Arch. & N. H. Soc.	
A chronological history of Somerset	W. G. Willis Watson	1925
Civil War and Interregnum	David Underwood	1973
County topographies	E. R. Kelly	1875
A description of England and Wales	Unknown	1750
Education in the West of England 1066 - 1548	Nicholas Orme	1976
General Directory for the County of Somerset	Somerset County Gazette	1840
General-At-Sea, Robert Blake	Michael Baumber	1989
The Great Revolt of 1381	Charles Oman	1969

Historic towns in Somerset	Michael Aston, Roger Leech	1977
The history and antiquities of Somersetshire	Rev. W. Phelps	1839
A history of Bridgwater	Sydney G. Jarman	1889
The history of part of West Somerset	C. E. H. Chadwych Healey	1901
The history of Somerset Yeomanry, volunteer and territorial units	W. G. Fisher	1924
History of the Sydenham family	Dr. G. F. Sydenham	1928
Kelly's directory of Somerset	Kelly's	1861-1910
Mixed moments	Heal	Unknown
The parish church and town of Bridgwater	Unknown	
Pilgrims in old Bridgwater	Thomas Bruce Dilks	1920
Place names of Somerset	James D. Hill	1914
Reverend Prince and his Abode of Love	Charles Mander	1976
River Parrett valley study	Bridgwater geography group	
Rough Passage	Commander R. D. Graham	1936
The Saxon conquest of Somerset	Daniel James Pring	1933
The Saxon conquest of Somerset and Devon	H. M. Porter	1967
Somerset Area review committee for non-accidental injury to children	Somerset County Council	1977
Somerset Archaeological Society annual reports		
Somerset harbours	Grahame Farr	1954
Somerset medieval wills	F. W. Weaver	1983
Somerset parishes	Arthur L. Humphries	1905
Somerset Roads - The legacy of the turnpikes	J. B. Bentley & B. J. Murless	1985
Somerset Worthies	Unknown	Unknown
The Somerset Year Book		1925
The Somerset Years	Florence Chuk	1987
The Statistics and Gazeteer of New Hampshire	Alonzo J. Fogg	1875
The story of Bridgwater Parish Church	Thomas Bruce Dilks	
The strange voyage of Donald Crowhurst	N. Tomalin and R. Hall	1970
The Victoria History of the County of Somerset		1969
War and peace in West Somerset 1620 - 1670	Douglas Stevens	

Index

Index

Index

Index

Index

Index

Index

Index

Index

Acknowledgements

Jeri C. Adams	Bryan Chamber of Commerce, Ohio
Denise Bradley	Town Clerk, Bridgewater, New York State
Norma Brownell	Town Clerk, Bridgewater, Vermont
C. A. Buchanan	For information on the Poor Laws and Somerset Workhouses
Phyllis Clements	Bridgewater Historical Society, New Hampshire, USA
Courtaulds Films	For permission to reproduce the sketch of Sydenham Manor
Thomas S. Curren	Author, Bicentennial History of Bridgewater, New Hampshire
Allan Doyle	Nova Scotia Tourist Board, Halifax, Canada
Mary Dunn	Fontanelle, Iowa
Graeme Elvey	Chief Executive Officer, City of Marong, Victoria, Australia
Jonathan Evans	For his drawing of the ship 'Britannia'
Betty Gregg	Bridgewater Public Library, Massachusetts, USA.
C. C. Hyland	Municipality of Brighton, Tasmania
Janice Jaquish	Bridgewater Town Historian, New York State
Bill King	For kind permission to use postcards from his collection
Donna Kingsbury	Town Hall, Bridgewater, Maine, USA.
Grace V. Meddaugh	Town Clerk, Bridgewater, Connecticut, USA.
Betty Nuse	Township Clerk, Bridgewater, New Jersey
Susan Paul	South Australia Research and Information, Adelaide
Neil Pierce	Newfound Lake, New Hampshire
Lisa Rhuland	Town Clerk, Bridgewater, Nova Scotia, Canada
Evelyn Shrogg	Bridgewater, South Dakota, U.S.A.
Chris Sidaway	For information relating to medieval Bridgwater and the castle
Lynn Walker	Canadian High Commission, London
Lisa Whipple	Courtaulds United States Inc., New York, USA.

Special thanks go to Chris Hocking and Bill Chedgey who painstakingly proof read every section of this publication. Thanks also to the staff of Bridgwater Public Library who without exception were so co-operative.

Whilst the author has endeavoured not to misrepresent any event or person in the preparation of this book, he acknowledges that errors can occur. He does not venture to claim that this publication is free from error and would appreciate being notified where inaccuracies may occur.